SE

WITHDRAWN
UTSA Libraries

PERSPECTIVES ON ATTRIBUTION RESEARCH AND THEORY

Participants of the Bielefeld Conference on Attribution Theory (from left to right): Siegfried Streufert, Bernard Weiner, Harold H. Kelley, Ernst H. Liebhart, Fritz Heider, Wulf-Uwe Meyer (partially hidden), Wolfgang Stroebe, Dietmar Görlitz, Kenneth J. Gergen, Grace Heider, and Heinz Heckhausen.

PERSPECTIVES ON ATTRIBUTION RESEARCH AND THEORY
The Bielefeld Symposium

Edited by
DIETMAR GÖRLITZ
Technical University, Berlin

With contributions by Martin Dobrick, Kenneth J. Gergen, Mary M. Gergen, Dietmar Görlitz, Heinz Heckhausen, Fritz Heider, Manfred Hofer, Harold H. Kelley, Ernst H. Liebhart, Wulf-Uwe Meyer, Fritz-Otto Plöger, Siegfried Streufert, Susan C. Streufert, Wolfgang Stroebe, Bernard Weiner, and Franz E. Weinert.

BALLINGER PUBLISHING COMPANY
Cambridge, Massachusetts
A Subsidiary of Harper & Row, Publishers, Inc.

Translation from the German and technical editing by David Antal.

Copyright © 1980 for English language version only by Ballinger Publishing Company. All rights reserved. No part of this publication may be reproduced, stored in a retrieval system, or transmitted in any form or by any means, electronic, mechanical, photocopy, recording or otherwise, without the prior written consent of the publisher.

International Standard Book Number: 0-88410-375-7

Library of Congress Catalog Card Number: 80-23629

Printed in the United States of America

Library of Congress Cataloging in Publication Data

Main entry under title:

Perspectives in attribution research and theory.

    Papers presented at a conference on "attribution" held June 28-30, 1977 at the Center for Interdisciplinary Research of the University of Bielefeld.
    Bibliography: p.
    Includes indexes.
    1. Attribution (Social psychology)—Congresses. I. Görlitz, Dietmar, 1937-   II. Antal, David. III. Bielefeld. Universität Zentrum für Interdisziplinäre Forschung.
HM251.P4259   302   80-23629
ISBN 0-88410-375-7

CONTENTS

List of Figures ix

List of Tables xi

Dedication to Professor Heider—*Bernard Weiner* xv

Preface xvii

PART I.   *HISTORY AND SCOPE OF THE THEORY*   1

Chapter 1
Perception and Attribution
—*Fritz Heider*   3

Chapter 2
On Balance and Attribution
—*Fritz Heider*   9

Chapter 3
Magic Tricks: The Management of Causal
Attributions—*Harold H. Kelley*   19

Definitions and Distinctions 21
Magic Tricks and Related Phenomena 24
The Nature of "Magic" Events 26
Elements of the Real Causal Sequence 29
Concealment of the Real Causal Sequence 31
Conclusion 34

PART II.   ATTRIBUTIONS OF SUCCESS AND FAILURE 37

Chapter 4
A Theory of Motivation for Some Classroom Experiences — *Bernard Weiner* 39

The Search for Causes 40
Dimensions of Causality 43
Consequences of Causal Properties 48
Stability 48
Locus 54
Control 60
Theoretical Range 65

Chapter 5
The Role of Causal Attribution of Pupils' Behavior in the Teacher's Control of Actions
— *Manfred Hofer and Martin Dobrick* 75

A Model of Social Behavior 76
Relations between Causal Attribution and Other Constructs
 of the Model 83

Comments on the Chapter by Hofer and Dobrick
— *Franz E. Weinert* 89

Chapter 6
An Attributional Analysis of the Relation between Expectancy and Incentive (Affect)
— *Wulf-Uwe Meyer and Fritz-Otto Plöger* 95

An Empirical Investigation 97
Conclusions 105

Chapter 7
Self-Esteem and Attribution: Individual Differences in the Causal Explanation of Success and Failure
— Wolfgang Stroebe — 109

Self-Esteem and the Causal Explanation of Success and Failure in the Area of Achievement — 111
Self-Esteem and Causal Explanation of Success and Failure in the Area of Interpersonal Relations — 114
Self-Concept and Social Reality — 118

PART III. ATTRIBUTION AND AFFECT — 121

Chapter 8
Perceived Autonomic Changes as Determinants of Emotional Behavior
— Ernst H. Liebhart — 123

Outline of the Model — 125
Motivation for Explanation Search — 126
Accessibility of Context Information — 135
Plausibility of the Attribution — 141
Behavioral Impact of Attribution — 146
Concluding Observations — 151

PART IV. METHODOLOGICAL PROBLEMS AND THE SOCIAL CONTEXT OF ATTRIBUTION — 157

Chapter 9
Attribution, Dimensionality, and Measurement: How You Measure Is What You Get
— Siegfried Streufert and Susan C. Streufert — 159

Experiment 1: Attributions of Responsibility and Causality — 162
Experiment 2: Attributional Dimensions of the Experimenter and the Subject — 176
Conclusions Based on the Two Experiments — 184

Comments on the Chapter by Streufert and Streufert — Heinz Heckhausen — 187

Attribution and Measurement: In Response
to Heckhausen — *Siegfried Streufert and
Susan C. Streufert* 193

Chapter 10
Causal Attribution in the Context of Social Explanation
— *Kenneth J. Gergen and Mary M. Gergen* 195

The Emergence of Sociorationalism 197
The Awareness of Mental Processes 203
Analytic Philosophy: Reasons and Causes 206
Toward an Ethnography of Explanation 208

Comments on the Chapter by Gergen and Gergen
— *Heinz Heckhausen* 213

Appendix to the Conference
— *Dietmar Görlitz* 219

Selected Bibliography 231

Author Index 255

Subject Index 261

About the Contributors 267

LIST OF FIGURES

3-1	Properties of the Magic Trick and Other Related Phenomena	24
4-1	Partial Representation of an Attributional Theory of Motivation	66
4-2	An Attributional Framework for the Parole Decision Process	70
5-1	Schematic Diagram of a Model of Social Behavior	77
6-1	Percentage Frequency of Attributions for Seven Levels of Difficulty	101
6-2	Percentage Frequency of Affects for Seven Levels of Difficulty	104
7-1	Attribution of Positive and Negative Evaluations to "Role Play" or "Sincere Behavior" by Subjects with High and Low Self-Esteem	118
9-1	Effect of Scale Characteristics and the Time Factor on Attributions of Causality and Responsibility	170
9-2	Dimensionality of Attribution as per Weiner et al. (1971)	177
9-3	Effects of Increasing Success and Failure on Attributions of Luck versus Ability	182

9-4 Seven-Point Forced-Choice Scale for the Internal–
     External Dimension Compared with Sum of the
     Scales for Task Difficulty, Effort, Ability, and Luck   183

LIST OF TABLES

3-1	Apparent and Real Causal Sequences of "The Whispering Queen"	22
3-2	Types of "Magic" Events in Apparent Causal Sequence	28
3-3	Aspects of the Apparent Causal Sequence That Promote Concealment of the Real Causal Sequence	32
4-1	Summary of Previous Coding Systems	42
4-2	Causes of Success and Failure, Classified According to Locus, Stability, and Controllability	46
4-3	Percentage of Respondents Stating a Particular Emotion for Success, as a Function of the Attribution for Success	57
4-4	Mean Likelihood of Helping as a Function of Perceived Locus of Causality and Controllability	63
6-1	Number of Own Hits and Hits of Others from Seven Distances with Twenty Throws from Each	98
6-2	Categories of Causal Factors for Success and Their Frequency	99
6-4	Categories of Affects for Success and Their Frequency	100
6-4	Percentages of Affects at Three Difficulty Levels Reported by Subjects Who Attribute Success to Luck	105
10-1	Explanatory Categories: A Preliminary Schema	209

CONTRIBUTORS

Dr. Martin Dobrick, Seminar für Pädagogik, Technische Universität Carolo Wilhelmina, Braunschweig, West Germany
Dr. Kenneth J. Gergen, Department of Psychology, Swarthmore College
Dr. Mary Gergen, Department of Psychology, Swarthmore College
Dr. Dietmar Görlitz, Institut für Psychologie, Technische Universität Berlin, West Germany
Dr. Heinz Heckhausen, Psychologisches Institut der Ruhr-Universität Bochum, West Germany
Dr. Fritz Heider, Department of Psychology, University of Kansas
Dr. Manfred Hofer, Seminar für Pädagogik, Technische Universität Carolo Wilhelmina, Braunschweig, West Germany
Dr. Harold H. Kelley, Department of Psychology, University of California at Los Angeles
Dr. Ernst H. Liebhart, Fachbereich Psychologie der Philipps-Universität Marburg, West Germany
Dr. Wulf-Uwe Meyer, Fakultät für Pädagogik, Philosophie, Psychologie, Abteilung Psychologie, Universität Bielefeld, West Germany
Fritz-Otto Plöger, Detmold, West Germany
Dr. Siegfried Streufert, Department of Behavioral Science, Pennsylvania. State University Medical School, Hershey
Dr. Susan Streufert, National Institutes of Health, Bethesda, Maryland
Dr. Wolfgang Stroebe, Psychologisches Institut, Universität Tübingen, West Germany
Dr. Bernard Weiner, Department of Psychology, University of California at Los Angeles
Dr. Franz E. Weinert, Psychologisches Institut der Universität Heidelberg, West Germany

DEDICATION TO PROFESSOR HEIDER
Bernard Weiner

It is a great pleasure and honor for us to dedicate this book to Professor Fritz Heider. Today, Professor Heider is known as the founding father of attribution theory. Born in Vienna in 1896 and raised in Graz, Professor Heider completed his doctoral studies in 1920 under the direction of Professor Meinong. In 1921 Dr. Heider went to Humboldt University in Berlin, where he came into direct contact with Lewin and other Gestalt psychologists. The following decade appears to have been a period of unrest for both Dr. Heider and Germany as a whole. In 1930 Professor Heider moved to the University of Hamburg, the psychology laboratory of which was under the direction of William Stern. Dr. Heider remained there only a year. In 1931 he left for Smith College in Massachusetts. Dr. Koffka, working there on a special five-year research project, had been in touch with Dr. Stern, who had suggested Dr. Heider to fill a one-year position at Smith.

At the same time, Grace Moore was working as an assistant to Dr. Koffka. She soon became Grace Moore-Heider, and Fritz Heider stayed in America. The two worked almost two decades at Smith College, then moved to the University of Kansas in Lawrence, which was one of the centers of Gestalt psychology in the United States. The Heiders still live in Lawrence. I would like to add that there are *two* Dr. Heiders. Dr. Grace Heider pursued her own independent career in the fields of developmental and personality psychology. She has made numerous contributions in her own right.

Dr. Heider has the gratitude of all the colleagues who have joined him in the field of attribution theory. Without his presence, this book would not have come into existence. Dr. Heider is not and has never been a dogmatic leader. Unlike some of the other outstanding people in the social sciences, he has encouraged others to be independent, even critical. I believe that the vitality and fruitfulness of attribution theory is in part due to this atmosphere. We are not part of a dogmatic tradition that prescribes what our approach has to be. We have Fritz Heider to thank for this, a very warm, inspiring, and patient man whom we all love and respect.

PREFACE

The present volume contains contributions to the conference on "attribution" held June 28–30, 1977, at the Center for Interdisciplinary Research of the University of Bielefeld. This conference would not have materialized had it not been for the fortunate circumstance that some of the outstanding researchers in this field were in Europe during the summer of 1977. Fritz Heider was visiting his native country, Austria; Harold Kelley had been invited to give a guest lecture at the Technical University of Berlin; Kenneth J. Gergen was a visiting professor at the universities of Marburg and Paris; and Bernard Weiner was working on a research project at the Technical University of Berlin while also serving as a visiting professor at the University of Bielefeld.

Special thanks goes to the Center for Interdisciplinary Research of the University of Bielefeld, which financed the conference and graciously provided the necessary facilities. The editor is particularly indebted to colleagues Bernard Weiner, whose initiative made this American edition possible, and Wulf-Uwe Meyer for their constant support and effort in preparing the conference and the report. The editor also extends his thanks to Klett-Cotta, Stuttgart, for its role in publishing this book. Special mention must go here to Ballinger Publishing Company, Cambridge, Massachusetts, in particular to Cynthia Insolio Benn, the copyeditor, who will long be remembered for the meticulous and insightful expertise invested in the difficult task of preparing the manuscript for publication in the United States. Finally, the editor expresses his deep appreciation to the secretaries of the Psychology Department at the Technical University Berlin and at the University of Bielefeld for their help in getting both language editions into print; to Daniele Paul and, especially, David Antal. Without their patience and active participation in the translating and editing process, and without the encouraging assistance of my wife, this book would never have been published.

Dietmar Görlitz

I HISTORY AND SCOPE OF THE THEORY

Part I of this book deals with the origins of concepts central to attribution theory and integrates other concepts that relate to attribution and its processes. The discussion is broadened to include investigation of neglected types of everyday atrributions. In the first chapter, Fritz Heider reflects upon the relation of "perception and attribution," analyzing the conditions underlying these phenomena and the nature of the environment that makes both necessary. Central to the discussion are considerations of how the causal hierarchy of things allows perception to give us information about distant objects, and how it facilitates attribution as the recognition of causes and effects.

Chapter 2, a second contribution by Heider, "On Balance and Attribution," brings together his early work on causality and perception of people. The balance concept is presented as a logical extension of statements pertaining to attribution. The tendency connecting the two is unit-formation, in which Gestalt laws of simplicity and order would be active—including some that are not restricted to perception.

Harold Kelley pursues the subject further with an analysis of unusual cause and effect relations exemplified by the magician's deliberate shaping of causal attribution in "magic tricks." Taking the course of a single event from the standpoint of the participants, he distinguishes between various causal sequences whose differences are specific for erroneous attributions. Kelley also points out the significant variations and conditions of unusual causal sequences and shows which techniques can contribute to concealing the true sequences of events.

1 PERCEPTION AND ATTRIBUTION
Fritz Heider

In the past few years I have often been asked about the origins of various ideas of mine—the roots of the balance idea, or the beginnings of attribution theory, for example. As a result, I turned to my older works; I read them and thought about them—an occupation that was sometimes eye-opening and sometimes accompanied by a feeling like homesickness. Two years ago I spoke about balance and attribution at a conference at Dartmouth College where I tried to show how these concepts were developed in works I had published in the 1940s. At that time, however, I did not mention that these works were in some ways the children and grand-children of my dissertation, which I wrote in the winter of 1919—20, and which I later expanded and published (in 1926) under the title "Ding und Medium" in the journal *Symposion*.

In 1919 when I was a student in Graz, the philosopher Meinong gave me—as a suggestion for a dissertation—a puzzle to solve. With this puzzle I was steered in a direction that I have followed for a long time. What I have written here stems from two sources: first, from this dissertation, and second, from later thoughts, particularly thoughts on attribution. Meinong's puzzle was the following: When the sun shines on a house and the light reflected by the house strikes our eye, why do we say that we see the house? Since the light is caused by the sun, why don't we say that we see the sun? This question and the attempts to answer it have finally led to the somewhat unhappily named concepts of distal and proximal stimulus; they have introduced basically new problems into perception research. One becomes attentive to the outside world which lies beyond the retina and to the conditions of perception, which lie in the environment and which make the knowledge of this environment possible. Brunswik later elaborated this and called it "ecology of perception."

When we look more closely at the causal structure of the environment, we find, first, a characteristic of great significance for our perception and for our life in general: the parts of the environment have differing degrees of causal importance—a kind of causal hierarchy exists. We find centers and offshoots; one might almost say that our environment is not very democratically arranged—in it there are masters and servants, parts that determine occurrences in the neighborhood and parts whose occurrence is externally determined. One could also say that there are active and passive parts of the environment and that the events of the passive parts can often be attributed to the active parts. The passive parts can also often mediate information about the active parts. The mediation of *information* and *attribution*, both of basic importance for our knowledge about the environment, presume a causal hierarchy. One could very easily imagine an environment with a minimum of causal hierarchy, a minimum of constraints, a minimum of entropy. It would be an environment composed of a homogeneous mixture of gases. Distant perception would be impossible since there would be no objects in this world and no mediation of information about distant events. It is good to imagine such a world because we can then understand more easily how much our perception and our whole life owes to the purely physical structure of the world. The fact that such a causal hierarchy exists, that causal centers and causal offshoots exist, allows our perception to extend beyond the limits of our bodies and allows us to learn something about the larger environment. It also makes it possible for us "to attribute" (*zuschreiben*) events and contents, that is, to relate them to other events and contents. We attach them, so to speak, to contents that are more permanent; we thereby fix them and have a better overview of the possibilities of future development.

If we examine this causal hierarchy more closely, we find two types of superordination and subordination. First there is the difference between solid things as causal centers and the light and sound waves in which the things are bathed and which transmit knowledge to us from them. This distinction is the central theme of my work in "*Ding und Medium.*" This wave movement per se is usually not important to us; it is important only as a messenger of the world of things and persons that is our primary interest. These messengers usually disappear completely in our picture of the environment. When we direct our gaze at things (or at persons), we believe that they directly reveal their nature to us in some way, and we are not aware of the mediation.

I will not go into problems of perception further; I only want to discuss certain observations that are related to perception and also to attribution, and that refer to the constancy phenomena. The proximal stimulus, this message from the object, is formed and determined not only by the object but also by facts that are really independent of the object and that therefore falsify or cloud the message. To these facts belong, of course, the illumination, the distance between the person and the object, and also the position of the object in relation to the person. One can say that these constancy phenomena are cases of attribution; it always concerns the question of whether a property of the proximal stimulus is ascribed to the object or to one of these other conditions. The perception is a victim of a delusion if the message is credulously taken literally. One could also say that it is a false generalization to believe that an object must always appear the way it does under certain conditions. Piaget has spoken about these things, and I believe that many years ago Whitehead called this mistake "false concreteness."

Because of the *second* type of superordination and subordination, however, we also find a causal hierarchy among the solid units themselves, and there the distinction between things and persons is particularly important. Persons are to a far greater extent than things the originators of events; they are the ones who direct changes and usually determine the occurrence of events. This is, of course, usually the case when simple movements or a change in location are involved. If one notices in a familiar room that something is in a different place, one wonders who did it. Tables do not move themselves. On the other hand, not all persons belong to the originator class to the same extent. In social events some people play more the role of causal centers and others the role of passive, "moved" parts. DeCharms used the expressions "origins" and "pawns" for this distinction.

I therefore repeat: In both cases, perception and attribution, we find a structure that contains on the one hand cores or centers, and on the other hand, offshoots, or passive parts; that is, a type of hierarchy seems to be significant here. In this way perception and attribution resemble each other. But we also find differences: the causal structure that is important for perception contains the difference between things and mediations—between the common, solid units, which appear as objects of perception, and the movements of light and sound waves, which occur as mediation. These roles are seldom exchanged; it is rare that solid units transmit information to us about waves.

The causal structure that is usually important for attribution is different. The passive parts that are moved by the active ones or that are forced into an event are often not mediations; that is not their main function. The event that happens to the passive parts and that is attributed to the active parts does not always serve to improve the cognition of this originator.

I would like to add only that this is a very inexact and rough analysis of the comparison of perception and attribution. For a more precise analysis one would also have to consider especially the attributions that use the network of interpersonal concepts.

Further, the relation between experimental results and reality, to which hypotheses and theories refer, can also be viewed as a relation between mediation and core event. The experiments stand between the researcher and the reality about which he would like to learn more. The experiments are like a telescope through which reality is looked at, and either this mediation can have a distorting effect or it can yield a true picture.

When one reads today's experimental works, one cannot help wishing that the writers would be somewhat more careful with generalizations. A relationship of X to Y is studied in a specific situation, and certain results are reported. At the end of the work we are told that X always behaves in this way toward Y, without consideration of the situation. It has now been perhaps thirty or forty years since Brunswik advised us to treat the sampling of situations as conscientiously as the sampling of subjects. It has not helped, and many researchers still behave like Piaget's child who believes that the mountain looks just the same from the other side as it does from his side. In both cases, that of the experimenter and that of the child, there is the same disregard of the influence of other factors on the mediation. To give one example: Someone wanted to study the influence of unit relations on balance. There are many different unit relations: marriage, blood relationship, working in the same group, living in the same room, and so on. One would expect that the researcher would test a representative number of relationships in order to come to a general result. But no, he took one relationship, and unfortunately a very weak one that is not very effective, namely, acquaintanceship, and thus came to the "general finding" that unit relations have a very minor influence on balance—an obviously false conclusion because it is based on a false generalization.

Another circumstance in our modern world that is gaining increasing influence is the significance of the media: the press, television, radio, and so forth. It is obvious that similar problems play a role there, problems of thing and medium or of reality and the way in which it is mediated to us. What is presented to us as reality by the newspapers is usually rather far away. It is a "distal stimulus" that is not reached directly by our perception. We recognize the object through the mediation of the newspaper. The newspaper therefore plays the role of a telescope through which we must look in order to gain knowledge about the object. The question comes up again: Does the mediation provide a true picture of the distant reality, or does it distort it?

A few years ago I gave some thought to the problem of violence, but I have published little about it so far. The question is why so many people are fascinated by murder and terror and passionately interested in it. And why do they want to read about it in the newspapers? An obvious answer is that they are full of repressed hatred and repressed aggression—but the obvious is not always correct.

It is possible that another factor also plays a role. A newspaper brings information about current events that cause important changes from one day to the next. It is a peculiarity of our environment that destruction and annihilation cause significant changes much faster than do construction and formation. Millions of years were needed to create the necessary conditions for the appearance of a person, but the destruction of this complex system can happen in seconds. Construction usually requires a long time, destruction a short time; and this is true of an organism, a building, or a machine like a clock. The step from order to disorder is short, from disorder to order, long. If an institution like a daily newspaper deals with "news," then it must necessarily deal with destruction, catastrophe, earthquakes, floods, murders. If a powerful magician were to appear and suddenly conjure up a big house, that would certainly also be a very interesting novelty. Many people would pay large sums of money in order to see it, and they would buy newspapers that reported it.

If one should ask why this great difference between the creation of disorder and the creation of order exists, then one would probably say that entropy somehow plays a role here, the directional nature of time.

But to the question as to whether the transmission of the media provides us with a true picture of distant reality or whether it in some way distorts this reality and simulates incorrect relationships, I must answer that in fact this coupling of newspaper with news and of news with destruction occasions a selection in presentation, a one-sidedness, so that the relation of constructive events to destructive events is totally falsified.

2 ON BALANCE AND ATTRIBUTION

Fritz Heider

The problems of balance are so closely connected in my thinking with the problems of attribution that I cannot completely separate the two, and I have to treat both at once. Both of these groups of problems, balance as well as attribution, have roots going back to my early life. I will try to be brief, but in order to get a better perspective on later developments I have to mention these more personal beginnings.

One of these roots is an early concern with perception that had its origin in an interest in art. I grew up in Austria where painting was, at least at that time, a favorite hobby. Almost all my relatives painted or sketched, and I got my first sketch book before I was seven years old. During my teens I wanted to become a painter. I still think that attempts to sketch, that is, to put on paper pictorial representations of the environment, are the best introduction to the remarkable processes involved in perception. It leads to an intimate familiarity with perception and a know-how about it. One would probably not be far wrong to say that such a know-how may provide the soil on which good theories of perception can flourish.

A second early concern that led to later theorizing was an interest in interpersonal relations. As far as I remember it developed gradu-

---

This chapter was originally delivered as a lecture in 1975 at a conference of the Mathematical Social Science Board at Dartmouth College supported by the National Science Foundation.

ally, but it was certainly very much intensified by the situation right after the First World War, when life in Austria became difficult because there were grave shortages of food, heat, and illumination. This led to an atmosphere thick with quarrels and irritability; people became touchy and petulant.

These two early concerns, the one with perception, growing out of painting and sketching, and the other with human relations, which was stimulated by a stressful social climate, soon merged and led into thoughts of what is now called person perception. In an environment of discord and petty squabbles, it often happens that we are confronted with troubling interpersonal situations. For instance, two people who are close and dear to us may come into conflict with each other, each one thinking that only his interpretation of the issue is the right one. We listen to one of them, we are sympathetic, and we think, yes that seems plausible—and then we listen to the other one and his view also seems justified. Thus we experience this conflict in ourselves, and one way to save oneself is by intellectualizing everything, by realizing that people often have very egocentric views of the events that concern them and that their personal perspective may distort our picture of the other person. In short, such experiences make us spend thought on person perception and make us aware of relations and events between other people. Anyway, this is how they affected me, and as early as 1920 or 1921 I gave a talk on person perception to a group of people who were interested in science. That was in Graz, the Austrian city in which I had grown up. This talk fell flat; I was not sure whether it was my fault or the fault of the audience.

Maybe I should remind you at this point that there seem to be two different kinds of problems within the field of social psychology. One deals with problems in which the concept of a group is prominent. Objects of study are relations between groups, or relations between a group and individuals. For instance, how does being part of a group influence the individual person, his beliefs, motivations, and achievements? Until quite recently, maybe ten or fifteen years ago, what was called social psychology dealt almost exclusively with problems involving groups, and only rarely was the second big class of problems considered—those that treat interpersonal relations, relations between one person and one or very few other persons. At present, this second field is growing very rapidly and has been accepted as another part of social psychology. The difference between these two parts of social psychology has some important consequences. First, the very rich folklore of commonsense psychology is mainly concerned with interpersonal problems and is much less specific about groups. Second, the study of relations between a few individuals soon leads one to consider questions of person perception and attribution.

Returning to the sketch of the origin of the balance idea, I have to mention three papers that I published in the forties and that trace a continuous development. The first one, prepared with Marianne Simmel, tried to show the importance of attribution and person perception. It appeared in 1944, and I will call it the "film paper." The second one, also from 1944, deals with some factors responsible for attribution and actually discusses cases of balance, though balance is not yet explicitly presented. I will refer to it as the "phenomenal causality paper." The third paper, published in 1946, contains the explicit formulation of the balance hypothesis. The first of these papers, the film paper, describes a little experiment with an abstract film. It has its origin in an attempt to study person perception. In 1930 I had come to the Research Department of The Clarke School for the Deaf in Northampton, Massachusetts. One of our projects was an investigation of the problem-solving processes of young deaf children who as yet had hardly any speech. How was it possible that they could somehow think without the help of words? We tried giving these children a number of language-free tests. One test that seemed especially interesting used a form board. I suppose you are familiar with tests like this that require fitting tiles of different geometrical forms into the appropriate openings. It was fascinating to watch the children work on them. One had the feeling that it was possible to follow a child's thinking when he picked up a piece, tried to fit it into different gaps without success, then picked up another piece, and so on. We made some moving pictures of this process, and soon found that we could dispense with the picture of the face. Most of the information was in the movements of the hands carrying the pieces. This led to the idea that one might make a film in which the geometric pieces move around by themselves—one could show how they try to find their proper places, how they attempt to fit themselves into their beds, to get a snug fit or not, and so on. That would be a film in which just the movements and some geometric forms portray thought and purposive behavior. Such a film might give clues to the main problem of our concern, clues namely to how we perceive thought in another being, how we get information about the so-called mental processes, how we perceive intention, wishes, abilities, and so on.

Following this idea still further, I thought of a little story, a succession of interpersonal events that are told by the motion of geometric figures that have no similarity to human beings. That is the origin of the film that I made with Marianne Simmel, in which a circle and two triangles move around in different ways. The subjects to whom we showed the film were asked to describe it and to answer a number of questions about it. There was hardly anybody who did not perceive the goings on in the film in terms of some kind of give and take between persons. As a matter of fact it was rather difficult to describe the events in purely spatial geometric terms, avoiding any anthropomorphizing.

A study of the answers of the subjects made one realize the great importance that attribution plays in person perception, attribution understood here as the *connection between a perceived change (Geschehen) and a person conceived of as causing this change* by some action. This attribution has the effect of connecting the perceived change with the significant environment and especially with its more invariant features. The relation to non-person perception and to constancy phenomena is also mentioned in the paper: "Phenomenal movements per se are comparable to reduction colors, and acts of persons are comparable to object colors" (Heider and Simmel 1944: 256). It is also suggested that a hypothesis of unit-formation might help us understand this organization in which movements are seen as actions of persons, and the question is asked: "Does this unit-formation follow some of the laws of purely figural unit-formation?" (Heider and Simmel: 257).[a]

The next paper, the one on phenomenal causality, carries out the suggestion at the end of the film paper. It deals with the way in which Wertheimer's laws of unit-formation influence attribution of actions to persons. Wertheimer says that parts of the visual field that are close together or that are similar to each other will be seen as belonging together, as forming one unit. Thus proximity and similarity are unit-forming factors, and he enumerates a number of others.

---

a. The distinction between reduction colors and object colors originated with Katz (1911: sec. I) [Ed.].

It is tempting to take a further step, namely, to assume the Wertheimer factors (similarity, proximity, and so on) not only bring about phenomenal belongingness, but that they can also bring about phenomenal causation. That is, when two parts of the cognitive field are similar (or proximal, and so on) this similarity can induce attribution, that is, one of these parts is likely to be seen as the origin or cause of the other part. For instance, a bad action will easily be seen as committed by a person who already has a bad reputation. It is shown in the paper that the opposite phenomenon has also been reported in the literature; that is, attribution can induce apparent similarity. A familiar case would be the prestige suggestion: the evaluation of utterances or artistic products can depend on the prestige of the person to whom they are attributed. This attribution not only can influence the value of the product, but may even change its meaning.

The first paragraph of the third paper makes the idea of balance appear to be a logical continuation of the paper on phenomenal causality—as if one had just to sit down and think through what is said about attribution and figural unit-formation, generalize a little, and out comes the balance idea. One might also suppose that the idea of balance came about by way of the *prägnanz* idea, which was very familiar to me and which is closely related to balance. Both are manifestations of a tendency toward simplicity or order, toward a distinguished state; we want to have our cognitive food prepared so that it is easy to swallow, to assimilate. But that was actually not the way in which I came to balance. I came to it empirically, one might say, not through experimental results, but rather through informal observations, and through Spinoza, the old rationalist, who had collected very shrewd observations about life and about liking and loving, and who tried to systematize these observations. He thought he could put them into some kind of logical order à la Euclid in the fashion of geometry.

I was greatly attracted by Spinoza, first because he treated important interpersonal phenomena (such as loving and hating), and then because he attempted to build a coherent theory about them. However, when I studied closely what he had to say and tried to think through all his propositions and derivations, I came to the conclusion that he did not quite succeed and that in the end his attempt was very unsatisfactory. Nevertheless, these propositions seemed to contain some kind of system. When one listed them and looked them over, they definitely did not give the impression of a random, chance medley; one had the feeling that there was some order in it, as if one were confronted with a kind of cipher. I cannot resist this opportunity to quote from the third book of Spinoza's *Ethics*, and in doing it I will simplify them a bit. I will use the letters p, q, and o for persons, x and y for non-person entities. For instance, proposition number 22 states that if p likes o, and q benefits o, p will like q. Number 16: If p likes x, and y is similar to x, p will like y. Number 45: If p likes o, and q dislikes o, p will dislike q. Number 33: If p loves o, he will try to make o love p.

I pored over the propositions. I tried all sorts of graphic representations, looked at them from different points of view and with different central concepts in mind, but for a long time they refused to disclose their pattern. It was tantalizing, since I had the conviction that all the information necessary for the solution of the problem was right in front of my eyes. Then, one afternoon, I realized that I had to bring in Wertheimer's unit-forming factors and that I had to treat unit relations on the same plane, so to speak, as attitudes. I do not remember whether I understood right away all the implications of this conception, but I had the feeling that the puzzle was solved. I stopped work and went for a walk.

Looking back now, it seems strange that it took me so long to consider units as relevant to my problem, since I had used this idea in the paper on phenomenal causality. Probably at that time I still thought that attitudes such as "to love" or "to like" belong in a compartment different from that in which unit-formation belongs. The mental blinders of textbook psychology imply that attitudes belong to social psychology whereas units belong to perception, and such artificial separations can often make trouble. These days I conceive of attitudes as interacting with unit-formation. But it was clear to me right away that a breakthrough had occurred, the kind of reorganization that Gestalt psychologists talk about.

It may be worthwhile to spell out in greater detail what this reorganization involved. Two facts seemed to be important: Spinoza uses a number of different expressions to characterize the relevant connections, as for instance, love, hate, benefit, similar. The relations between these expressions are not specified. In contrast to that, the connections in the balance formulation form two large groups, the positive connections and the negative connections. The relation between them is clear, and one can put them together in a quasimathematical calculus, for instance by multiplication. On the other hand, it would be impossible to multiply "p loves o" by "o dislikes p." This means that the balance calculus is based on a certain kind of classification that considers connections as equivalent that offhand would seem very different and incommensurable. Not only different kinds of attitudes are treated as equivalent—at least in the first approximation—but also positive attitudes are treated as belonging to the same class as positive unit relations.

There is one other aspect of the balance calculus that does not appear in Spinoza's formulations, and that is the importance of the loop arrangement, or the "cycle," as Cartwright and Harary called it. Why is the cycle necessary? I am puzzled by it, and I have suspicions that it is in some way akin to the mathematical concept of group, in which again a kind of cycle arrangement plays an important role.

I will now go back to the paper on phenomenal causality and explain what I meant when I mentioned the implicit presentation of balance in this paper. May I remind you that one of the main results of this article was that similarity and proximity (or other Wertheimer factors) favor the attribution of acts to persons. This means that if the relation of a certain act a to a certain person p is one of similarity, then there is a tendency to attribute a to p, that is, to connect a with p by a causal relation as well. Or, if a has one positive relation to p, there is a tendency to connect the two by another positive connection. Two relations of the same sign between two items that would be "path balance" according to Cartwright and Harary. It appears that what the paper on phenomenal causality really treats is the influence of the balance tendency on attribution.

We have here a case of two *different formations* of the same observations, the one formulation given in the paper on phenomenal causality and the other in terms of balance. The first does not allow one to go much beyond oneself; it leads to a more restricted view, whereas the second suddenly makes many new considerations possible. Unsuspected new relations, similarities, categories, or possibilities of combinations are brought to one's attention. They have been inaccessible and invisible, but now they abruptly come within reach.

The difference between the two formulations can probably best be shown by an example. Let us take the statement: "Bad actions will often be attributed to people thought of as bad." In the formulation of phenomenal causality that means that similarity seems to induce attribution. One would not expect that this statement is in any way related to the statement that a person will generally try to meet people that he likes. The formulation in terms of balance would be the following: both similarity and attribution refer to positive relations, and one positive relation will often tend to bring about another positive relation. We see right away the equality in structure of "Similarity produces attribution" and "Liking produces proximity."

I have to add another point in regard to the role balance plays in the paper on phenomenal causality. Attitudes (liking and disliking) are not considered, but only interactions between unit relations, that is, only interactions between causal units and other units. For instance, how may the appearance of a causal unit be induced by similarity or how may a belief in a causal unit induce phenomenal similarity?

As long as we stay within the frame of the narrow formulation of the paper on phenomenal causality, this will raise no questions—but according to the new formulation in the paper on balance, we now consider it possible to treat any unit as functionally equivalent to any other, at least to some degree. This leads right away to the question whether there exist interactions between other unit relations, for example, between similarity and proximity, that are comparable to the interactions between similarity and causal connections.

During the last years I have followed up this idea off and on and have come to the conclusion that there is indeed a tendency toward balance that concerns arrangements of unit relations alone, without attitudes. I have collected numerous examples, and so far, in my notes, I have spoken of the tendency toward coinciding unit-formations. Usually, when unit factors coincide, we have the impression of an orderly set-up, and where a pair of items is connected with one unit factor, often the appearance of a second is induced. Things that are similar to each other often seem to be closer to each other than dissimilar things; and vice versa, there is often an influence of proximity on similarity. I will not go into that; I only want to remind you of what it means to "make order." Usually it means to make the factor of proximity coincide with the factor of similarity: We tend to put similar things together.

But whether we include attitudes in our considerations or not, it is probably safe to say that the tendency toward harmony is not merely reactive, that it is not only a matter of repairing the disturbances and attempting to get back to a state of restful peace. Often it implies a reaching out, a changing of more and more parts of the cognitive field and of the environment to bring them into consonance with important seminal ideas and attitudes. This acquisitive growth spreads out over the environment a network of relations that are in balance with the founding source-relation. A good illustration is the progress of changes that start with a fortunate love affair.

The original attitude is like a seed in a crystal formation. If, for instance, a man A loves a woman B he will try to make B love A, in case this symmetrical attitude did not arise simultaneously with A's love. If the mutual love between A and B is once established, they will both work toward adding more positive relations since these are in harmony with the seed attitude. They will want to be together as much as possible; they will want to start sexual relations, to live together, to marry. Then a host of common relations to further people and things will develop. They may acquire common property, which both like; their tastes and values may get more and more alike; they may have children to whom they are connected by blood relation and by love; they have friends in common; they share many experiences and have a stock of common memories; and so on. In short, a great many attitude and unit relations are clustered around the original seed element, and all these relations combine in cycles that are in harmony with the original attitude and therefore in harmony with each other.

If the mutual sentiment of A and B changes from love to dislike or hate, then the whole network of relations becomes at once discordant in all its parts. A and B will feel that all the unit-formations that grew up in harmony with love are fetters that tie together two persons who repel each other. They will try to separate, and the separation will lead to many difficulties because it is in conflict with the developed cluster. They will want to cut the bands of common property, divide up the children, and so forth.

The fact that the change in sign of just one relation can produce such a massive disharmony seems to speak against the assumption that "the amount of balance . . . can be measured by the number of lines . . . whose sign must be changed in order to achieve balance" (Harary, Norman, and Cartwright 1965: 348). At the same time, this case makes one skeptical about the hypothesis that balanced structures can always be learned more easily than unbalanced ones. True enough, ease of learning and redundancy go together, and balance represents one kind of redundancy. However, imbalance can also be redundant, as is shown by the cluster of relations that becomes unbalanced when the seed relation changes.

The significant feature of this kind of network of relations is that one relation, namely, the relation of A to B, is part of many cycles. One might speak here of a polycycle relation. Then, of course, this relation is a factor in the balance of all the cycles, and one would assume that it has much greater influence on the amount of balance than a relation that is part of only one cycle.

In conclusion I want to describe briefly once more the roles that attribution and balance play in our cognitive makeup. Attribution is a relative of perception; it serves to anchor our impressions and the perceived changes in the conception of the more invariant sphere of relevant entities. It serves to make happenings understandable and to get as much useful information about the environment as possible from them. Attribution often means a unit-formation, a relation of belonging together between an event and a person.

The tendency toward balance is a tendency of the parts of the cognitive field not to quarrel with each other, to be accommodating, and to make up a harmonious family. Parts that are connected in some way should fit each other, should be concordant; and so it is very plausible that parts that are connected as cause and effect will also be seen as fitting each other. Balance deals with relations of relations; and dyadic arrangements in which the relations of the two items are all positive or all negative will be harmonious.

3 MAGIC TRICKS
The Management of Causal Attributions

Harold H. Kelley

For some years I have had the hunch that an analysis of the procedures used by professional magicians in performing their magic tricks would prove enlightening for social psychology. I have begun that analysis here. It should be emphasized that this chapter is a progress report. I have not made a thorough survey of magicians' procedures, and I am not yet entirely satisfied with the conceptual framework for my analysis.

In keeping with the theme of this volume, I have focused particularly upon the attributional aspects of magic tricks. This, of course, is a natural and obvious approach to take. The successful magic trick intimately involves the causal attribution process. The observers of the trick, the audience, see some sort of extraordinary cause-and-effect relation apparently occur. The magician in some way manages things so that, for example, a certain effect seems to occur in the absence of any of its usual causes. Or, a cause of known efficacy seems not to have its usual consequences. In all such cases, the causal attribution process of the observers has been led astray by the procedures of the magician. This abstract description of the magic trick suggests that an attributional analysis is particularly appropriate to its understanding. It also suggests that from this analysis we may

Preparation was facilitated by National Science Foundation Grant BNS—76—20490.

hope to learn something about the general processes whereby causal attributions are managed.

In a sense this might be regarded as a review of an experimental literature. The successful magic trick is an experimental procedure that "works," that is, that produces the desired effect upon the subjects (the members of the audience). It is replicable: it has worked in the past and presumably will work in the future. The instructions for how to perform the trick, to be found in a book of magic, are, in a sense, the description of the *experimental* treatment in the *method* section of a research paper. True, the *control* treatments are not described, but they can easily be imagined. And we can plausibly assume that the described procedure produces the desired effect significantly more often than do various alternative procedures.

From a different perspective, my analysis of magic is in the tradition of Heider's analysis of common sense. I examine the beliefs and practices of certain laymen for what can be gleaned about their explicit or implicit understanding of the attribution process. Of course, magicians are different from the typical lay or nonscientific person. Their activity consists primarily of the control and management of causal attributions rather than simply making such attributions. More importantly, they are highly experienced and expert in their activity and very self-conscious about it. Consequently, magicians may have an implicit understanding of the attribution process that in some ways is superior to that of their audience and even to our own.

From the perspective of social psychology in general, the magic trick is always an interpersonal event—there is always a magician and an audience. It makes no sense to think of a magician doing a trick except to have some sort of effect on an audience. The only exception would be where he is practicing alone, in order to have such an effect. Even then, he is his own audience, a stand-in for future real audiences. (Magic books strongly advise practicing before a mirror.) So magic is always interpersonal. Moreover, in many of the most interesting cases, the relationship is an interactive one. The audience (or members of it) are brought into the act in various roles and for various apparent and hidden purposes. We may expect, then, to find in the magician's arcanum some important ideas about the structure and organization of interpersonal behavior.

DEFINITIONS AND DISTINCTIONS

It is necessary first to give some definitions and to make some distinctions. These will serve to specify the particular phenomena under analysis and to make clear what phenomena are excluded from our consideration. The definitions will also form the basis for our analysis. In presenting these general concepts, it will be extremely helpful for us to have a concrete example. Consider first a very simple trick, "The Whispering Queen." The "effect" is as follows: A member of the audience chooses a card from a deck of ordinary playing cards. Without anyone seeing it, this card is shown to the member's "favorite queen," previously set aside from the deck. Subsequently the queen "whispers" the name of the chosen card to the magician who announces it. Upon comparison, the queen's whispered identification is found to correspond to the chosen card.

With that example in mind, as summarized in Table 3−1, let me turn to some definitions and distinctions. To remind us of the special setting of the magic trick, I will use the term "audience" to refer to the one or more observers of the particular event. I will use the term "magician" (M in the table) to refer to the individual who is identified as such by the audience and who is managing the event.

As suggested earlier, one essential property of the magic trick is that to the audience there appears to occur a sequence of events that involves an extraordinary or supernatural cause−effect relation. I will refer to this as the *Apparent Causal Sequence*, or ACS. This is shown in the left column of Table 3−1. The supernatural aspect of this sequence, as stated in step 8, is that the queen, a playing card, has seen, remembered, and whispered the identity of the chosen card. An inanimate object has apparently been able to do something that ordinarily only humans can do.

A second essential property of the magic trick is that the audience believes there to be an underlying causal sequence involving natural or ordinary cause−effect relations. In addition, in all the cases I will be considering, there is, in fact, such an underlying causal sequence. I will refer to it as the *Real Causal Sequence*, or RCS. For "The Whispering Queen" the real sequence is shown in the right-hand column. (A comparison of the two columns of Table 3−1 also shows the temporal correspondences between ACS and RCS). It should be emphasized that this is the true "real causal sequence," and not necessarily the one any member of the audience believes to be the real one.

Table 3-1. Apparent and Real Causal Sequences of "The Whispering Queen."

Step	Apparent Causal Sequence (ACS)	Real Causal Sequence (RCS)
1.	Magician (M) asks member of audience to shuffle deck for him.	
2.	M asks member to name favorite queen. M runs through deck until he comes to the designated card. M takes it from deck and lays it on table face up.	M notes and memorizes top card on deck, e.g., seven of hearts.
3.	M squares deck and cuts it into three face-down piles, arranged in a row.	M places portion of deck with top card in the middle position in the row.
4.	M asks member to choose a pile and push its top card onto table without showing the face.	M asks, "Which do you want, an end pile or a middle one?" If member chooses middle pile, M removes two end ones. If member chooses end pile, M says, "Alright, take either one you want, and I'll take the other." Top card of remaining pile, always the middle one, is pushed off onto table.
5.	M slides face-up queen under corner of chosen card. This "gives queen a chance to look at the index corner of the card."	
6.	M holds queen to member's ear saying that she will whisper the name of the card. Member fails to hear it.	
7.	M holds queen to his own ear and hears and announces the whispered message, e.g.: "seven of hearts."	M announces the card he had seen in Step 2.

Table 3-1. continued

Step	Apparent Causal Sequence (ACS)	Real Causal Sequence (RCS)
8.	M flips over the face-down card and it is shown to be the named card, the seven of hearts. Apparently the queen has seen, remembered, and whispered the chosen card.	

Source: Adapted from W.B. Gibson, *Card Magic Made Easy*, New York: Barnes and Noble, Division of Harper & Row, 1976.

The second essential property of the magic trick is that the audience believes there to exist such a sequence and, indeed, such does exist. In the successful trick, despite the audience's belief in the existence of a Real Causal Sequence that differs from the apparent one, they are not able to detect the true one.

There is a third property of the magic trick. I do not regard it as an essential property, but it is an exceedingly interesting one. This is the *story* that is woven through the Apparent Causal Sequence. The story in the "Whispering Queen" is a particularly charming one. The whispering card could be any one of the 52, but one of the face cards makes a better story. The face cards symbolize persons and these persons are pictured as having the necessary capabilities to make the ACS work: eyes, minds, mouths. The queens are particularly appropriate as helpers in the scenario: They are pictured as open (there are no one-eyed queens as there are jacks!) and, by virtue of their sex, they might be expected to be particularly helpful. And of course, a *favorite* queen is especially appropriate, especially for a male representative from the audience, because she might be expected to reciprocate his liking and be willing to whisper secrets in his ear.

I am not yet sure of the role that the story plays in a magic trick. Presently, I regard it as a nonessential property of the trick, for the reason that a given Apparent Causal Sequence can form the basis for a number of different story lines. Thus, the ACS seems a more basic concept, and it seems important to begin our analysis with it. However, there is no question that the story greatly affects the entertainment value of the trick. For this reason, magicians give great care to the development of their stories for each trick. And from a social psychological view, the story may play an important role in the central feature of the trick, which is the concealment from the audience of the true RCS.

In my present analysis, I am setting aside the story aspect and focusing upon the other two, more essential properties of the magic trick:

1. An Apparent Causal Sequence involving a supernatural cause–effect relation
2. An audience belief, justified by the facts, that there is an underlying Real Causal Sequence that involves a natural cause–effect relation.

MAGIC TRICKS AND RELATED PHENOMENA

These two properties enable us to locate our realm of analysis in relation to certain other similar phenomena. Considering only those cases where objectively there is a discrepancy between the Apparent Causal Sequence and the real one, we may form a 2 × 2 table as in Figure 3–1. One distinction is whether the apparent effect is a supernatural one or a natural one, and the second distinction is whether or not the audience (observers of the effect) believes that the apparent sequence is different from the real one. A magic trick consists of a supernatural effect that is believed to be based on an underlying Real Causal Sequence that is different from the apparent one. "Real"

Figure 3–1. Properties of the Magic Trick and Other Related Phenomena.

		Audience's Belief about Causal Sequence	
		Apparent ≠ Real	Apparent = Real
Nature of Apparent Effect	Supernatural	Magic trick	Real magic
	Natural	Science	Confidence game

MAGIC TRICKS: THE MANAGEMENT OF CAUSAL ATTRIBUTIONS   25

magic would be the case where the apparent supernatural effect is taken to reflect the real, underlying causal structure of the world. This would be illustrated by "believing" observers of a parapsychological effect (ESP or PK), who take the Apparent Causal Sequence to be the real one.

The case where the apparent effect is natural and the Apparent Causal Sequence is taken for the real one is illustrated by a confidence game. In this "game," a victim is shown that someone (the "inside man") can predict or control the outcome of a contest (horse race, stock market) through natural but corrupt means such as bribery or illegally obtained information. The victim is induced to finance a large wager on the "sure" outcome of the contest in return for a share of the winnings. In the end, something goes wrong so that the victim's money is lost. It is actually shared by the inside man and his confederates, who have staged the whole situation; ideally this is never known to the victim. In this case, the victim (the audience) has no sense that anything of an extraordinary nature is being played out and takes the Apparent Causal Sequence (by which they have an opportunity to capitalize on the corrupt knowledge or control) to be the real one.

Science often provides illustrations of the fourth cell of the figure, where there is observed a natural effect, but the audience (the scientist) suspects that the underlying real causal structure may be different from the apparent one (that the elementary structure of matter is discontinuous rather than continuous as it appears; or that observed properties are not transmitted as such from parents to progeny, as they appear to be, but that phenotypical properties reflect underlying genotypes that are the transmitted causal factors).

While Figure 3-1 suggests that the boundaries between the magic trick and its neighbors are clear, this is not the case. The line between the trick and real magic seems to blur. It is possible for an audience at least temporarily to suspend its disbelief in the ACS (its belief in a separate RCS) and to take the observed phenomena more or less at face value. It seems likely that members of the audience thereby contribute to their own entertainment, being able to experience at least briefly a sense of thrill or awe at "seeing" the supernatural in action. However, too extended or complete a suspension of disbelief probably creates some discomfort. Perhaps the greatest pleasure is derived from the trick when its ACS is taken at face value but in a "pretend" or "role-playing" way, with there being in the background a confident belief in a natural RCS that does not require confirmation or explication. A strong "problem-solving" response with a focused attempt to figure out the RCS is probably incompatible with the kind of enjoyment of the trick described (though not without its own possible rewards).

The procedures of magicians have often been used in confidence games, including the sleight of hand involved in three-card monte and procedures for switching the valise containing the victim's money, as well as the arrangements whereby the victim appears to "find" a particular thing or decides voluntarily to take some action. The con man is often simply a magician who does not reveal himself as such and who performs, not for the price of admission, but for more significant gains.

The relation between science and magic is an interesting and ever-changing one. Magicians often employ cause–effect relations known to science but unfamiliar to the layman. These encompass chemical effects (self-lighting cigarettes, color changes), topological and mathematical facts (knots, magic number squares), and even some psychological phenomena (sensory thresholds, visual illusions). With changes in the layman's knowledge and beliefs about science, the magician's problems have changed. At an earlier time, his tricks might have been confused with those of real magic. Now, they are more likely to be confused with scientific effects. That is, the apparent effect (the mysterious color change, the dissolving coin, the self-untying knot) is likely to be seen as natural rather than supernatural, and as reflecting special scientific rather than arcane knowledge. Consider, for example, the trick in which the magician M pretends to identify a card that the audience member A "chose" by detecting a fingerprint A placed on its face. The actual identification is based on a procedure similar to that in "The Whispering Queen." M's trick is not very impressive if, for all that A knows, M actually is able to see a fingerprint.

THE NATURE OF "MAGIC" EVENTS

I have defined the magic trick in terms of two essential properties: (1) an Apparent Causal Sequence involving a supernatural cause-effect relation, and (2) an audience belief, justified by the facts, that there is an underlying Real Cause Sequence that involves a natural cause-effect relation. These properties suggest several questions for our analysis: First, what Apparent Causal Sequences appear to be *supernatural*? That is, what kinds of effects appear to be "magic"? Second, what are the elements of the Real Causal Sequence? That is, what is the real basis for the trick? And third, how are the Real Causal Sequence and the key elements in it concealed from the audience? This will lead to the central question of how the structure of the ACS promotes the concealment of the RCS.

I will now turn to these three questions, taking them up in order. Space does not permit a thorough consideration of each one, but we can at least see the general form of each set of answers and in that way understand in broad outline what a thorough analysis of magic tricks may eventually tell us.

Let us first consider the nature of "magic" events. The question here is what kinds of events will appear to be supernatural—that is "... outside the normal experience or knowledge of man; not explainable by the known forces or laws of nature."

Although I cannot claim to have evolved an ideal classificatory system, at present it seems to me that two large classes of such events can be distinguished. These are shown in Table 3—2 along with some examples of each. The two large categories correspond roughly to the two types of phenomena with which attribution theory and research have dealt. These have to do with *cause-effect sequences* and *entity properties*. Certain "magic" effects constitute violations of the audience's expectations about cause-effect sequences, and others involve violations of the properties that entities are assumed to have.

Under the heading "Violations of cause-effect expectations" shown in Table 3—2 there are first the six possible ways in which the expectation that specific cause C leads to specific effect E can logically be violated. C can lead to the opposite of E (as when a fire produces something fresh and alive, like flowers, rather than something dry and dead such as ashes), or C can have no effect (as when the saw leaves no mark on the young lady who is apparently sawn in half), or C can have an unexpected effect different from E. The opposite of C leading to E is perhaps illustrated by "The Whispering Queen." It is usually animate objects that convey information by speaking, but here an inanimate object appears to do so. The case where E occurs without any apparent cause is one of the magician's favorites, illustrated by the many routines in which things appear out of thin air, candles light themselves, and so on. The case of (not C)

Table 3-2. Types of "Magic" Events in Apparent Causal Sequence.

I. Violations of cause-effect expectations

   A. Logical violations: Given an expectation that $C \to E$, then

$$C \to \text{opposite of } E$$
$$C \to \text{no effect}$$
$$C \to F \text{ (not } E\text{)}$$
$$\text{opposite of } C \to E$$
$$\text{no cause} \to E$$
$$(\text{not } C) \, D \to E$$

   B. Formal violations:
     1. Spatial or temporal contiguity (causation at distance or displaced in time)
     2. Magnitude correspondence (small cause has large effect, or vice versa)
     3. Figural similarity (effect differs figurally from cause)

II. Violations of entity properties

   A. Attributional criteria violations: Given an entity assumed to have thinglike properties, there is:
     1. Temporal inconsistency
     2. Intermodality inconsistency
     3. Lack of consensus
     4. Lack of distinctiveness

   B. Violations of thing-medium distinctions
     1. Thing is a medium
     2. Medium is a thing

$D \to E$ involves events where a familiar effect occurs for some previously irrelevant reason, as when the light bulb glows when the magician passes his hand over it.

Some of the violated expectations are more *formal* in nature, having to do not with specific $C \to E$ expectations but with formal relations and correspondences between causes and effect. Three types of this kind of effect are described in Table 3-2.

For me it is interesting to find that violations of entity properties are in part derivable from the several attributional criteria. Given an entity that is assumed to have thinglike properties, there are instances of temporal inconsistency (it disappears and reappears, or changes shape or color, for example), intermodality inconsistency (you feel it and hear it but don't see it), lack of consensus (the magician alone can perceive something that, subsequently, all can confirm), and lack of distinctiveness (an entity fails to show properties characteristic of its class or type or shows properties characteristic of some contradistinctive class, as with hypnotic effects in which a person exhibits anesthesia or amnesia or when an inanimate object moves by itself as if it were animate.) Finally, some effects seem to violate common thing–medium distinctions. On the one hand, we are able to see through a solid object, it serving as a medium for visual images in the way that the air ordinarily does. On the other hand, a medium is found to impress itself upon other things in the way that things act upon media, as when an impalpable substance leaves its mark upon a mirror or piece of paper.

From these types of effects, it will be clear that what appears to be supernatural depends upon the prior beliefs and knowledge of the audience. It is only as *their* expectations are violated that the effect can be a magic one. Thus, the nature of "magic" effects will depend upon the mental development, the cultural and scientific sophistication, and the historical era of the audience.

ELEMENTS OF THE REAL CAUSAL SEQUENCE

The key element in the Real Causal Sequence is what makes the magic trick work. Such elements are too numerous to list or classify, because almost any cause–effect relation can be employed in one trick or another. So my treatment of this topic is necessarily a superficial one.

To give a few examples; in "The Whispering Queen" the Real Causal Sequence contains two key elements: (1) the magician's observation of the top card and (2) his leading or "forcing" the member of the audience to designate that card. In card tricks generally, the magician usually either gains certain information about the deck or makes certain arrangements in it, either before or during the trick. It is also common for him to force a participant either to look at a certain card or to place a selected card in a certain position in the deck where the magician can later find it. The procedures by which a participant is led to do something while still feeling he is making a choice are obviously of interest to social psychologists inasmuch as they relate to the "illusion of freedom" that has been discussed in connection with certain social psychological experiments.

Some other key elements that I have found of particular interest have to do with manipulating thing and medium properties. A number of effects are based on presenting different but identical things as being the same thing. By presenting one coin on the left and then an identical but different one on the right, the appearance can be given of a single coin that mysteriously moves from one location to another. This effect relies on a kind of apparent movement as in the phi-phenomenon. The medium through which something is perceived is commonly manipulated as a basis for magic effects. Thus, the visual line of sight is imperceptibly disrupted or deflected in order to make things appear or disappear. Occasionally, the property that a thing imparts to a medium is mistaken for a property of the medium itself. For example, water is changed to wine and then back to water again by inserting and then removing a red plastic card, which is invisible because it exactly fits the glass and which through refraction makes the contents of the glass appear to be red.

These comments are simply to mention a few of the key causal elements that may in themselves be of special interest to psychologists. Whatever its specific nature, an important aspect of the key element is its *familiarity* to members of the audience. As we will see, this factor is important in determining the locus of the element (whether hidden or in full view) and in the structuring of the Apparent and Real Causal Sequences. In some cases, the key element is a cause–effect relation wholly unknown to the audience. This is the case with tricks based on scientific or esoteric knowledge. If the effect is strange enough to appear to be supernatural, it can be presented simply and openly, with attribution to supernatural powers or perhaps to the magician's own power. The credibility of this attribution will, of course, depend upon the knowledge of the audience about such matters. Here again we see that the ingredients of the successful magic trick must be carefully matched to the knowledge and beliefs of the audience.

In other cases the trick involves a gimmick or device that is totally unknown to the audience but that is based on familiar causal principles. An example is the "pull" device by means of which things are made to "disappear," though in fact they are drawn up the sleeve by an elastic string. And finally, in some cases, the key element is a simple device or procedure that is part of the audience's everyday experience. This is illustrated in "The Whispering Queen" by the magician's simply looking at the top card, "forcing" the member to take it, and then, later, announcing it. This last sort of causal element must, of course, be concealed from the audience. Clearly, some of the most interesting tricks are those in which the key causal element is (1) wholly familiar to the audience and (2) out in the open but, for various reasons, unnoticed.

CONCEALMENT OF THE REAL CAUSAL SEQUENCE

My third and final question concerns how the magician manages to conceal the key elements in the Real Causal Sequence.

The RCS need not always be concealed. If the key causal element is unfamiliar to the audience and if the effect is strange, the magician may simply show it to the audience and perhaps take credit for it himself.

Concealment itself means several different things in magic. In some cases the key causal element is literally concealed; it is hidden from view, up the sleeve, or invisible to the naked eye (a fine string or wire that pulls something). In other cases the key element is out in the open but not noticed for reasons I will give. And of course the audience need not literally *see* the crucial element for the trick to be spoiled. They need only vividly *imagine* or figure out the underlying mechanism, correctly or incorrectly, in order not to be "fooled." In this connection, some of the gimmicks of the magic art are interesting because they are difficult to imagine. In a sense they are unthinkable. This property seems to derive from there being a sharp *incongruity* between the audience's conception of a particular object and a property it is constructed actually to have, as is the case with a folding coin or hollow dice.

Although the gadgetry of magic holds a certain fascination, as a social psychologist I find much more interesting the structure of the Apparent Causal Sequence, and particularly its interpersonal aspects, as these promote the concealment of the Real Causal Sequence. In Table 3-3 I have listed seven aspects of the ACS that I have identified thus far as serving this concealment purpose.

First, the magician often gives false cues as to when the trick starts. These demarcate the beginning of the ACS and strongly suggest that the RCS also begins at (or after) that point in time. Thus, the audience is encouraged to process only the events from that

Table 3-3. Aspects of the Apparent Causal Sequence That Promote Concealment of the Real Causal Sequence.

1. False demarcation of start of trick
2. Providing for pseudodisruption of Real Causal Sequence
3. Discouraging relevant hypotheses about Real Causal Sequence
4. Encouraging false hypotheses about Real Causal Sequence
5. Sequence contingent on audience's behavior
6. Misdirecting attention
7. Commonplace and cooperative actions

point on in interpreting the sequence. There is no need, of course, for the RCS to be temporally coterminous with the ACS. Often the RCS has begun well before the trick is begun. Tricks can be classified on this basis. In some cases the key causal element has already been set in motion beforehand. In other cases, as in "The Whispering Queen," the sequence starts with a truly clean slate and the key causal element is introduced thereafter.

Second, the magician often provides for what appears to be a disruption of the RCS but which, in fact, is not. This procedure is particularly important when the audience suspects that the RCS is already in motion when the trick begins. The purpose of the pseudodisruption is to show that certain plausible real causes for the eventual effect are not in fact operative. Thus, in the card trick, the magician may shuffle the cards, though without truly disturbing them, or he may even risk a shuffle by a volunteer, the latter in cases where the location of the critical card is multiply indexed so it is unlikely to become detached from all its indicators.

Third, the preceding procedure illustrates a more general one, which involves steps taken to discourage various relevant hypotheses about the RCS. The magician may tap the dice to show that they are solid, when in fact they are not. Members of the audience are shown or even allowed to inspect the cabinet to show that it is empty and contains no hidden compartments, though in fact neither may be true.

Fourth, the magician may encourage a false hypothesis about the RCS. By an obvious and perhaps awkward move, he may suggest that he is managing the effect in a particular way. The audience is led to believe they are seeing through his trick — that they understand the

RCS. The denouement comes when he springs the trap on them and they discover they have been following a false, decoy RCS and have no inkling of the real one. This adds markedly to the entertainment value of the trick but, more importantly, seems to be one of the interesting ways in which attention is diverted from the true RCS.

Fifth, the sequence of events is sometimes made contingent upon the audience's behavior. This is well illustrated by "The Whispering Queen," in which the magician's instructions to the participant depend upon which one of the three piles of cards the participant chooses. The clear purpose here is to give the person a sense of having chosen a pile when in fact his choice has been neutralized and he has been forced to choose a *particular* pile. Inasmuch as the trick is only done once, this contingency is never evident to the audience. We may guess that, to the contrary, they probably have a retrospective sense that the way the sequence unrolled was the only way it could have. In other words, they probably have a sense, in relation to the trick, of the "inevitability of history."

Sixth, the misdirection of attention is an important part of the magician's art. His movement, gaze, and posture draw the audience's attention to one part of the field while he or an assistant executes effective actions elsewhere. One hand holds the attention while the other picks up, drops, or manipulates whatever is necessary for the next step in the RCS.

Finally, commonplace and cooperative actions, of the sort that go unnoticed, are often used to introduce key elements in the RCS. Here, attention is controlled not by misdirection but by the fact that these innocent and familiar actions rarely draw the attention. Examples are when the magician looks through the deck to locate the person's favorite queen for him, or when he looks through the deck "to make sure it's a full one." In either case, the magician has an opportunity to note certain key facts about the deck such as the top and bottom cards. On other occasions, the magician will use one card one he has a special interest in, to scoop up the rest of the cards. In the course of this very natural, instrumental act, he places that card in a special location. In such cases, the banality of the actions, their simple service in the common interest of having the conditions right and having the trick proceed expeditiously, enable the actions also to be used for hidden purposes without drawing any notice.

These ideas—the ones summarized in Table 3-3 and others I have mentioned in this section—are the most important outcome of our analysis. They bear on the central question of this chapter, which is how causal attributions are managed. The answer is to be found in a variety of things, even including taking credit for things that happen naturally (as Mark Twain's Connecticut Yankee proved his magic powers by "causing" an eclipse). Other instances involve inventing things with effective but incongruous properties. Most important is the management of the sequence of events, especially its interpersonal aspects, as summarized in Table 3–3.

As is true of all "experimental" work, we must be somewhat cautious in generalizing from the magic context to other attribution management settings. As I have emphasized, the management here occurs for an audience that is rather confident there is a natural explanation for the supernatural event. Furthermore, they are strictly observers of the phenomena, and the context is one of the theater. So involvement with the phenomena is rarely high, yet one must be impressed with the trick that is successful under such cool, intellectualized conditions. May not these principles be doubly effective under circumstances in which the audience has high emotional involvement in a phenomenon that has serious consequences?

CONCLUSION

Although my analysis of magic tricks is far from complete, it suggests some of the things we may eventually learn from this effort. The ideas we gain about attribution management suggest ways in which persons other than magicians—political leaders, salesmen, and others—can create false scenarios of the causes of events. Because people's reactions to events are greatly affected by their understanding of why those events occur, such attribution management can have important effects on the acceptability or unacceptability of real life experiences. If our analysis tells how some people can fool others, it may also tell us something about how nature "plays tricks" on us, leading scientists to interpret the causal structure of the world in false ways.

The magic trick may have special merits as a setting in which to study the attribution process. One central question in attribution research concerns the interplay between recent or current *information*, about a particular cause–effect relation, and preexisting conceptions or *beliefs*, pertaining to that same cause–effect relation. Magic tricks provide a variety of ways in which current evidence can be put into opposition to causal preconceptions and expectations. Therefore, tricks may provide a useful research site for investigating the basic nature of causal evidence and its collision with prior causal beliefs.

Also in relation to attribution theory, we are led to consider one of the most basic but least studied questions in our domain. This question is: "When do people ask why?" In analyzing what effects appear to be supernatural or "magic," we must certainly be identifying phenomena that stimulate people to raise attributional questions. In response to the magic trick, these questions commonly involve *how*—"How is it done?", and the explanations are sought in terms of mechanisms or processes. These correspond more closely to the physical scientist's questions than to the psychologist's motivational or intentional questions. Yet it is possible that the same basic principles apply to the two sets of questions, these being the principles, as outlined in Table 3–2, that define an event as being "unusual" or "extraordinary" and, hence, requiring explanation.

From a broader perspective, the varieties of audience reactions to magic tricks may provide useful evidence for research on motivational processes. I have only hinted at some of the motives and interests that may be involved for the audience, including the desire to be entertained (magic tricks seem to have much in common with humor), to be thrilled (perhaps), and to be challenged (in an intellectual or cognitive sense). The motives satisfied by successfully taking the role of magician also seem potentially to be important. There are certainly special satisfactions to be gained from fooling other people or even, perhaps, from placing them in awe of one's powers. There may even be derived some sense of real control over supernatural powers, particularly if the audience reaction is qualitatively one of bewilderment and respect.

Finally, our analysis has led us beyond questions of attribution management. It has raised issues of the perceived versus the real organization of behavior, and particularly the perception of social interaction. More generally, we are led to examine how the social and physical environment controls the individual's attention to and memory for events.

These brief remarks will suggest some of the benefits that social and personality psychology may derive from an analysis of magic tricks. I intend to pursue this analysis further and welcome other psychologists' similar efforts.

II ATTRIBUTION OF SUCCESS AND FAILURE

The four contributions in this part treat one of the most popular subjects in attribution research, a subject that has long attracted attention particularly in the context of achievement motivation: causal explanations of success and failure. Bernard Weiner's new chapter (which replaces his Bielefeld contribution) offers a comprehensive review of the present state of development of his theory in attributional motivation psychology, presenting, but also reformulating and updating, some earlier positions in the light of new empirical results. Weiner proceeds from a central assumption in attribution theory that the search for causes is a primary source of an individual's action, that many effects of action related mainly to achievement in the school setting and other environments of daily life call for attributional analysis. He brings to mind the variety of relevant causes and expands a taxonomy of causes he designed earlier by adding to the dimensions of locus and stability the factor of control as a third dimension. Weiner further postulates that each of these dimensions possesses both primary and secondary consequences for subsequent phenomena. He supports this portion of his model with empirical findings for *stability* (the link with expectancy change; relations to the maintenance of self-concept, resistance to extinction, and programs of achievement change), for *locus* (the relations to affect, which represent here only one of three possible sources of affects), and for *control* (in connection with the perceived control in others, he explores the relations to helping behavior, evaluation, and sentiments; in connection with the self-perception of control, he points to different relations). The contribution closes with a discussion of the theoretical range of this more general theory of motivation and documents other areas to which the theory is applicable, areas such as hyperactivity, mastery, parole decisions, affiliation, and depression.

The next chapter, by Manfred Hofer and Martin Dobrick, outlines a complex model for the teacher's control of pupil actions. In this model the teacher's attributions represent an important part of the system. The authors explain their model at the construct level and suggest ways in which their hypothesis can be verified empirically. Franz Weinert's commentary subsequently examines the model's range of generality.

The contribution by Wulf-Uwe Meyer and Fritz-Otto Plöger (which updates and replaces Meyer's Bielefeld contribution) discusses and tests the relation between expectancy and incentive that is central to Atkinson's theory of motivation. The authors propose that few of the components as Atkinson conceived them have yet been empirically represented thoroughly enough, then describe their own experiment, which is more closely allied with the assumptions of the theory. The results indicate a variety of achievement-related affects and point out the limits of provability of the relation between expectancy and incentive postulated by Atkinson. The authors also inquire into the role and the content of attribution-dependent affects.

This part's final chapter, by Wolfgang Stroebe, transcends the narrowly defined scope of achievement research to deal also with attributions of success and failure in social interaction. Stroebe demonstrates the mediating function of self-esteem in both the achievement and the social spheres, presents related concepts, and supports his hypothesis with empirical results.

4 A THEORY OF MOTIVATION FOR SOME CLASSROOM EXPERIENCES

Bernard Weiner

The attributional approach to classroom motivation and experience has proven exceedingly rich. In this chapter I examine the particular attributional path I have followed and document its richness by outlining a few of the empirical and theoretical relations that appear to be conclusive. The extensity of the theoretical network suggests that a general theory of motivation is under development.

Some of the thoughts expressed here have been voiced in previous reviews (Weiner 1972, 1974, 1976). With each opportunity to take stock of where we are, some ideas become more firmly fixed, others are discarded, and new presumptions take their place, some earlier evidence grows in stature, and other prior data require reinterpretation. There certainly is some advantage to the dictum of publish and perish, which allows one to convey his or her ideas in a single, self-contained, and final package. Like most others, however, I communicate my thoughts as they evolve, and prior questionable truths give way to new, equally uncertain laws, while other notions remain unchanged.

This article was written while the author was supported by Grant MH—25687—04 from the National Institute of Mental Health. Copyright (1979) by the American Psychological Association. Reprinted from the *Journal of Educational Psychology*, 1979, vol. 71, no. 1, 3—25.

THE SEARCH FOR CAUSES

A central assumption of attribution theory, which sets it apart from pleasure-pain theories of motivation, is that the search for understanding is the (or a) basic "spring of action." This does not imply that human beings are not pleasure-seekers, or that they never bias information in the pursuit of hedonic goals. Rather, information-seeking and veridical processing are believed to be normative, may be manifested in spite of a conflicting pleasure principle, and, at the least, comprehension stands with hedonism among the primary sources of motivation (see Meyer, Folkes, and Weiner 1976).

In a school setting the search for understanding often leads to the attributional question, "Why did I succeed (or fail)?" or, more specifically, "Why did I flunk math?" or "Why did Mary get a better mark on this exam than I?" But classrooms are environments for the satisfaction of motivations other than achievement. Thus, attributional questions also might pertain to, for example, interpersonal acceptance or rejection, such as "Why doesn't Johnny like me?" However, for the time being attention will be centered upon achievement.

Among the unknowns of this attributional analysis is a clear statement of when people ask "why" questions. It has been demonstrated that this search is more likely given failure (rejection) than success (acceptance) (Folkes 1978). Furthermore, it is plausible to speculate that unexpected events are more likely to lead to "why" questions than expected events (Lau and Russell 1978) and that subjective importance also will influence the pursuit of knowledge. Finally, it has been demonstrated that during task performance "failure-oriented" or "helpless" students especially tend to supply attributions (Diener and Dweck 1978). Diener and Dweck also intimate that a subset of students, called "mastery-oriented," do not engage in attribution-making. However, I suspect that attributional inferences often are quite retrospective, summarize a number of experiences, take place below a level of immediate awareness, and are intimately tied with self-esteem and self-concept. Thus, I believe that attributions are supplied by the mastery-oriented students as well, although not necessarily during or immediately following all task performances.

An initial statement by myself and Frieze, Kukla, Reed, Rest, and Rosenbaum (1971) regarding the perceived causes of success and failure was guided by Heider (1958) as well as by our own intuitions.

We postulated that in achievement-related contexts the causes perceived as most responsible for success and failure are ability, effort, task difficulty, and luck. That is, in attempting to explain his or her prior success or failure at an achievement-related event, the individual assesses his or her level of ability, the amount of effort that was expended, the difficulty of the task, and the magnitude and direction of experienced luck. We assumed that rather general values are assigned to these factors and that the task outcome is differentially ascribed to the causal sources. In a similar manner, future expectations of success and failure would then be based upon one's perceived level of ability in relation to the perceived difficulty of the task (labeled by Heider as *can*), as well as an estimation of the intended effort and anticipated luck.

In listing the four causes we did not intend to convey that they were the *only* perceived determinants of success or failure, or even that they were the most salient ones in all achievement situations. In later work (e.g., Weiner 1974; Weiner, Russell, and Lerman 1978), we explicitly indicated that factors such as mood, fatigue, illness, and bias could serve as necessary and/or sufficient reasons for achievement performance. Research restricting causality to the other four causes at times might give rise to false conclusions. For example, assume that one is testing the hedonic bias notion that success primarily is self-ascribed. By not including help from others, for example, among the alternative causes, the hedonic bias hypothesis might be supported because the given external causes (task difficulty and luck) do not adequately capture the phenomenology of the subject.

In the last few years intuition has given way to empirical studies attempting to identify the perceived causes of success and failure. At least four investigations of *academic* attributions (Elig and Frieze 1975; Frieze 1976; Bar-Tal and Darom 1977; Cooper and Burger 1978) have been conducted, and there undoubtedly are many more unknown to me. There have been a number of studies that examine attributions outside of the classroom context, dealing with work experiences and athletics, for example. The methodologies of the classroom inquiries have minor variations, with students or teachers stating the causes of success or failure at real or imagined events and judging themselves or others. The responses are then categorized and tabulated.

Cooper and Burger (1978) provide a concise summary of the data from three of the studies (see Table 4–1). It is evident that ability, effort (both typical and immediate), and task difficulty are among

Table 4-1. Summary of Previous Coding Systems (adapted from Cooper and Burger 1978).

Frieze (1976)	Bar-Tal and Darom (1977)	Cooper and Burger (1978)
Ability	Ability	Academic ability
Stable effort	Effort during test	Physical and emotional ability
Immediate effort	Preparation at home	Previous experience
Task	Interest in the subject matter	Habits
Other person	Difficulty of the test	Attitudes
Mood	Difficulty of material	Self-perceptions
Luck	Conditions in the home	Maturity
Other		Typical effort
		Effort in preparation
		Attention
		Directions
		Instruction
		Task
		Mood
		Family
		Other students
		Miscellaneous

Source: *The Journal of Educational Psychology*, 1979, vol. 71, no. 1, p. 5. Reprinted by permission.

the main perceived causes of achievement performance. Thus, the prior intuitions of Heider (1958) and my colleagues and me were not incorrect. In addition, Table 4-1 shows that others (teachers, students, and family), motivation (attention and interest), and what Cooper and Burger label acquired characteristics (habits and attitudes) and physiological processes (mood, maturity, and health) comprise the central determinants of success and failure. Luck is not included with the dominant causes but could be prominent on specific occasions, particularly in career or athletic accomplishments (see Mann 1974).

In sum, there are a myriad of perceived causes of achievement events. In a cross-cultural study it was even reported that patience (in Greece and Japan) and tact and unity (in India) are perceived as causes of success and failure (Triandis 1972). But there is a rather small list from which the main causes repeatedly are selected. Furthermore, within this list ability and effort appear to be the most salient and general of the causes. That is, outcomes frequently depend upon what we can do and how hard we try to do it. A clear conceptual analysis of only ability and effort would greatly add to our knowledge, given an attributional perspective.

Before moving on to this conceptual formulation, it should be recognized that Table 4-1 presents only a description of the perceived reason for success and failure in achievement settings. Although attribution theory often is referred to as a naive conception, using the language of the person on the street, it also has been appreciated that science has to go beyond mere phenomenology. That is, order must be imposed using scientific terminology that may not be part of the logic of the layperson. This is implicit in, for example, the work of Kelley (1967, 1971). Heider also clearly acknowledged the distinction between a naive psychology and a scientific psychology when he stated, "There is no prior reason why the causal description (scientific language) should be the same as the phenomenal description (naive language), though, of course, the former should adequately account for the latter" (Heider 1958: 22).

I now turn from the layperson's perception of causality to the scientific language that is imposed on these causes. In this chapter I completely neglect the process by which causal beliefs are reached, although this is the most common problem in the attributional field and is what is meant by the attribution process (see Kelley 1967, 1971; Weiner 1974). This void is left so that full space can be devoted to the psychological consequences of perceived causality, the topic most central to my concerns.

DIMENSIONS OF CAUSALITY

Inasmuch as the list of conceivable causes of success and failure is infinite, it is essential to create a classification scheme or a taxonomy of causes. In so doing, similarities and differences are delineated and the underlying properties of the causes are identified. This is an indispensable requirement for the construction of an attributional theory of motivation.

The prior theoretical analyses of Rotter (1966) and Heider (1958) were available to serve as our initial guides in this endeavor. Rotter and his colleagues proposed a one-dimensional classification of causality. Causes were either within (internal) or outside (external to) the person. In a similar manner, Heider (1958) as well as De Charms (1968), Deci (1975), and many others have articulated an internal–external classification of causality. Rotter labeled this dimension locus of control, whereas in the present context locus is conceived as a backward-looking belief and therefore is referred to as *locus* of causality. Indeed, I contend that the concepts of locus and control must be separated.

The causes listed in Table 4–1 can be readily catalogued as internal or external to the individual. From the perspective of the student, the personal causes include ability, effort, mood, maturity, and health, while teacher, task, and family are among the external sources of causality. But the relative placement of a cause on this dimension is not invariant over time or between people. For example, health might be perceived as an internal ("I am a sickly person") or as an external ("The 'flu bug' got me") cause of failure. Inasmuch as attribution theory deals with phenomenal causality, such personal interpretations must be taken into account. That is, the taxonomic placement of a cause depends upon its subjective meaning. Nonetheless, in spite of possible individual variation, there is general agreement when distinguishing causes as internal or external.

A second dimension of causality, which we have come to perceive as increasingly important, is labeled *stability* (Weiner et al. 1971). The stability dimension defines causes on a stable (invariant) versus unstable (variant) continuum. Again Heider (1958) served as our guide, for he contrasted dispositional and relatively fixed characteristics such as ability with fluctuating factors such as effort and luck. Examining Table 4–1, ability, typical effort, and family would be considered relatively fixed, whereas immediate effort, attention, and mood are more unstable. Effort and attention may be augmented or decreased from one episode to the next, whereas mood is conceived as a temporary state. However, as indicated previously, the perceived properties of a cause can vary. For example, mood might be thought of as a temporary state or as a permanent trait. In addition, experimenters can alter the perceived properties of a cause. For example, although difficulty level of a task generally is considered a stable characteristic (Weiner et al. 1971), Valle and Frieze (1976) portrayed task difficulty as unstable by anchoring this concept to assigned sales territory, which could be shifted for any salesperson. At times task difficulty is classified as stable, while the experimental manipulation strongly suggests that subjects would perceive this factor as unstable (see Riemer 1975).

Still a third dimension of causality that was identified by Heider and later incorporated into the achievement domain by Rosenbaum

(1972) was labeled *intentionality*. Causes such as effort or the bias of a teacher or supervisor were categorized as intentional, whereas ability, the difficulty of the task, mood, and so on were specified by Rosenbaum to be unintentional.

In prior writings this distinction was accepted (e.g., Weiner 1974, 1976). But following a suggestion of Litman-Adizes (1977), it is now apparent that Rosenbaum (1972) mislabeled this dimension. Rosenbaum argued that the dimension of intentionality is needed to differentiate, for example, mood from effort. Both of these are internal and unstable causes, yet intuitively they are quite distinct. Rosenbaum invoked the intent dimension to describe this difference, with mood classified as unintentional and effort classified as intentional. However, it seems that the dimension Rosenbaum had identified was that of control. Failure attributed to a lack of effort does not signify that there was an intent to fail. Intent connotes a desire, or want. Rather, effort differs from mood in that only effort is perceived as subject to volitional control. Hence, I propose that a third dimension of causality categorizes causes as *controllable* versus *uncontrollable*.

Causes theoretically can be classified within one of eight cells (2 levels of locus × 2 levels of stability × 2 levels of control). Among the internal causes, ability is stable and uncontrollable; typical effort is stable and controllable; mood, fatigue, and illness are unstable and uncontrollable; and temporary exertion is unstable and controllable. Among the external causes, task difficulty is stable and uncontrollable; teacher bias may be perceived as stable and controllable; luck is unstable and uncontrollable; and unusual help from others is unstable and controllable (see Table 4−2).

Some problems with this classification scheme remain unsolved, particularly among the external causes. For example, can an external cause be perceived as controllable? The answer to this question depends on how far back one goes in a causal inference chain as well as whether controllability assumes only the perspective of the actor, which is not the case in Table 4−2 (for instance, teacher bias may be controllable from the vantage point of the teacher, but not given the perspective of the pupil). These questions, as well as the proposed independence of the dimensions, are difficult issues for future thought and research.

Although the main dimensions of causality in achievement-related contexts may have been identified, other dimensions are likely to emerge with further analysis and will raise additional problems about

Table 4-2. Causes of Success and Failure Classified According to Locus, Stability, and Controllability.

Controllability	Internal		External	
	Stable	Unstable	Stable	Unstable
Uncontrollable	Ability	Mood	Task difficulty	Luck
Controllable	Typical effort	Immediate effort	Teacher bias	Unusual help from others

Source: The Journal of Educational Psychology, 1979, vol. 71, no. 1, p. 7.

the independence of the dimensions. Intention may be one of these dimensions and logically could be separable from control (although causes are certain to correlate highly on these two dimensions). A causal statement regarding a neglected homework assignment illustrating the separation of intent from control is "I wanted to study, but could not control myself from going out." A conceptually similar example disassociating intent from control concerns a criminal who does not want to commit a crime but cannot control the compulsion. Criminal justice also accepts the possibility of control without intent, as in negligence.

Still another possible dimension of causality, identified by Abramson, Seligman, and Teasdale (1978), has been labeled *globality*. The global versus specific ends of this dimension capture the concept of stimulus generalization (while stability expresses temporal generalization). For example, one's ability may be perceived as task-specific ("I failed because I am poor at math") or as a general trait influencing performance in a wide variety of settings ("I failed because I am dumb").

The dimensions of causality introduced above were derived from a logical examination of perceived causes. More recently, a number of investigators have employed techniques such as factor analysis or multidimensional scaling to discover the dimensions of causality (see, for example, J.P. Meyer 1978; Passer 1977; Michela, Peplau, and Weeks 1978). In the inceptive study by Passer, male and female subjects rated the similarity of the causes of either success or failure. Eighteen causes were presented in all possible pairs to the subjects. The similarity judgments provided the input for a multidimensional scaling procedure. This method is akin to a cluster analysis and depicts the underlying judgment dimensions.

Passer found two clear dimensions of causality: (1) a locus dimension, anchored at the internal end with causes such as bad mood and no self-confidence and at the external extreme with causes such as "bad teacher" and "hard exam"; and (2) an intentional-unintentional dimension (which I will call controllable-uncontrollable), anchored at the controllable end with causes such as "never studies," "hard," and "lazy," and at the uncontrollable extreme with "nervous" and "bad mood." The findings reported by Passer (1977) were similar for males and females in both the success and failure scaling solutions.

The proposed third dimension of causality, stability, was not displayed. Nevertheless, Passer's results are encouraging in that two of the three dimensions that had been presumed did emerge, and other unanticipated dimensions that had not been part of the logical analysis did not appear.

The data reported by Michela, Peplau, and Weeks (1978) were equally promising. Although they were concerned with the causes of loneliness, two familiar dimensions emerged in their study: stability and locus. There was some indication that control also appeared in the data, although it did not come through as an independent dimension and was more evident among the internal causes. This suggests that perhaps control cannot be paired with externality.

The investigation by J.P. Meyer (1978) provides the best evidence for the dimensions portrayed in Table 4-2. Meyer gave subjects information relevant to the judgment of the causes of success and failure, such as past history and social norms (Kelley 1967). The subjects then rated nine possible causes of the outcomes, including ability, effort, task difficulty, luck, mood, and teacher. A factor analysis of these ratings yielded the three dimensions suggested in Table 4-2.

It therefore appears that what dimensions emerge in part depends on the empirical procedure that is used. Given a multidimensional scaling method where subjects rate the similarity of the causes, the dimensions generated by the logical analysis may not be identical to those emerging with the empirical procedure. For example, as shown in the Passer (1977) data, a naive person may not spontaneously recognize that mood, luck, and effort are similar because they are unstable, and thus a stability dimension of causality will not be evident. On the other hand, factor-analytic procedures are not subject to this limitation, and as J.P. Meyer (1978) has demonstrated, this procedure has yielded results fully supporting the logical analysis. For the scientist these dimensions are second-order concepts (Schütz 1967: 59); they are concepts used by attribution theorists to organize the causal concepts of the layperson.

CONSEQUENCES OF CAUSAL PROPERTIES

I turn now from the dimensions of causality to the consequences or the implications of these dimensions for thought and action. I contend that each of the three dimensions of causality has a primary psychological function or linkage, as well as a number of secondary effects. The primary relation of the *stability* dimension is to the magnitude of expectancy change following success or failure. The *locus* dimension of causality has implications for self-esteem, one of the emotional consequences of achievement performance; affect also is a secondary association for causal stability. The dimensional linkages with expectancy and affect (value) integrate attribution theory with expectancy-value formulations of motivation as outlined by Atkinson (1964), Lewin (1935), and others (see Weiner 1972, 1974), although this unification is not examined here. Finally, perceived *control* by others relates to helping, evaluation, and liking. The theory thus addresses both self- and other-perception and intra- as well as interpersonal behavior. The locus and control dimensions have a number of secondary effects that also will be very briefly considered.

STABILITY

The primary conceptual linkage of the stability dimension with expectancy of success was first explored by Weiner et al. (1971) and has not greatly changed since that time (see Weiner 1972, 1974, 1976). I now more fully perceive the implications of this association, other secondary linkages with causal stability have been uncovered, and the empirical data have grown in clarity. But the following discussion is consistent with prior statements and is partially redundant with these earlier writings.

Research in the attributional domain has proven definitively that causal ascriptions for past performance are an important determinant of goal expectancies. For example, failure that is ascribed to low ability or to the difficulty of a task decreases the expectation of future success more than failure that is ascribed to bad luck, mood, or a lack of immediate effort. In a similar manner, success ascribed to good luck or extra exertion results in lesser increments in the subjective expectancy of future success at that task than does success ascribed to high ability or to the ease of the task. More generally expectancy shifts after success and failure are dependent upon the perceived stability of the cause of the prior outcome; ascription of an outcome to stable factors produces greater typical shifts in expectancy (increments in expectancy after success and decrements after failure) than do ascriptions to unstable causes. Stated somewhat differently, if one attains success (or failure) and if the conditions or causes of that outcome are perceived as remaining unchanged, then success (or failure) will be anticipated with a greater degree of certainty. But if the conditions or causes are subject to change, then there is some doubt that the prior outcome will be repeated.

Empirical Evidence

A large number of research investigations support the foregoing theoretical contentions (see Fontaine 1974; McMahan 1973; J.P. Meyer 1978; Ostrove 1978; Rosenbaum 1972; Valle 1974; Valle and Frieze 1976; Weiner, Nierenberg, and Goldstein 1976; W.-U. Meyer 1970; Pancer and Eiser 1975). In the Weiner et al. (1976) investigation, it was demonstrated that expectancy changes are related to the dimension of stability and are not associated with the locus of causality. This is an important finding, not only because two attributional dimensions are discriminated, but also because a vast competing literature relates expectancy changes to the dimension of locus (see Weiner et al. 1976 for a review).

Weiner et al. (1976) gave subjects either zero, one, two, three, four, or five consecutive success experiences at a block-design task, with different subjects in the six experimental conditions. Following the success trial(s), expectancy of success and causal ascriptions were assessed. Expectancy of future success was determined by having subjects indicate "How many of the next ten similar designs you believe that you will successfully complete" (Weiner et al. 1976: 61). To assess perceptions of causality, subjects were required to mark four rating scales that were identical with respect to either the stability or locus dimensional anchors but differing along the alternate dimension. Specifically, one attribution question was, "Did you succeed on this task because you are always good at these kinds of tasks, or because you tried especially hard on this particular task?" "Always good" and "tried hard," the anchors on this scale, are identical on the locus of causality dimension (internal), but they differ in perceived stability, with ability a stable attribute and effort an unstable cause. In a similar manner, judgments were made between "lucky" and "tried hard" (unstable causes differing in locus), "these tasks are always easy" and "lucky" (external causes differing in stability), and "always good" and "always easy" (stable causes differing in locus). Thus, the judgments permitted a direct test of the locus versus stability interpretation of expectancy change.

Expectancy estimates were examined separately for each of the causal judgments. The data revealed that within both the internal and the external causes, expectancy increments were positively associated with the stability of the ascription; that is, there were higher expectancies given ability and task ease ascriptions than given effort or luck attributions. Contrasting locus of causality differences within either the stable or the unstable ascriptions disclosed that the disparate causal locus groups did not differ in their expectancies of success.

Locus of Control Controversy

One of my disappointments has been that investigators associated with social learning theory and locus of control have failed to recognize or admit the stability-expectancy linkage and the existence of other dimensions of perceived causality. Some researchers (such as Lefcourt, von Baeyer, Ware, and Cox 1978) are incorporating the stability dimension into perceived causality scales. But this is in contrast with the position of other investigators. For example, Phares states, "At the present time there does not appear to be a convincing body of data supporting the utility of adding the stability dimension.... Even should the addition of stability find support in laboratory studies of expectancy changes, it is not at all clear that ...

[broader] demonstrations of utility will be forthcoming" (1978: 270).

In opposition to this statement, the literature associating stability with expectancy change is unequivocal, and the findings generalize outside of the laboratory as well as beyond the achievement domain (as will be documented later). It may indeed be that the concept of locus of control has great utility; my modest hope is that individuals in this area will acknowledge some of the prior shortcomings in their conceptual analysis of expectancy shifts at skill and chance tasks and in their limited approach to causality (for a fuller discussion of these issues, see Weiner et al. 1976).

Formal Analysis and Self-Concept Maintenance

McMahan (1973) and Valle and Frieze (1976) have developed formal models of expectancy shifts based upon the concept of causal stability. Valle and Frieze postulate that predictions of expectancies P are a function of the initial expectancy E plus the degree to which outcomes O are attributed to stable causes S:

$$P = f\{E + O \ [f(S)]\}$$

In addition, Valle and Frieze (1976) also note that the perceived causes of success and failure are related to the initial expectancy of success. It has been clearly documented that unexpected outcomes lead to unstable attributions, particularly luck (Feather 1969; Feather and Simon 1971; Frieze and Weiner 1971). Hence, Valle and Frieze conclude, "There is some value for the difference between the initial expectations and the actual outcome that will maximally change a person's predictions for the future. If the difference is greater than this point, the outcome will be attributed to unstable factors to such a great extent that it will have less influence on the person's future predictions" (1976: 581).

These ideas have important implications for the maintenance of one's self-concept and for attributional change programs (see Weiner 1974, 1976). For example, assume that an individual with a high self-concept of ability believes that he or she has a high probability of success at a task. It is probable that failure then would be ascribed to unstable causes such as luck or mood, which may not reduce the subsequent expectancy of success and sustains a high ability self-concept. On the other hand, success would be ascribed to ability, which increases the subsequent expectancy (certainty) of success and confirms one's high self-regard. The converse analysis holds given a low self-concept of ability and a low expectancy of success: Success would be ascribed to unstable factors, and failure to low ability. These attributions result in the preservation of the initial self-concept (see Ames 1978; Fitch 1970; Gilmore and Minton 1974; Ickes and Layden 1978). In addition, the preceding analysis suggests that in change programs involving expectancies or self-concept the perceived causes of performance must be altered, and a modification in self-perception would have to involve a gradual process (Valle and Frieze, 1976).

In one research investigation guided by the foregoing reasoning, Ames, Ames, and Garrison (1977) had children of high or low social status in the classroom attribute causality for positive and negative interpersonal outcomes. For example, the children were given situations such as, "Suppose you meet a new student at school and you become friends quickly"; or "Imagine you ask someone to play with you after school, but they say they cannot play." The children then attributed causality for each situation either to an internal, an external, or a mutual cause. The data indicated that given negative interpersonal outcomes, high-social-status children made greater use of external causal ascriptions, and given positive interpersonal outcomes, they made more internal attributions than the low-social-status pupils.

Resistance to Extinction and Achievement Change

The stability concept is generalizable to the body of psychological literature concerning experimental extinction (see Rest 1976). Experimental extinction often is defined as the cessation of a previously instrumental response following the permanent withholding of the reward. It is reasonable to presume that when a response is perceived as no longer instrumental to goal attainment, the organism will cease making that response. Hence, any attribution that maximizes the expectation that the response will not be followed by the goal should facilitate extinction. On the other hand, attributions that minimize goal expectancy decrements after nonreward should retard extinction.

As discussed already, the stability or instability of the perceived causal factors influences the expectancy that the outcome of an action might change in the future. Therefore, I suggest that resistance to extinction is a function of attributions to the causal dimension of stability during the period of nonreinforcement. Ascriptions of nonreinforcement to bad luck, lack of immediate effort, or other unstable causes are hypothesized to minimize expectancy decrements and result in slower extinction than attributions of nonattainment of a goal to perceived stable factors, such as teacher bias, high task difficulty, or lack of ability. Rest (1976) has presented strong evidence confirming these hypotheses. Inasmuch as random reinforcement schedules elicit unstable causal attributions (Weiner et al. 1971), they also should (and do) increase resistance to extinction. In a similar manner, chance rather than skill instructions also increase resistance to extinction (Phares 1957), presumably because failure is ascribed to unstable causes only given the chance instructions.

A related notion is that information generating lack-of-effort ascriptions for failure also should result in response maintenance (see Rest 1976). There are data in the infrahuman experimental literature that may be interpreted as supporting this hypothesis. Lawrence and Festinger (1962), marshalling evidence to support their cognitive dissonance explanation of extinction, report that resistance to extinction is positively related to the effortfulness of a response. Our analysis suggests that when great exertion is required to attain a reward the salience of effort as the cause of goal attainment is augmented. Thus, the expectancy of reward following nonattainment of the goal should be comparatively unchanged and extinction prolonged. With repeated nonreward, however, the ascription shifts from effort to ability and/or task difficulty, thus decreasing expectancy and promoting extinction.

These ideas have more than just a passing relevance to educational practices. Many of the burgeoning achievement-change programs make direct or indirect use of attributional principles. These programs often attempt to induce students to attribute their failures to a lack of effort, which is both unstable and under volitional control (see Andrews and Debus 1978; Chapin and Dyck 1976; Dweck 1975). This goal is expressly established for "failure-oriented" children who apparently ascribe their failures to a lack of ability, which is a stable and uncontrollable cause (see Diener and Dweck 1978). Presumably, inasmuch as effort can be increased volitionally, ascriptions of nonattainment of a goal to lack of effort will result in the sustaining of hope and increased persistence toward the goal. On the other hand, since ability is stable and not subject to volitional control, ascription of nonattainment of a goal to low ability results in giving up and the cessation of goal-oriented behavior.

In sum, it is suggested that the relations between diverse independent variables (reward schedules, effortfulness of the response, and certain attributional biases) and the dependent variables of resistance to extinction or persistence in goal-related behavior are mediated by perceptions of causality:

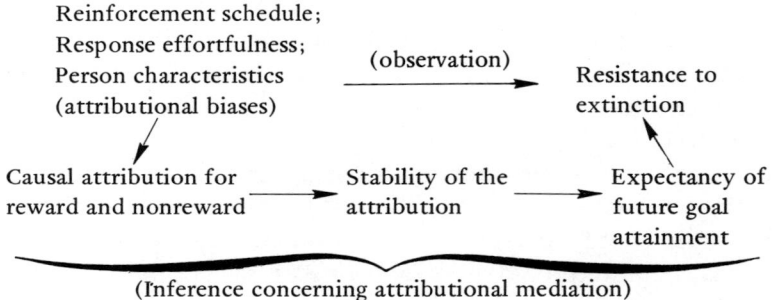

LOCUS

In contrast with the rather stable beliefs about causal stability, our thoughts concerning locus of causality have fluctuated greatly. A temporary resolution is proposed here that is a synthesis of our previous antithetical positions and better accounts for the complexity of human affective responses.

Initially, my colleagues and I (Weiner et al. 1971) postulated that locus of causality is related to the affective consequences of success and failure. Emotional reactions were believed to be maximized given internal attributions for success and failure and minimized given external attributions. Thus, for example, pride and shame, the alleged dominant affects in achievement situations (Atkinson 1964; McClelland, Atkinson, Clark, and Lowell 1953), would be most experienced given personal responsibility for success and failure, as opposed to instances in which external factors such as luck or others were perceived as the causal agents. This postulated relation seemed intuitively reasonable, was consistent with Atkinson's (1964) formulations concerning the incentive value of success and failure, and found support in a variety of research investigations. Because I have presented a detailed account of this position elsewhere (Weiner 1977), I will not discuss it in any further detail.

Subsequently, it became evident that it is incorrect to presume an invariant positive relation between internality and the magnitude of emotional reactions in achievement settings. For example, failure ascribed to others, such as the bias of a teacher or hindrance from students or family, will presumably generate great anger and hostility. In this event, externality is positively related to emotional intensity. Thus, the position expressed in Weiner et al. (1971) cannot be correct (see Weiner 1977; Weiner et al. 1978).

We therefore initiated a series of studies to determine the relation between attribution and affect (Weiner et al. 1978; Weiner, Russell, and Lerman 1979). In our first investigation, subjects were given a scenario that depicted a success or failure experience at an exam, along with a causal attribution for that outcome (for example, Joan failed because she did not have the ability). The subjects then reported the affects that they surmised would be experienced in this situation. About 100 affects for success and 150 for failure were provided, with responses made on rating scales indicating the intensity with which the affects would be experienced.

There were two general findings of interest. First, there was a set of outcome-dependent, attribution-independent affects that represented broad positive or negative reactions to success and failure, regardless of the "why" of the outcome. Given success, feelings of pleasure, happiness, satisfaction, goodness, and so on were reported as equally experienced in the disparate attribution conditions. In a similar manner, given failure, there were a number of outcome-linked emotions, such as feeling uncheerful, displeased, and upset. The outcome-dependent affects for both success and failure were reported as the ones that would be most intensely experienced.

But for both success and failure there were many emotions discriminably related to specific attributions. Given success, the unique attribution-affect linkages were the following: ability-competence and confidence; typical effort-relaxation; immediate effort-activation; others-gratitude; personality-conceit; and luck-surprise. That is, if one perceived that success was caused by ability, then competence and confidence were reported as intensely experienced; if one succeeded because of help from others, then the dominant reported affect was gratitude; and so on. In a similar manner, for failure, the attribution-affect linkages were the following: ability-incompetence; effort-guilt and shame; personality-resignation; others-aggression; and luck-surprise (see Weiner et al. 1978).

It is of interest to point out that at times causal attributions yield opposite reactions for success and failure, as would be expected given diametric outcomes (respectively, competence versus incompetence given ability attributions; gratitude versus aggression for attributions to others). But at times the same emotion accompanies both positive and negative outcomes (surprise given a luck attribution); and given still other ascriptions, such as typical or immediate effort, the emotions that accompany success (respectively, relaxation and activation) are unrelated to the failure-tied affects (guilt and shame).

These data suggested we should reject the supposition that locus of causality mediates affective reactions in achievement contexts. Rather, emotions appeared to be either outcome-generated or attributionally generated, without any intervening dimensional placement.

Additional evidence, however, has resulted in a synthesis of our prior antithetical stances. In a recent study (Weiner, Russell, and Lerman 1979) subjects recreated a "critical incident" in their lives in which they succeeded (or failed) at an academic exam because of ability, typical effort, immediate effort, help (or hindrance) from others, personality, or luck. They then listed three affects they experienced in this situation. Table 4-3 includes only the emotions that were reported for *success* by more than 10 percent of the respondents for any particular attribution. The table shows the percentage of subjects in all the attribution conditions reporting these relatively shared experiences.

The data in Table 4-3 are consistent with our previous findings. The most dominant affect, happiness, is expressed regardless of the reason for the success. In addition to this outcome-linked emotion, there are significant attribution-affect linkages. These associations are as follows: ability-competence and pride; other people-gratefulness and thankfulness; stable effort-contentment; personality-pride; and luck-surprise, relief, and guilt (the linkages are based on comparisons within an emotion but across attributions).

The failure data also revealed systematic patterns. There were significant outcome-linked emotions including disappointment, as well as attribution-affect associations consistent with prior research;

Table 4-3. Percentage of Respondents Stating a Particular Emotion for Success, as a Function of the Attribution for Success.

Emotion	Causal Attribution					
	Ability	Unstable Effort	Stable Effort	Personality	Others	Luck
Competence	30	12	20	19	5	2
Confidence	20	19	18	19	14	2
Contentment	4	4	12	0	7	2
Excitement	3	9	8	11	16	6
Gratefulness	9	1	4	8	43	14
Guilt	1	3	0	3	2	18
Happiness	44	43	43	38	46	48
Pride	39	28	39	43	21	8
Relief	4	28	16	11	13	26
Satisfaction	19	24	16	14	9	0
Surprise	7	16	4	14	4	52
Thankfulness	0	1	0	0	18	4

Source: The Journal of Educational Psychology, 1979, vol. 71, no. 1, p. 13.

ability-incompetence and resignation; effort-guilt; other people-anger; and luck-surprise.

Additional analyses of these data also demonstrated that causal dimensions play an essential role in affective life. Given internal attributions for success (ability, effort, personality), the affects pride, competence, confidence, and satisfaction were reported more frequently than they were given external attributions (others, luck). Internal ascriptions for failure generated the emotions of guilt and resignation. In sum, particular affects clustered with the internal causes. Reanalysis of Weiner et al. (1978) revealed virtually identical results.

It therefore appears that in achievement situations there are (at least) three sources of affect. First, there are emotions tied directly to the outcome. One feels "good" given success and "bad" given failure, regardless of the reason for the outcome. These probably are the initial and strongest reactions. Second, accompanying these general feelings are more distinct emotions, such as gratitude or hostility if success or failure, respectively, is due to others, surprise when the outcome is due to luck, and so on. Third, the affects that are associated with self-esteem, such as competence, pride, and shame, are mediated by self-ascriptions. Many emotional reactions are shared given success due to ability or effort, the two dominant internal attributions. It therefore may be that the central self-esteem emotions that facilitate or impede subsequent achievement performance are dimensionally linked, referred by the actor to himself or herself. Some affects thus seem to be mediated by the locus dimension, but in a manner much more complex than was originally posited. It is likely that these dimension-linked affects have the greatest longevity and most significance for the individual.

Stability and Affect

In addition to the locus–affect linkage, there also is a relation between causal stability and emotions. My colleagues and I (Weiner et al. 1978) found that the affects of depression, apathy, and resignation were reported primarily given internal and stable attributions for failure (lack of ability, lack of typical effort, personality deficit). This suggests that only attributions conveying that events will not change in the future beget feelings of helplessness, giving up, and depression. Perhaps the control dimension also plays a role in generating these particular emotions. Hence, the dimensions of causality relate to different sets of emotions.

In another research investigation supporting a stability–emotion union, Arkin and Maruyama (1979) assessed students' attributions for their success or failure in a college course. In addition, anxiety associated with school performance was measured. It was found that among successful students, the stability of their attributions was negatively correlated with anxiety. That is, when success was ascribed to stable causes, students reported relatively little anxiety. On the other hand, among the unsuccessful students, attributional stability and anxiety correlated positively; most fear was reported when failure was perceived as likely to recur in the future.

Cognition-Emotion Sequence in Achievement Contexts

On the basis of the foregoing discussion, I suggest that in achievement-related contexts (and, in particular, school settings), the actor progresses through something like the following cognition-emotion scenarios:

1. "I just received a D in the exam. That is a very low grade." (This generates feelings of being frustrated and upset.) "I received this grade because I did not try hard enough" (followed by feelings of shame and guilt). "There really is something lacking in me, and it is permanent" (followed by low self-esteem or lack of worth and hopelessness).

2. "I just received an A on the exam. That is a very high grade" (generating happiness and satisfaction). "I received this grade because I worked very hard during the entire school year" (producing contentment and relaxation). "I really do have some positive qualities, and will continue to have them in the future" (followed by high self-esteem and feelings of self-worth, as well as optimism for the future).

Some Thoughts about Feelings

Psychology is completing two movements that have relatively neglected the study of affect. The first is the behavioristic period, which denied verbal report data; the second is the cognitive movement, which focuses on intellective structures. In contrast to these periods, I believe that psychologists and educators now will turn to the study of affect.

At present many of the investigations of affect in the schools measure some global feeling state such as "satisfaction." But for the study of emotions greater differentiation must be allowed. For example, one might speculate that differential classroom "atmospheres" provide the opportunity for the experiencing of disparate emotions. Perhaps settings that promote internal ascriptions maximize positive or negative self-images and feelings of pride and shame. On the other hand, environments that permit more student interaction enhance feelings such as gratitude and anger, inasmuch as attributions of success and failure to others are promoted. Overall satisfaction ratings mask distinctions between, for example, pride and gratitude. It is time that closer attention was paid to affective life in the classroom.

Secondary Linkages

Because of the vast literature in the locus of control area, it might be anticipated that causal locus is directly linked with many pychological reactions in addition to esteem-related affects. This indeed is likely to be the case. For example, it has been reported that locus of control relates positively to behaviors such as information-seeking and to experiences such as feeling like an "origin" [as opposed to feeling like a "pawn" in DeCharms' (1968) terminology of personal causation—Ed.]. In most of this research, however, the concepts of locus and control are united. It is not reasonable to expect individuals who attribute failure to a lack of ability, which is internal but uncontrollable, to seek out information or feel like origins. Rather, it seems that the experiential state of an origin and correlated behaviors are exhibited because of the perceived personal control of the situation, or the belief that causality is both internal and controllable. Thus, the discussion of the secondary linkages with locus is postponed until the presentation of the control dimension of causality.

CONTROL

Attribution theory as formulated by Heider (1958), Jones and Davis (1965), and Kelley (1967) primarily concerns person perception, or inferences about the intentions and dispositions of others. But thus far in this chapter I have only been concerned with self-perception. I believe that one of the main contributions of work in this field has been the adaptation of some principles of social perception for the construction of a theory of motivation that has the individual as the unit of analysis.

In the discussion of the implications of causal dimensions, self- and other-perception were not distinguished. Considering changes in the expectancy of success, the same cause–effect logic pertaining to causal stability should hold when considering oneself or others. The discussion of affect also is equally applicable to both the self and others, although of course the emotional experiences are limited to the self and inferred about others. But if success or failure is perceived as being due to certain causes, then particular affective experiences should follow.

The following examination of the dimension of control centers upon inferences about others and how beliefs about another's responsibility for success and failure influence an actor's reactions toward that person. The reactions examined are helping, evaluation, and sentiments.

Helping

Ickes and Kidd (1976), guided by Weiner et al. (1971) and Rosenbaum (1972), proposed an attributional analysis of helping behavior. A number of investigators prior to Ickes and Kidd (1976) had established that the tendency to help is influenced by the perceived cause of the need for aid (see Berkowitz 1969; Ickes, Kidd, and Berkowitz 1976; Piliavin, Rodin, and Piliavin 1969; Schopler and Matthews 1965). The majority of these experiments concluded that help is more likely when the perceived cause of the need is an environmental barrier, as opposed to being internal to the person desirous of aid. For example, Berkowitz (1969) reported that individuals are more inclined to help an experimental subject when the experimenter caused a delay in the subject's response, in contrast with a condition in which the subject is perceived as personally responsible for falling behind in the experiment.

In their review, Ickes and Kidd (1976) argued that this locus of control explanation of helping confounds the causal dimensions of locus and intentionality (which I again will call controllability). They suggest that in the study conducted by Berkowitz (1969), the causal ascription to the experimenter is both external and uncontrollable (from the perspective of the actor), whereas an attribution to the subject's own mismanagement is internal to the actor and is perceived by the potential helper as under volitional control. Hence, two dimensions of causality are confounded, and it is impossible to determine which of the two causal dimensions is responsible for the differential help-giving. Ickes and Kidd, in contrast with Berkowitz, suggest that it is the controllable aspect of the perceived cause, and not the locus, that mediated the disparate help-giving. The reader should note how similar this analysis is to the one pertaining to expectancy shifts in skill and chance tasks. Both controversies point out that the locus-of-control literature has been plagued by an inadequate analysis of perceived causality. Furthermore, what is required is research that separates the various causal dimensions.

Other data support the Ickes and Kidd (1976) interpretation of helping behavior. For example, Piliavin et al. (1969) found that there is a bias to aid an ill person in distress as opposed to helping a drunk. According to the preceding argument, this is because drunkenness is perceived as subject to volitional control, whereas illness is not. When a failure is perceived as controllable, then help is withheld; the persons presumably should help themselves. For this reason, it is much easier to raise charity funds for battered children or the blind than for alcoholism centers.

Guided by the prior research of Barnes, Ickes, and Kidd (1977), Simon and Weiner (in press) applied these ideas to one instance of altruism in the classroom: lending class notes to an unknown classmate. In this investigation, two themes were created for a student's failure to take class notes. One theme involved a professor, and the second concerned an employer. In the professor theme, the student always (stable) or sometimes (unstable) did not take notes because of something about himself (internal) or something about the professor (external). Either he was unable to take good notes (uncontrollable) or he did not try (controllable), while the professor either was unable to give a clear lecture or did not try. Thus, for example, an internal, stable, and uncontrollable cause was that the student never was able to take good notes (low ability), while an external, unstable, and uncontrollable cause was that the professor at times could not give a clear lecture. Each story within the eight possible causal combinations (2 levels of stability × 2 levels of locus × 2 levels of control) elaborated the basic scenario. The second theme involved a work situation in which the student did not have the notes because he (or the boss) always (sometimes) was responsible for his coming late to school, which could (could not) have been avoided.

Following each causal statement the subjects rated the likelihood of lending their notes to the student. Judgments were made on a ten-point scale anchored at the extremes with "definitely would lend my notes" and "definitely would not lend my notes."

The mean helping judgments for four conditions (2 levels of locus × 2 levels of control) are shown in Table 4-4. Stability did not affect the judgments and thus is ignored in the analysis. Table 4-4

Table 4-4. Mean Likelihood of Helping as a Function of Perceived Locus of Causality and Controllability.

Locus of Causality	Controllable	Uncontrollable
Internal	3.13	6.74
External	7.35	6.98

Source: Data are from Simon and Weiner (in press). Higher numbers indicate greater likelihood of note lending.
Table reprinted from *The Journal of Educational Psychology*, 1979, vol. 71, no. 1, p. 17.

reveals that helping is reported to be relatively equal and reasonably high in all conditions except when the cause is internal and controllable, in which case aid is unlikely to be given. That is, if the student did not try to take notes (professor theme) or could have avoided being absent (employer theme), then help is withheld. The findings concerning the influence of intent information on moral judgments and criminal justice support this line of reasoning (see Carroll and Payne 1976, 1977, discussed later in this chapter).

Evaluation

Some of the early experimental work conducted by me and my colleagues was undertaken to promote the distinction between various causes of success and failure. In particular we attempted to provide evidence that ability and effort should be distinguished, although both are internal in locus of causality.

In one reference experiment that was employed, subjects were asked to pretend that they were teachers and were to provide evaluative "feedback" to their pupils (see Eswara 1972; Kaplan and Swant 1973; Rest, Nierenberg, Weiner, and Heckhausen 1973; Weiner and Kukla 1970; Weiner and Peter 1973). The pupils were characterized in terms of effort, ability, and performance on an exam. The data from these investigations conclusively demonstrated that effort is of greater importance than ability in determining reward and punishment. High effort was rewarded more than high ability given success, and lack of effort was punished more than lack of ability given failure. To explain these findings, I stated,

> There appear to be two reasons for the discrepancy between ability and effort as determinants of reward and punishment. First, effort attributions elicit strong moral feelings—trying to attain a socially valued goal is something that one "ought" to do. Second, rewarding and punishing efforts is instrumental to changing behavior, inasmuch as effort is believed to be subject to volitional control. On the other hand, ability is perceived as nonvolitional and relatively stable and thus should be insensitive to external control attempts (Weiner 1977: 508).

Thus, both the moral and control aspects of evaluation were considered. But it was not realized that evaluation is conceptually similar to behaviors and feelings such as help-giving, altruism, liking, and blame. That is, there is a pervasive influence of perceived controllability or personal responsibility on interpersonal judgments in achievement-related contexts, including how students are graded.

Sentiments

Investigations linking liking to perceptions of controllability primarily have been conducted in the area of loneliness (see Peplau, Russell, and Heim in press). Michela, Peplau, and Weeks (1978) found that persons lonely for reasons thought to be controllable (e.g., "does not try to make friends") are liked less than individuals lonely for uncontrollable reasons (e.g., "no opportunity to meet people"). In addition, when a lonely person puts forth effort to make friends, that person is liked and elicits sympathy (Wimer and Peplau 1978). In contrast, if it is believed that the lonely individual is responsible for his or her plight, then sympathy is not forthcoming, and respondents indicate they would avoid such persons. I assume that this pattern of results will also be evident in achievement-related contexts. Surely a teacher will not particularly like a student who does not try, and failure perceived as due to lack of effort does not elicit sympathy.

Self-Perception of Control

Whereas perceived control in others relates to interpersonal judgments, self-perceptions of control have quite a different array of consequences. These intrapersonal effects appear to be vast, ranging from experiential states, such as feeling like an "origin" (DeCharms 1968) and perceiving freedom of choice (Steiner 1970), to specific behaviors, such as information search (see Rotter 1966) and normal functioning rather than learning, cognitive, and motivational deficits that are postulated to accompany the loss of control (Seligman 1975). This is a complex subject matter in need of systematic examination and synthesis that goes well beyond the scope of our present knowledge.

Summary

A variety of sources of information (not discussed here) are used to reach causal inferences in achievement-related contexts. The perceived causes of success and failure primarily are ability and effort but also include a small number of other salient factors such as home environment and teacher, and a countless host of idiosyncratic factors. These causes can be comprised within three primary dimensions of causality: stability, locus, and control. There also are an undetermined number of subordinate causal dimensions, including perhaps intentionality and globality. The three main dimensions, respectively, are linked to expectancy changes, esteem-related affects, and interpersonal judgments (decisions about helping, evaluation, and sentiments). In addition, there are secondary linkages between the causal dimensions and psychological effects: Stability relates to depression-type affects, and control is associated with particular feeling states and behaviors. The dimension-consequence linkages influence motivated behaviors such as persistence and choice. This theory is depicted in Figure 4-1.

THEORETICAL RANGE

The theory rather sketchily conveyed in Figure 4-1 has been shown to be relevant to many classroom-related thoughts and actions. The topics already examined in this chapter include the perceived reasons for success and failure, expectancy change, self-concept maintenance, achievement-change programs, reinforcement schedules, hopelessness, sources of emotion, self-esteem, helping, evaluation, and

Figure 4-1. Partial Representation of an Attributional Theory of Motivation.

Antecedent conditions →	Perceived causes →	Causal dimensions →	Primary effects →	Other consequences
	Ability	Stability	Expectancy change	Performance intensity
	Effort (typical and immediate)	Locus	Esteem-related affects	Persistence
	Others (students, family, teacher)	Control	Interpersonal judgments	Choice
				Etc.
	Motivation (attention, interest)	Intentionality		
	Etc.	Globality		

Source: The Journal of Educational Psychology, 1979, vol. 71, no. 1, p. 18. Reprinted by permission.

liking. Still other achievement-related topics have been demonstrated to be encompassed within this attributional conception (see Weiner 1974, 1976). The breadth of the phenomena incorporated within our attributional framework intimates that a general theory of motivation is being constructed. In the remainder of this chapter I document other areas to which the theory is applicable. Some of the theoretical extensions are germane to the school setting, whereas other topics are of interest to an audience of educational psychologists primarily because they demonstrate the range of the conception.

Hyperactivity and Psychostimulants

Whalen and Henker (1976) have outlined an attributional analysis of the effects of drug treatment for hyperactive children. They contend that when hyperactivity is combated with a drug, the belief is conveyed to both the child and his or her parents that the cause of hyperactivity is a physiological dysfunction. Hence, the involved individuals are not responsible for or in control of the maladaptive behavior that is exhibited. Because this physiological deficit is perceived as an uncontrollable cause, neither the child nor the parents need feel guilty or blame themselves for the aberrant behavior. That is, the shift in perceived causality from "lack of effort" minimizes self-blame, low self-esteem, and negative evaluations from others. This appears to be a benefical and an unanticipated side effect of the treatment technique.

On the other hand, Whalen and Henker also state that "the reputed physiological dysfunctions used to explain the failures of hyperactive children are frequently viewed as stable and relatively unresponsive to behavior change effects" (1976: 1123). Thus, the perception of fixed causation might lead to "demoralization about problem solutions ... and interferes with effective coping" (p. 1124).

In sum, again this is an analysis of a psychological phenomenon from the perspective shown in Figure 4-1. Individuals utilize information (treatment technique) to infer causation about an event (hyperactivity). The perceived cause (a genetic deficit) is perceived as uncontrollable and stable. This minimizes certain negative affects and unfavorable evaluations (benefical effects) but also weakens the perceived possibility of recovery (a harmful consequence). These two factors, in turn, influence the long-range influence of the treatment (negatively, according to Whalen and Henker 1976, inasmuch as they perceive expectancy to be the more potent determinant of long-term behavioral change).

Mastery

The labels mastery and competence are prominent among the writings of many psychologists (such as Nissen 1954; White 1959). However, in my opinion systematic experimental work elucidating these alleged motivators of behavior has not been conducted. An investigation by Nuttin (1973), described as demonstrating "causality pleasure," could provide an important experimental paradigm for this area. Nuttin placed five-year-olds in an experiment room containing two machines. The machines each had colored lights and movable handles. For one machine (A), the onset of the lights was preprogrammed by the experimenter. The lights in the alternate machine (B) went on or off only when the handle was moved beyond a certain point. Thus, although both machines stimulated the viewer perceptually, the children were the producers or the cause of the stimulation only with machine B.

The subjects in this experiment were free to spend their time with either machine. The experimenters recorded various indexes of choice or preference, such as the time spent with each machine and verbal reports of liking. Both observational and self-report data revealed that the children strongly preferred machine B over machine A. These findings have been replicated by Weiner, Kun, and Weiner (in press).

From the theoretical perspective shown in Figure 4–1, the experiment by Nuttin (1973) illustrates a temporal sequence involving the use of information, inferences concerning locus of causality, positive affect, and some behavioral consequences of emotional states. That is, on the basis of the observed covariation between their own actions and the onset of the lights in machine B, the children infer that they are personally responsible (ability and effort) for the stimulation from that machine. Self-attribution for the outcome increases positive-esteem-related affects, and the augmented affect increases the probability of engaging in the action again as well as increasing "liking" about playing with the machine.

This interpretation is applicable to another developmental study that has not been conceptualized as involving mastery-type behavior. Watson (1966, 1967) demonstrated that eight-week-old infants can learn an instrumental response (a head turn) to increase stimulation (the movement of a mobile). He also reported that infants in the instrumental response condition apparently displayed more instances of positive affect (smiling and cooing) than children in a condition in which the mobile movement was controlled by the experimenter. This again suggests the following temporal sequence: response-outcome covariation→perceived internal causation→positive affects of competence and pride→choice. That is, the enhanced positive affect and subsequent performance of the instrumental response are mediated by perceptions of self-responsibility (perhaps the control dimension also plays a role here).

The underlying premise of this interpretation of Watson's (1966, 1967) research is that affect and choice can be used to infer cognitive processes (perceptions of causality). It may seem far-fetched to draw the inference that eight-week-olds have the cognitive capacities to make causal deductions. However, it also may be that a differentiation between the self and the environment has developed by that age, and that primitive inferences about locus and control can be made using proprioceptive feedback information. If this interpretation has any validity, then Watson perhaps has identified the existence of attempts at mastery among very young infants. Note also that one may consider the contribution of the Watson investigations from a light somewhat different from what is usual for psychologists: the observation of the behavior is of interest primarily because it tells us something about the contents of the mind!

Parole Decisions

A parole decision is a complex judgment in which causal attributions play a major role. Figure 4-2 depicts the parole decision process as conceptualized by Carroll and Payne (1976, 1977). The figure indicates that the decisionmaker is provided with a variety of information about the criminal, the crime, and other pertinent facts. This information is combined and synthesized, yielding attributions about the cause of the crime. The causal attributions, in turn, influence

70 ATTRIBUTIONS OF SUCCESS AND FAILURE

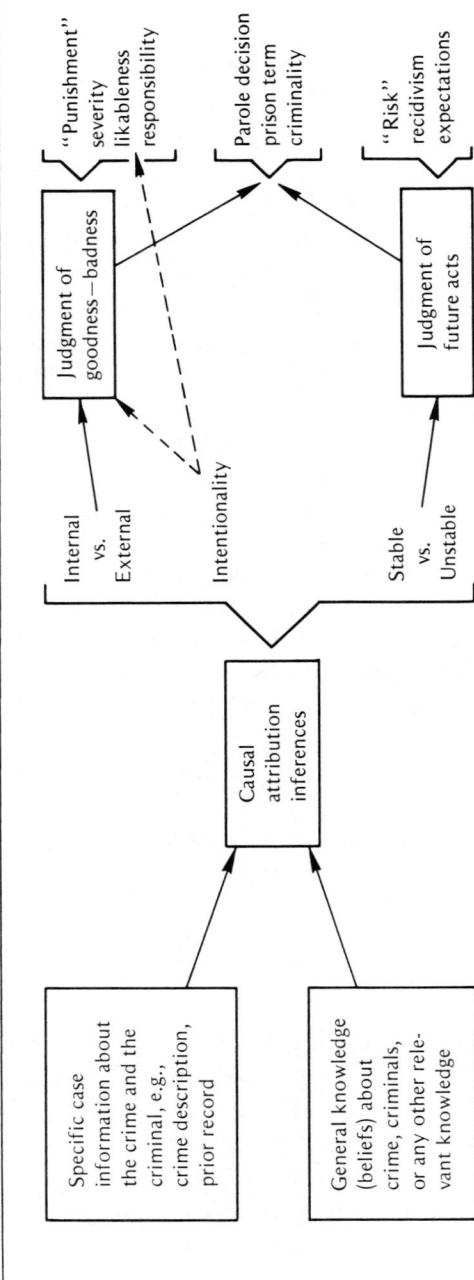

Figure 4-2. An Attributional Framework for the Parole Decision Process. (In this case, an attributional analysis of perceptions of crime and criminals.)

Source: From Carroll and Payne, 1977, p. 200. Copyright 1977 by Plenum Press, Inc. Reprinted by permission.

judgments about deserved punishment and social risk, which are believed to be the basis for the final parole decision.

Carroll and Payne, after reviewing an extensive literature, contend that the parole decision process is "based on a simple two-part model. In the first part, the primary concern of the decision maker is to make the punishment fit the crime. . . . At the second part . . . the primary concern . . . is with parole risk, i.e., the probability that the person being considered for release will again violate the laws of society" (1976: 15).

According to Figure 4-2, crimes that are ascribed to internal and/or intentional (controllable) factors (such as personality characteristics or evil intents) should result in harsher evaluation (punishment) than crimes attributed to external or unintentional (uncontrollable) causes (such as economic conditions or bad friends). In addition, the risk associated with parole should depend on the stability of the perceived cause of the crime. If, for example, the crime is attributed to some fixed personality trait, then the decisionmaker will expect that a crime again will be committed if the prisoner is paroled. On the other hand, if the cause of the crime has been or can be altered (if economic conditions have improved or a job can be found) then the criminal will be perceived as a good parole risk.

Given this analysis, a criminal is least likely to be paroled if the cause of the crime is perceived as internal or controllable but stable ("He is an evil person"). Conversely, parole will tend to be granted when the crime is perceived as caused by external and/or noncontrollable and unstable factors (such as prior economic conditions). The remaining causal combinations should fall between these extremes in terms of parole probability.

Carroll and Payne have furnished support for these hypotheses, examining professional parole decisionmakers and the judgments of college students when given simulated criminal cases. They find, for example, that perceptions of the locus, stability, and controllability of causes significantly relate to perceived responsibility for the crime, likelihood of recidivism, likability, prison term, and the purpose of the sentence.

In sum, according to Carroll and Payne (1976, 1977) the parole decision procedure is conceptually identical to the perceived sequence of events in the achievement domain: Antecedent information is processed, a causal judgment is reached, and the cause is placed within the locus, stability, and intentionality (control) dimensions. This influences evaluation and expectancy, which are the main determinants of the parole decision.

Affiliation and Loneliness

It has been reasoned that in our culture two sources of motivation are most dominant: achievement and social recognition (or, in Freud's more general terms, *Arbeit* and *Liebe*). Hence, affiliative motivation is a natural area to turn toward in the development of a theory of motivation.

An attributional analysis of affiliative motivation guided by the theory shown in Figure 4–1 conceives of loneliness as a social failure (Gordon 1976; Stein and Bailey 1973). Hanusa (1975) and Heim (1975) examined the perceived causes of social success and failure and found them to be similar to the causes of achievement success and failure. As already indicated, Michela et al. (1978) used scaling procedures to discover the dimensions of the causes of social failure and found them to be similar to the dimensions uncovered in achievement contexts.

The question that then remains is whether the attributional dimensions in the affiliative domain relate to psychological factors in the same manner as in the achievement domain. Research reveals that is indeed the case (see Peplau et al. in press). Stability relates to the perceived probability of remaining lonely in the future, locus is associated with esteem-related affects, and as previously stated, control is linked with liking and sympathy toward the lonely person (also see Folkes 1978).

Depression and Learned Helplessness

In accordance with the trend in loneliness research, recent explanations of depression have focused upon the cognitive, rather than the affective, aspects of this disorder (see Beck 1976). The work of Seligman (1975), captured under the label of *learned helplessness*, has been especially influential. I will not dwell upon Seligman's use of this construct or the supporting empirical evidence in this context. Rather, my goal is to convey the pertinence of the literature on learned helplessness to the attributional model depicted in Figure 4-1 (see Abramson et al. 1978; Weiner and Litman-Adizes in press).

Learned helplessness communicates the belief that there is no perceived association between responding and environmental outcomes. That is, the actor believes that the likelihood of an event is independent of what he or she does. The belief in helplessness is alleged to produce deficits in motivation and learning, negative affect, and a syndrome that has been labeled "depression."

As this work has progressed from infrahuman to human research, it has become evident that it also is essential to consider why actions and outcomes are perceived to be independent. For example, Klein, Fencil-Morse, and Seligman (1976) found that only individuals making internal attributions for response-outcome independence exhibited aspects of the learned helplessness syndrome. Attributions of response-outcome independence to external factors did not produce any learning deficits. In a similar manner, Tennen and Eller (1977) found learned helplessness only under conditions that promote low-ability attributions for prior lack of control.

Partially because of these data, Abramson et al. (1978) adopted an attributional framework for helplessness. I have extracted the following statements from the Abramson et al. article, piecing the statements together into new paragraphs to illustrate their thinking.

> Our reformulated hypothesis makes a major new set of predictions. The helpless individual first finds out that certain outcomes and responses are independent, then he makes an attribution about the causes. This attribution determines the chronicity, generality, and intensity of the deficits. Depressed people seem to make more global, stable, and possibly internal attributions about the cause of their helplessness and as a consequence show more general, chronic, and intense deficits than nondepressed people.
>
> Depression occurs when an individual expects that the probability of a highly preferred outcome is low and he expects that he is helpless to increase it. If the attributions for the present state of affairs are to stable and global factors, the future will look dark to the individual. He expects that he will find himself helpless again and again. This is what is usually meant by "hopelessness." Another implication of the formulation is that individuals will show the greatest loss of self-esteem when they make internal, global, and stable attributions for their failures (Abramson et al. 1978: mainly pp. 52, 55, 56).

In sum, it is argued that depressed individuals attempt to make sense out of perceived evidence that their responses do not affect outcomes. A cause is determined that often is classified as stable, internal, and global. This leads to a low expectancy of success across a wide array of environments and a heightened negative affect (loss of self-esteem), which are sufficient precursers of depression.

Conclusion

I have selectively reviewed the extensive literature outside of the achievement domain, including hyperactivity, mastery, parole decisions, loneliness and affiliation, and depression. The data strongly suggest that a general conception of motivation, as well as a particular method of psychological analysis, is evolving.

5 THE ROLE OF CAUSAL ATTRIBUTION OF PUPILS' BEHAVIOR IN THE TEACHER'S CONTROL OF ACTIONS

Manfred Hofer and Martin Dobrick

Since Heider (1958), the process of causal attribution has been seen in the whole context of the control of behavior by the individual. Usually an attempt is made to predict behavior in very specific situations with the help of induced or inferred causal explanations. Thus, helping behavior (Ickes and Kidd 1976), judicial action (Carroll and Payne 1976), or moral behavior (Dienstbier et al. 1975) are referred to as dependent variables. Intended teaching behavior (praise or punishment) is also predicted (Rheinberg 1975). In the framework of the theory of achievement motivation, causal explanations are related to behavior intensity, frequency of reaction, duration of or persistence in problemsolving, and choice behavior (Meyer 1976, Weiner 1974). This chapter will discuss two points:

1. Usually, the variable of causal attribution is used as sole predictor. Certain significant theoretical and practical interrelations were discoverable in this way, of course. Nevertheless, we believe that it is necessary to go beyond this unidimensional approach. Human actions can rarely be explained satisfactorily through a single independent variable. In addition to causal attributions, a number of other important cognitions determine actual behavior. In recent

---

This contribution is based on work conducted in the framework of a project partially financed by the German Research Association (Deutsche Forschungsgemeinschaft) (Ref. no.: Ho 649/1).

years, attitude research has emphasized the necessity of taking into consideration multiple attitudes as determinants of behavior. Furthermore, recent developments in the field of achievement-motivation theory have introduced additional constructs to explain motivation and action (Heckhausen 1977).

2. Behavior is also usually conceived unidimensionally in a quantitative manner. The individual is asked to make decisions only in a specific subarea. For example, the extent of helping behavior is chosen as a dependent variable. In experiments on achievement motivation, performance, persistence in task solution, or the choice between tasks of varying levels of difficulty are included. Human action is further limited to artificial situations. The theories are still too narrow for actions in different natural settings with their many types of valences.

At present we are trying to design a more comprehensive theory of social action based on the example of teacher behavior in the classroom.[a] In this theory the teacher's causal explanation of pupil actions plays an important role in addition to other cognitions. The teacher's actions in the natural social field of the school are treated as the result of a decisionmaking process. Above all, we pursue the question as to why teachers behave differently in different situations (for example, toward different pupils).

A MODEL OF SOCIAL BEHAVIOR

Figure 5–1 is a schematic overview of a process model we developed on social behavior in the classroom.[b] The explanation is to be treated in a step-by-step manner on the basis of this overview (see Figure 5–1). Let us assume that the frame of events or the state of the situation that the teacher encounters is the first link in the chain to be explained.

    a. A (partially) empirical check of the model is conducted in the aforementioned research project, whereby the actual behavior of teachers is described with the help of an observation system. We developed questionnaires and scaling procedures for measuring the cognitive constructs. The illustrations used in this chapter are taken from this project.

    b. In order to avoid misunderstandings, we point out that it is not an attempt to represent the processes that actually take place in the teacher (in the sense of so-called naive theories). Rather, it is a hypothetical construction in which the relations between cognitive variables of the teacher as antecedents and the teacher's behavior as a consequence are brought together in a scientific explanatory context so as to permit the prediction of teacher behavior.

THE ROLE OF CAUSAL ATTRIBUTION OF PUPILS' BEHAVIOR

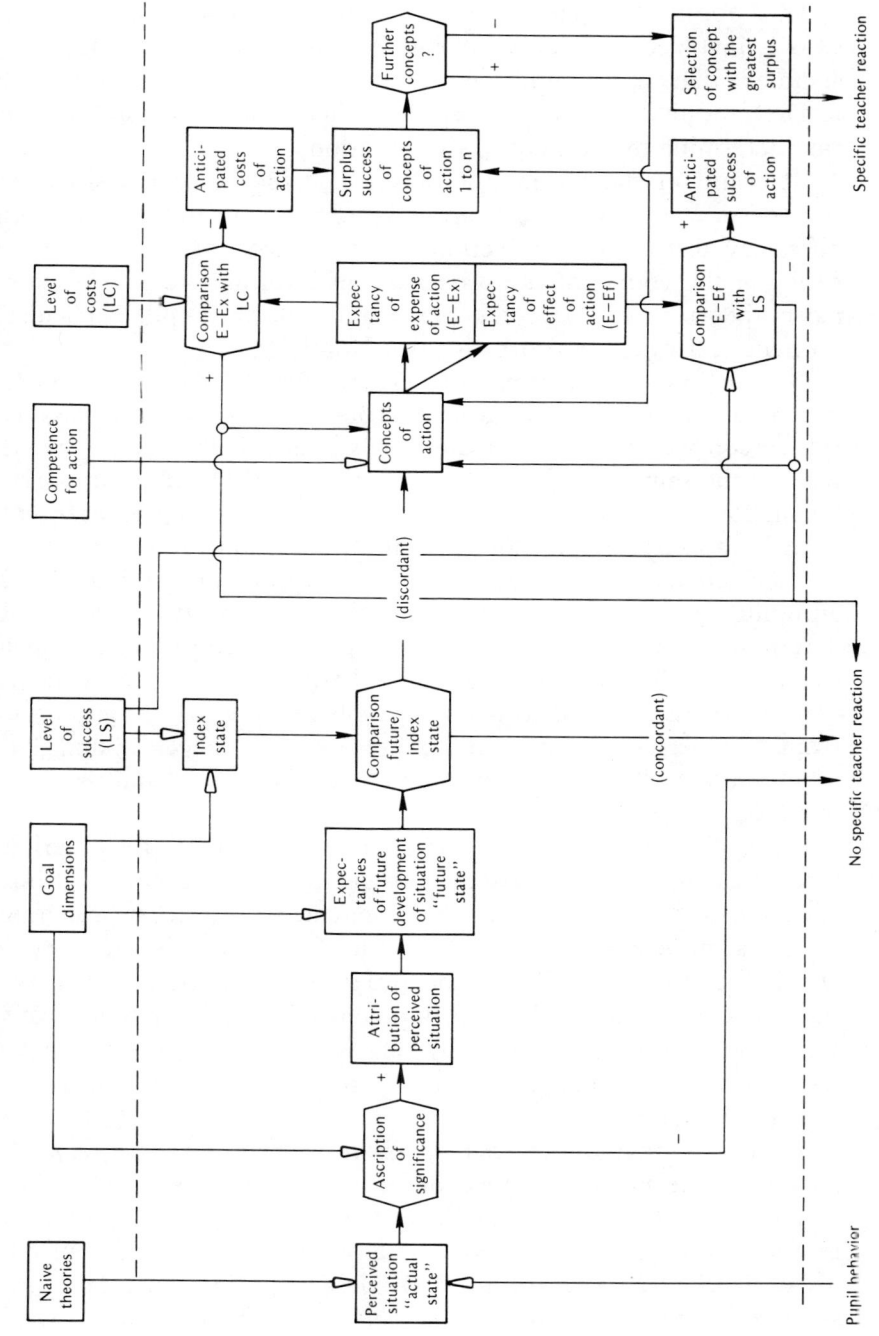

Figure 5-1. Schematic Diagram of a Model of Social Behavior.

This point of departure is characterized primarily by the pupil who is involved in it or was causally implicated in its origin. It is assumed that each pupil defines an individual situation for the teacher and that the characteristics and behavior of the pupil in question determine the content of the situation.

Relevant for the action is, however, not the "objective situation" but the *situation as it is perceived by the teacher*, which can be significantly distorted by selection, fixation, accentuation, and structuring in the course of the processing of information. The teacher's naive theories, as about the personality of the pupil, particularly influence information processing (see Hofer 1974).

On the basis of Silberman (1969) and Brophy and Good (1974), it can be assumed that the teacher groups the pupils in the class. For this reason we presume that the pupils in a group determine for the teacher the same, or at least a similar, situation. The literature on the Pygmalion effect (Brophy and Good 1974) analyzes teacher interactions with extreme types of good and poor pupils. In order to avoid the dangers of establishing an a priori typification or limiting the grouping criteria to the achievement dimension, groupings can be determined empirically with the help of processes of automatic classification. This can be done on the basis of the teacher's personality trait assessments. In this way, we obtained up to five pupil types from the perspective of the teacher: the "intelligent pupil," the "worker," the "inconspicuous pupil," the "agitator," and the "poor pupil."

Proceeding from the situation of the moment or the situational fact (such as a pupil's talking to a neighbor), the teacher will build expectancies as to the further development of the situation. Of particular significance for this expectancy formation is the cause to which the teacher attributes the situational fact. Before discussing the expectancies of further development of the situation and causal attributions as well as their interrelations in detail, the concept of ascription of significance should be introduced, since it is important for causal attribution.

We assume that the teacher makes an *ascription of significance* referring to the perceived situation. This ascription is closely related to the teacher's goals ("goal dimensions"). Situational facts that the teacher cannot relate to his goal dimensions are of no significance for his goal-oriented behavior and have no further influence on him. A situational fact can become significant, for example, if it is a condition for the possibility of achieving the goal, or if in the teacher's experience it is related to the achievement of the objective. The blinking of a pupil, for example, is of no importance to the teacher, assuming that he does not assess it to be a particularly subtle way of undermining his authority, in which case it takes on an indicator function.

The causal explanation provided by the teacher for the occurrence of the situation is referred to as *attribution*. A pupil's talking with his neighbor can be seen by the teacher as having been caused by, for example, general disinterest on the part of the pupil in school-related things or by a distraction just caused by the neighbor or something else. It can be assumed that causal attribution occurs only in significant situations.

The teacher's attribution represents the basis for the formation of his expectancies about the further development of the situation. The *expectancies of the situation's future development* comprise the totality of the teacher's experiences about the events that will most probably occur given the presence of a particular constellation of stimuli (situation) — or that are related to it. Expectancies of the situation's future development comprise both relatively general if–then relations about the school environment and specific if–then relations that develop for individual pupils in the course of the school year. For example, the teacher may have the general experience that when a pupil fools around, the restlessness transfers to the rest of the class. A specific example would be: "A joke told by pupil X to his neighbor soon spreads, and since the joke is usually at my expense, the whole class is soon laughing at me." Expectancies of the situation's future development are learned and are influenced by new experiences. Ascriptions of significance operate in such a way that the teacher does not apply expectancies of the situation's future development to the situations irrelevant to his goals. If he accords no significance to a pupil's blinking, then he will not derive any expectancies for future developments. On the other hand, the disinterest the pupil shows for the teacher's goals is of utmost relevance, and the teacher will therefore make presumptions about the further development of the situation.

These presumptions will differ according to the causal factors the teacher uses to explain the situation. If the teacher in the preceding example attributes the pupil's talking to the distraction just caused by his neighbor, then he is more likely to expect the talking to stop (because the pupil is otherwise interested) than if he attributes it to the absolute disinterest of this pupil. Therefore, the relevant experiences applied to the present situation are drawn from the store of experiences according to the choice of causal factors.

The perceived situation represents the *actual state* onto which a corresponding *future state* is projected. The latter is the situation that, according to the teacher's experience and the attribution made, will most probably result from the present situation if the teacher does not actively intervene. If the anticipated future state deviates from the teacher's desired *index state*, then the teacher must come up with appropriate strategies that will avoid the future state or which will facilitate its transition into the index state. The index state that the teacher strives for results partially from the teacher's goals, which are contained in the concept of *goal dimensions* (Mischel 1973: 272 speaks of "stimulus values").

The goals of the teacher that are significant for teaching range from general pedagogical ideals to that which he considers achievable within the classroom, from long-term instructional objectives (related to thematic content) to shorter term lesson objectives, and from rough goals to specific goals in the sense of the didactic organization of what he intends to communicate. Just as our discussion has centered around the primary goal of pupil qualification, a number of concepts can be subsumed under the heading of the acquisition of social affection. This can be partially confirmed empirically. In a pilot study we conducted teachers were asked to indicate the goals they pursued for different pupils. We were able to identify a hierarchy of goals. The two most common clusters were performance in the school (knowledge and comprehension) and behavior (discipline and active participation).

It must be noted that the teacher's goal dimensions partially determine the index state, albeit only its qualitative aspect. This qualitative determination suffices to permit the goal dimensions to be applied to the ascription of significance. The examples of relations that impart significance are likewise qualitative, not quantitative. The quantitative aspect of the degree in the determination of the index state is included in the concept of the level of success.

Whereas the goal dimensions represent the basis for the decision of whether expectancies of future development are applied to a given situation and provide the dimensions for the comparison between the future state and the index state, the levels of success represent the index state's fixed points in these dimensions.

The *level of success* set by the teacher defines, among other things, when he regards a pupil's performance as a success or a failure. Assuming that the teacher sets a relatively high level of success for a pupil, then that pupil must give a relatively highly qualified response (an answer) before the teacher registers a success. If the teacher has several, noncovarying subject areas (say, language, natural sciences, and social studies), he will derive several levels of success (one per subject area and pupil).

Thibaut and Kelley's "comparison level" (1959) is somewhat comparable to our level of success. To Thibaut and Kelley it is the expectancy against which the actually resulting effect is measured. We consciously avoid the concept of expectancy here because of the danger of confusion with other expectancy concepts. Instead we use the concept of level of success. Since the demands of the teacher on a poor pupil will be lower than those on a good pupil, there are two index states, depending on the pupil, according to which the anticipated future state is measured.

If the future state and the index state are in concordance, no teacher reaction follows. If a comparison of the future and index states results in discrepancies, then the teacher is faced with the problem of transforming the actual state into the index state (avoiding the future state). In order to achieve this, the teacher needs concepts of actions. It is assumed that a certain pool of possible action strategies is available to him. In this context Mischel (1973: 267) speaks of "behavioral construction capability." We call it *competence for action*.

During his training period the teacher learned problemsolving behavior, teaching strategies, didactic concepts, and the like; he also has his own teaching experience to draw on. In principle all these are possible patterns of behavior for all possible situations. Together with the capability of building new behavior from available parts, they form the pool from which a limited subarea is activated in the situation at hand; that is, it is considered by the teacher as a possible behavior.

The concepts of actions are the subarea out of the repertoire of possible behaviors that are brought into play in the particular situation. The delimitation or choice of the subarea results from the specificity of the particular expectancies of the situation's future development and the goal dimensions. The concepts comprise actions that in the teacher's opinion are suitable for transforming the given situation into the desired one or for avoiding an unpleasant development of the situation in the direction of a threatening future state.

Concepts of actions must also be differentiated according to qualitative and quantitative aspects. A given concept of action is thought of as a variable that can assume different degrees. Praise and punishment as measures of intervention, for example, can be increased by the teacher from "a little" to "a lot" (actions to which this does not apply can, under certain circumstances, be intensified by repetition).

Goal dimensions that are relevant at the moment affect the choice of concepts of actions. In certain situations, such as in reaction to an incorrect response, praise can thus be considered a means of getting the pupil's affection (as an example of a short-term goal) but not a means of achieving progress in learning (goal of qualification). On the other hand, reprimand as an alternative concept of action will not serve the goal of maximizing the student's liking.

Since the literature reports no findings on implicit teacher strategies of action other than didactic recommendations of action by educational theorists and specialists, we conducted a number of broad-based interviews with teachers. We asked the teachers what they did in particular situations of interaction and what this activity might be called. The following six concepts of actions resulted: motivating, demanding, helping, disciplining, restraining, indulging.

For each of the concepts of actions considered, the most probable pupil reactions are anticipated. These *expectancies of the effect of action* are compared with the level of success. Since the level of success defines success and failure for the teacher, the comparison produces the success or failure anticipated for each plan of action. The more the expectancy of the effect of action exceeds the standard of the level of success, the greater is the anticipated success.[c]

Rotter (1964: 82ff) introduces the concept of "freedom of movement" in connection with expectancies of success for particular types of behavior. Freedom of movement is reduced by raising the

---

c. This reveals the appropriateness of variable concepts of actions. They can be applied with successively increasing degrees of distinctiveness until the achievement of the standard set by the success level is foreseen. The same can occur for qualitatively different concepts of actions simultaneously. Concepts of actions with which the established standard cannot be achieved will not be dealt with.

level of success. In our research, too, the number of the originally considered concepts of actions is restricted when their associated future state is compared with the level of success. In fact, the higher the level of success, the more they are reduced because the probability increases that even the greatest quantitative intensity of a special concept of action no longer suffices to meet the standard.

In a way similar to that in which the teacher arrives—via expectancies of the effect of action and the levels of success—at an *anticipation of success* for a given concept of action, he will draw up a somewhat contrary account. The action can only be carried out with a certain amount of effort and may have additional undesired side effects.

For this reason the expectancy of the target result is accompanied by the expectancy of negative concomitant conditions. When they are compared with a *level of cost* analogous to the level of success, the costs of the action concept in question can be anticipated. The weighing of the anticipated success with the anticipated costs for each of the concepts of actions under consideration finally leads to a decision about the action to be carried out. The action that combines the lowest costs with the greatest success is chosen.

Checking this model requires the measurement of teacher behavior as a dependent variable in addition to a correct representation of the cognitive constructs. We consider the observation of classroom behavior to be suitable for objectifying teacher behavior. Drawing on Brophy and Good (1969), we develop a comprehensive system of teaching observation that focuses on the aspects of the dyadic teacher–pupil interaction.

RELATIONS BETWEEN CAUSAL ATTRIBUTION AND OTHER CONSTRUCTS OF THE MODEL

Causal Explanation and Goal Dimensions

The relation between causal attribution and goal dimensions is touched upon in the foregoing model description by the concept of ascription of significance. This concept was introduced in order to permit the clarification of why the teacher attributes only particular events that are striking to him. In accordance with this conceptualization, particular events (correct or incorrect responses, for example) take on significance for the teacher only when he can associate them with his goal dimensions. This serves to explain why the teacher does not attribute many of the events that occur in the course of a lesson; they are irrelevant to his objectives.

Situation and Causal Explanations Concerning the Selection of Causes

There are a number of studies concerning the question of which causal factors teachers refer to in the attribution of pupil-related events (Beckman 1973: Meyer and Butzkamm 1975; Rheinberg 1975). For our purposes the following viewpoints are decisive:

1. The catalogue of causes cannot be limited to causes that the teacher uses to explain the performance of the pupils at the end of the year (Meyer and Butzkamm 1975). In such a case, factors such as task difficulty, mode of presentation or other teacher factors, momentary distraction, or chance are omitted because they are probably not constantly operative throughout the year. Liebhart (1977) recently showed that these factors are rarely applied even in explaining performance on particular class assignments. They do, however, play a role in the explanation of actual individual events (e.g., Beckman 1973; cf. Brophy and Good 1974: 262ff). On the other hand, specific causal factors are omitted in the consideration of smaller units of time. For example, it appears rather improbable that a teacher will attribute a pupil's incorrect answer to the fact that the pupil is obese (particularities of constitution). We therefore consider it necessary to take the catalogue of causes by Meyer and Butzkamm (1975), which is based on the entire school year, and reduce it in certain places and expand it in others, depending on the situation at hand.

2. Research to date restricts itself to the study of causal factors that the teacher applies in the explanation of pupil *performance*. Another important goal dimension, however, can also be the area of pupil work conduct (discipline in the classroom and active participation) so that for the prediction of teacher behavior it is necessary to consider the causes of this constellation of events also. We applied the following list of causes in our research: ability, effort, power of concentration, difficulty of the task for this pupil, mode of presen-

tation of the material in the lesson, shyness of the pupil, aggressiveness of the pupil, chance (good or bad luck).

Dimensions of the Catalogue of Causes

Three dimensions are particularly relevant to our question: stability over time, the degree to which the teacher can modify the causes, and the direction of effect of the attributed cause. These dimensions are discussed below in relation to the associated variables of the model.

Causal Explanation and Future State

Applying considerations of Weiner and his colleagues (Weiner 1976), the more past successes and failures of *one's own* action are traced back to the stable causal factors of ability and task difficulty—as opposed to the variable factors of effort and chance—the more they are likely to be expected to recur. It may be assumed that this empirically validated relation between the dimension of stability over time and the expectancy of future results in explaining the outcome of one's own performance also applies to the causal explanation of the behavior of *others*.

If a teacher attributes a pupil action that he considers relevant to stable factors, he will (without intervening) anticipate a continuation of the action or other similar actions. If this future state is identical to the index state, then he will regard an intervention as superfluous. This is the case if the teacher attributes a pupil's correct answer to a difficult question to stable factors such as ability and therefore anticipates good performance from that pupil at the end of the term. He will not consider taking action. If the future state deviates from the index state in an undesired way—such as disruption by a talkative (stable cause) pupil—then action will be considered in order to eliminate the discrepancy.

On the other hand, if the teacher attributes the event to variable causes, he will consider a continuation of the event to be less likely. If the future state agrees with the index state—a pupil talks because he is distracted (variable cause): he will soon be quiet—then the teacher can refrain from intervening under certain circumstances. This differs from the case in which a poor pupil's good performance is attributed by the teacher to variable causes such as luck. Here the future state can deviate from the index state and place the teacher under pressure to act.

Causal Explanation and Motivation to Act

When there is a discrepancy between the future and the index state, the extent of the motivation to act depends on another dimension: the perceived extent to which the teacher can modify the causes. In contrast to Rheinberg (1975) we emphasize the perceived *extent to which causes can be modified* by the teacher rather than by the pupil. This dimension is important for the teacher because he has both a decided interest in the realization of the index state and certain possibilities to exert influence.

It is thus a matter of assessing whether or not the means of influence available to the teacher are effective with a given cause, whether or not anything can be changed with their help. If the teacher attributes the behavior of a pupil to causal factors that he perceives as unmodifiable, then intervention for the purpose of realizing the index state must appear pointless. Ability is one such cause for many teachers. On the other hand, one factor that the teacher can modify is the mode of presentation of the lesson material, for example.

Causal Explanation and the Selection of Concrete Concepts of Actions

If the teacher intends to intervene, he faces the question of which action he should choose. Among other considerations, such as which concepts of actions are available to him, his choice depends on the type of causes that have brought about the situation. If the teacher attributes a pupil's poor performance to shyness, he will exhibit a different behavior to this pupil than if he attributes the weak performance to a lack of effort. In the first case he is more likely to "help" or "indulge," in the second, to "motivate." He will behave still differently if he believes aggressiveness is the cause. He will then presumably exhibit "punishing" or "demanding" behavior.

There are presently only unspecific hypotheses about the relations in this area. For this reason we must be satisfied with these approaches to the concept of the situation- × action- × outcome-expectancies. Like Weiner, Russell, and Lerman (1978), we consider it necessary to tie directly into the specific causes in addition to using the dimensional approach.

The Effect of Attribution Tendencies

Proceeding from the principles in attribution theory of covariation, discounting, and augmentation (all according to Kelley 1971), we consider the distinction between unequivocal and equivocal attribution situations (see Mischel 1973) to be important for the explanation of interindividual differences in teacher behavior.

Equivocal situations are characterized by the fact that several competing causes for the explanation of pupil behavior are available to the teacher. Unequivocal situations are characterized by the fact that on a rational level, i.e., with the help of the aforementioned principles, *one* specific cause can be identified or inferred as the main determinant of pupil behavior. In equivocal situations the behavior of the teacher depends on individual attributional tendencies because they decide the relative weight given to the explanatory causes that are ultimately relevant to the action.

In order to identify unequivocal and equivocal situations, information is needed about the type of effect (inhibiting or facilitating) of the causes under discussion. Only in those cases in which at least two causes facilitating the action are considered equally operative can one speak of equivocal situations. Depending on the bias of his assessment, the teacher will exhibit a different behavior, namely, one related to the favored cause. This is therefore a condition for model-dependent inexact predictions since the construct of attributional tendencies has not yet been integrated.

The key relations of causal explanations can be summarized as follows: teachers form expectancies of the situation's future development on the basis of causal attributions of pupil-related events and on the classification of these causes according to the dimensions of stability/variability. These indicate a future state. If there is a discrepancy between the future state and the index state, the teacher is under pressure to act. The extent to which the pressure to act becomes motivation to act depends on the degree to which the teacher perceives the causal factors to be modifiable. The more modifiable the cause, the more likely the teacher is to plan actions; the less modifiable the cause, the less likely he is to plan actions. The possible individual actions he considers depend on the specific cause (or constellation of causes) that the teacher perceives to characterize the situation in question.

COMMENTS ON THE CHAPTER BY HOFER AND DOBRICK

Franz E. Weinert

Many teachers judge the results of attribution research to be particularly plausible, interesting, and helpful as compared to those of other psychological theories. This is not surprising, since they find the methods of such studies to be closely related to reality. The causal explanations of pupil performance that are requested of them are familiar from experience, and the relations reported in the results between causal attribution, assessment of performance, prediction of behavior, and their own intended actions appear simple and evident. Another contributing factor might be that teachers often feel that they are misused as objects of psychological research in trait-centered or behaviorist-oriented theories, which assume from the outset that they (must) act without insight, reflection, or real responsibility. In contrast, cognitive theories use and communicate the image of a person who judges and acts in a rational fashion. Even if scientific analysis convincingly proves the deficits and flaws of naive theories in the assimilation and processing of information, it changes nothing in the basic postulate of rational action inherent in cognitive theories.

The overall positive assessment of attribution research among scientists and practitioners, however, should not be permitted to camouflage the fact that the available empirical results are distinguished more by their plausibility than by their clarity and precision. Certainly researchers have, in agreement with the theory, been able to confirm empirically a number of linkages between the type of explanation for pupil performance given by the teacher and his pupil-specific explanations and plans of action, but we are far from being able even to approximate valid explanations and predictions of teachers' didactic behavior in specific interaction situations on the basis of knowledge about their typical or specific explanations of pupil performance.

Hofer and Dobrick quite correctly proceed on the premise that the behavior of a teacher toward individual pupils does not depend only on the causes he ascribes to the performance of children. They therefore develop a more comprehensive theory of social action in which causal attributions are integrated as important component processes. How are pupils perceived by the teacher? According to which characteristics does the teacher group them? To which situations does he ascribe pedagogical significance—and on the basis of which affinities to his overall and short-term goals? How does he explain the behavior and the performance of the children? What does he expect if he does not intervene pedagogically? On the basis of which implicit reference systems and standards of behavior does he assess the present and anticipated behavior of the pupils? What competencies for action are available to him and which plans of action are actualized in a concrete situation? Hofer and Dobrick do not see these as isolated questions but rather, with the help of a system of theoretical constructs and linkage rules integrating these constructs in a model-like way, as questions so interrelated that the answers to them should be a necessary condition for predicting teacher behavior in defined situations. The model's criterion for verification is not the accuracy of the prediction of questionnaire data by the actual questionnaire data of the same teachers, but the prediction of variable teacher behavior in real classroom situations. In my opinion both the development of the model and the choice of the verification criterion (reported on only briefly in the chapter) represent important innovations in the area of attribution research that is oriented to educational psychology. In spite of the foreseeable methodological difficulties in simultaneously processing data that stem from the operationalization of different but related theoretical constructs, the results of the empirical study can be awaited with great interest.

Although we are restricted to discussing primarily at the theoretical level for the time being, certain problems can already be identified that must encumber the model and its empirical checking.

A first problem lies in the theoretical specification of the model's units of analysis, which can be clarified in the example of the postulated attribution processes. Which events (patterns of behavior and performance of the pupils) does the teacher explain? What is the time frame and the thematic boundary of the situations to which causal explanations are ascribed? Depending on whether it is the grades on a report card, achievement changes in the course of the school year, the results of a class assignment, or behavior in teaching that must be explained, the ascription of stable and unstable causal factors is always related to the specific formulation of these questions. Which factors are used to explain an event does not depend only on the explanatory capacity ascribed to a single cause, however; it also depends on the distribution of the judge's attention to the potential causal factors (see Arkin and Duval 1975; Taylor and Fiske, 1975).

Additional difficulties obstructing a precise definition of the unit of analysis "teacher attribution" appear when one considers that attribution behavior is influenced by the perspective of the teacher (for example by dominance of the individual or social standard of reference—see Liebhart, 1977). Hofer and Dobrick attempt to avoid the related problems by assuming "that each pupil defines an individual situation for the teacher and that the characteristics and behavior of the pupil in question determine the content of the situation." Such a definition appears useful when it is the basis for a study in which the teacher sits at his desk and writes down for the experimenter causal explanations, assessments, and predictions of performance for each of his pupils as well as his intended reactions. It is highly questionable whether this assumption is also valid for real teaching conditions. In these circumstances, the situation is defined for the teacher by the behavior of the whole class, the course taken by the lesson, and the individual pupil to whom the teacher turns his attention for a time. It is doubtful whether the causal attributions made on the basis of restricted situational definitions are suited to predicting teacher behavior in real teaching conditions.

This raises the question as to the (demanded) range of generality of Hofer and Dobrick's model. Closely related to this is the second theoretical problem to be discussed briefly in this commentary.

The principal prerequisite of Hofer and Dobrick's model is the assumption that teachers behave rationally; that is, that necessary and sufficient conditions for explaining and predicting teacher behavior toward a specific pupil can be explained by a system of theoretically postulated cognitive mediating processes. Cognitive theories were developed and became popular because, as Miller, Galanter, and Pribram note, "It is so reasonable to insert between the stimulus and the response a little wisdom. And there is no particular need to apologize for putting it there *because* it was already there before psychology arrived" (1960: 2). I question, however, whether Hofer and Dobrick's cognitivistic model does not theoretically presuppose and postulate a little too much wisdom between the stimulus and the response. In other words, do teachers in practice really behave as rationally as the model prescribes so that even their mistakes can still be systematically (cognitively) explained? There are basically two reasons that lead me to doubt this:

1. A part of everyday behavior cannot be theoretically conceived as the outcome of decision processes—that is, as a reasoned choice between different options for action. This is particularly true of largely automatized routine behavior when learned cues release relatively rigid patterns of action. The utility of an elaborated cognitive theory is assessed differently depending on whether a situation is a part of such an automatized process or whether it takes on a behavior-controlling function. This is also true for impulsive behavior where circumscribed stimuli release reactions that are closely associated with it. Under these conditions theoretically hypostatized cognitive processes are probably better suited to the clarification of subjective justifications for behavior than for the explanation of internal behavior control.

It is therefore assumed that cognitive theories are particularly suited to explaining behavior when hypostatized mediating processes lead to the choice of one possible action among many. On the other hand, explanations based on association theory appear to be useful when a relatively unequivocal and stable link between a circumscribed stimulus and a resulting behavior is to be expected. A distinction is therefore drawn between two types of behavior: actions whereby different reactions by the same individual are observed longitudinally in spite of externally identical constellations of stimuli; and patterns of behavior whose probability of occurrence under conditions of circumscribed stimuli approaches $p = 1$. In my opinion the validity of Hofer and Dobrick's model is limited to the behavior situations of the first type.

2. The explanation of the outcome of one's own action or the action of others depends, of course, on which conditions are available to the judge in principle and which are actually available. In contrast to typical experimental situations, the actor has in practice no ready-made catalogues of causes available. For this reason the question as to which possible explanations of an action's effect are available to an individual becomes very important for a theory of causal attribution. The interindividual differences may be expected to be significant for both the availability and the accessibility of potential causal factors. This could, for example, be demonstrated in experiments in developmental psychology (see Weiner and Kun 1977; Robinson and Robinson 1976). There are also reasons to assume that typical differences in development can also partially be identified as interindividual differences among adults. The relation between this question and research on metacognition (Flavell 1977) is obvious. Causal attribution presumes not only knowledge about one's own behavior and that of others but also knowledge about this knowledge. Which situations are considered pedagogically significant, which causes are held responsible for success and failure, and which prognoses are derived about the further development and effectiveness of one's own options for actions also depend on whether and how one can make use of relevant knowledge, experiences, and operative capabilities. If such interindividual differences in metacognition, in information-processing, in anxiety, in dogmatic convictions, and so on are not taken into account in a social-cognitive model of action, the accuracy of the model's predictions will be affected.

6 AN ATTRIBUTIONAL ANALYSIS OF THE RELATION BETWEEN EXPECTANCY AND INCENTIVE (AFFECT)

Wulf-Uwe Meyer and
Fritz-Otto Plöger

One of the most widely known theories of achievement-oriented behavior was developed by Atkinson (1957). According to this model, the strength of the tendency to approach or to avoid an achievement-related activity is a function of the individual's motive strength and of perceived characteristics of the situation. The situational variables are the expectations of success and failure and the incentives of success and failure. The strength of the expectancies is represented by the subjective probability of success and failure, which can be assigned values between 0 and 1.00. The incentives of success and failure are specific anticipated affects that will accompany the incidence of success or failure. The incentive of success is defined as "pride in accomplishment" (Atkinson 1964: 241) and the incentive of failure as "shame and embarrassment" (Atkinson 1964: 244).

According to the model, the strength of these incentives is completely determined by the subjective probabilities. The incentive value of success I_s is a linear inverse function of the subjective probability of success P_s, that is, $I_s = 1 - P_s$. The incentive value of failure I_f is a linear negative function of the subjective probability: $I_f = -P_s$. That is, anticipated pride for succeeding increases with decreasing probabilities of success, while anticipated shame for failing de-

---

The work was supported by research sources from the University of Bielefeld, West Germany (Grant no. 1976/OZ2729).

creases with decreasing probabilities of success. Although the model (Atkinson 1957) has been revised and expanded several times by Atkinson and his colleagues (Atkinson and Cartwright 1964; Atkinson and Birch 1970, 1978; Raynor 1974), the definition of the incentives and the assumptions about their dependency on the subjective probability of success has remained unchanged.

A number of studies have examined the relation between expectancy and incentive (Brown 1963; Feather 1967; Karabenick 1972; Litwin 1966; Schneider 1971, 1973). Although it is often assumed that the findings of these studies confirm Atkinson's assumptions, a close examination of the methods used and the data obtained raises doubts on this matter (see also Schneider 1971). For example, in some of these experiments the incentives assessed were not related to subjective probabilities, as required by the model, but to the objective difficulty of the tasks (Brown 1963; Feather 1967). However, task difficulty and subjective probability are not necessarily the same. A very difficult task can certainly be assigned different subjective probabilities, depending on a person's perception of his ability level for the specific task (Kukla 1972; Meyer 1973, 1976). Feather also assessed subjective probabilities for each difficulty level. The mean subjective probability was 38 percent for the most difficult task and 87 percent for the easiest task. A linear relation between expectancy and incentive therefore was demonstrated (if at all) only for half of the total span of subjective probability (see also Schneider 1971). The same conclusion applies to the experiment conducted by Litwin (1966).

Furthermore, in none of the studies were the incentive values assessed according to Atkinson's definition (pride and shame). Litwin (1966) let his subjects assign money prices for success in a ringtoss game. Feather (1967) asked for the number of points one would assign to another person (not oneself) for success at tasks differing in difficulty. Both authors provide no information about why money or points are supposed to indicate the specific affect of pride and why they could not indicate the strength of any other affects like joy or pleasure. In the other three pertinent studies affects were assessed. Brown (1963) asked for the strength of the feelings "pleasure" and "displeasure," Schneider (1971, 1973) about "contentment" and "disappointment," and Karabenick (1972) about "satisfaction" and "dissatisfaction." However, these affects are not identical with pride and shame and they do not necessarily covary with them. For example, success experienced as a lucky strike at an extremely difficult task might evoke a strong feeling of pleasure or joy, but not a feeling of pride about one's own accomplishment. In sum, none of the pertinent studies satisfactorily represents the incentives of success and failure as defined by Atkinson. The more or less linear relations found between subjective probability or task difficulty and the different indicators of incentive therefore cannot be considered as unequivocal confirmations of Atkinson's conception.

Meyer (1973) pointed out that Atkinson's assumption of a linear relation between expectancy of success and the incentive of success (pride) might not hold for all achievement tasks. He stated that "pride about one's own accomplishment presumes a prospective internal attribution of the outcome of an action (as does shame about one's own incapability). Otherwise, the occurrence of such esteem-related affects is not possible, but rather joy or anger will result over the fact that an effect has or has not occurred" (Meyer 1973: 143). Meyer assumed that a curvilinear relation between expectancy and incentive value (pride or shame) will exist at tasks where positive outcome at levels very low in subjective probability and negative outcomes at levels very high in subjective probability give rise to attributions of luck. These are tasks that, for their solution, do not require a sequence of interrelated steps of action (like solving a complex mathematical problem), but where the solution can be reached in one step (like throwing a ring onto a stick). For these tasks, which were often used in order to test Atkinson's model, the incentive should be highest in the area of intermediate subjective probabilities, since in this area success and failure should be attributed to internal factors like ability or effort.

AN EMPIRICAL INVESTIGATION

These assumptions were partially tested in an experiment by Meyer and Plöger (1978).[a]

Method

Subjects were ninety male students from the University of Bielefeld, West Germany. They were provided a sheet with the description of a

---

a. An expanded version of this paper is available from the first author.

ring-toss game. This task was chosen because it has often been used to test Atkinson's theory (for example by Atkinson and Litwin 1960; Damm 1968; Hamilton 1974; Litwin 1966). Subjects were asked to imagine that, after a period of practice, they had thrown twenty rings at a stick from each of seven distances. The number of own hits reported in the questionnaire increased with decreasing distance from the target. In one experimental condition ($n = 30$), the subjects received information only about the number of their own hits. In two other conditions additional information was provided about the hits of others who performed this task. In the condition "high social norm" ($n = 30$), the number of hits by others from each distance was higher than one's own; in the condition "low social norm" ($n = 30$), the respective numbers were lower. This information is summarized in Table 6-1. The number of own hits was the same for all three experimental conditions.

To assess the dependent variables, three questionnaires were distributed in a randomized order. In these questionnaires a separate sheet was provided for each distance. The questionnaire on *subjective probability* asked the subjects to imagine that for each distance they had one more throw. They had to indicate how certain they would be to hit from each distance described. An 11-point scale was provided for the responses, ranging from 0 (definitely will not hit) to 10 (certainly will hit). The questionnaires on *attributions of success* and on *affects* asked the subjects to imagine that for each distance they made one more throw and that they hit the target. The subjects had to indicate what cause for this success and what affect

Table 6-1. Number of Own Hits and Hits of Others from Seven Distances with Twenty Throws from Each.

Distance	Own hits	Hits of Others	
		High norm	Low norm
A	1	10	0
B	4	12	0
C	8	13	0
D	11	16	4
E	14	20	7
F	17	20	8
G	20	20	10

they would experience. Attributions and affects were assessed as free responses. This procedure imposes heavy restrictions on the statistical analyses of the data. But these difficulties were tolerated in order to find out which attributions and affects are evoked given a free response procedure, rather than employing the more predominant reactive measures.

Categorization of Attributions and Affects

Attributions. Nine categories were established for classification. The 630 responses (90 subjects × 7 levels of difficulty) were assigned to one of the categories by a single rater. (If two causes were stated for an outcome, only the first one was considered.) To assess rater reliability, the responses of 15 subjects for the 7 difficulty levels were classified independently by a second rater. Interrater reliability was 85 percent.

Of the 630 responses, 67 (11 percent) were descriptions of achievement results; they were excluded from further analyses. The remaining 8 categories, and their overall frequencies, were: luck 35 percent, practice 25 percent, ease of the task 17 percent, skill 15 percent, effort 5 percent, ability 1 percent, external conditions of the situation 1 percent, momentary psycho-physical states 1 percent. Ability and skill were then combined, as were effort and practice. The categories: external conditions of the situation and momentary psycho-physical states were not considered further because of their low frequency of occurrence. The percent frequencies of the remaining categories are summarized in Table 6-2.

Affects. Eleven categories of affect were established. The 630 responses (90 subjects × 7 levels of difficulty) were assigned to one of

Table 6-2. Categories of Causal Factors for Success and Their Frequency.

	Percent
Luck	35
Practice, effort	30
Ease of the task	17
Ability, skill	16

these categories by a single rater. The responses of 25 subjects were then independently classified by a second rater, with an interrater reliability of 74 percent. (If two affects were stated for an outcome, only the first one was considered.)

Of the total 630 responses, 198 (31 percent) contained no descriptions of feeling states, and 29 (5 percent) were nonclassifiable responses. These responses were excluded so that the following percentages of affects are based on 403 responses. The affective classification and frequencies for the remaining nine categories are summarized in Table 6-3.

Results

Subjective Probability. An analysis of variance revealed a significant main effect for the task difficulty factor: with decreasing distance from the goal (and therefore higher numbers of own hits) the probability of success rises ($F(6/516) = 710.90$; $p < .001$). The effect for the social norm factor was insignificant, as was the interaction of both factors. When averaging over the three social norm groups, the mean probabilities were: 0.97 (A), 2.35 (B), 4.06 (C), 5.45 (D), 7.11 (E), 8.58 (F), and 9.63 (G). This represents the spectrum of subjective probabilities quite well when given an 11-point anchored scale.

Attributions. Concerning differences between the social norm groups there are but two consistent trends: In the low social norm

Table 6-3. Categories of Affects for Success and Their Frequency.

	Percent
Joy, enthusiasm	28
Indifference, no particular feeling	18
Satisfaction, gratification	17
Feeling of expectancy confirmation	11
Joy about luck	7
Surprise, amazement	7
Relief, security	6
Happiness	3
Pride	3

condition, at each difficulty level success is explained more often with ability/skill than in the high social norm condition. In addition, the ease of the task is reported less often at each level in the low social norm than in the high social norm condition. For each causal factor and difficulty level, it was determined whether the frequencies differ between the social norm groups. Of the total of 84 comparisons, only three proved to be significant. The frequencies were therefore combined over the social norm groups.

In Figure 6-1 the combined attributional frequencies are represented as percentages of the total attributional responses (the per-

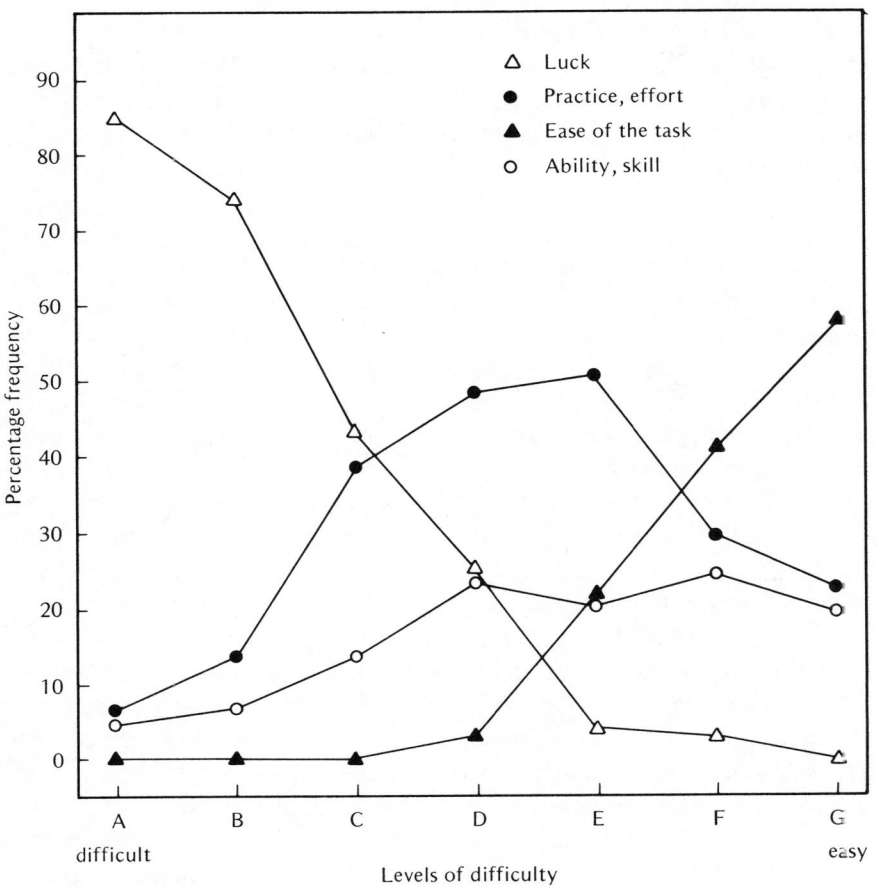

Figure 6-1. Percentage Frequency of Attributions for Seven Levels of Difficulty.

centages of the four categories total 100 percent at each difficulty level). The distributions of the response frequencies deviate at each difficulty level from an equidistribution ($p < .01$). Figure 6-1 indicates that attributions to luck, practice/effort, and ease of the task are a function of the consistency of anticipated success with the number of one's own previous hits (the subjective probability of success). Attributions to luck are most frequent when anticipated success is inconsistent with previous results, and with decreasing inconsistency attributions to luck decrease. On the other hand, attributions to the ease of the task occur most frequently when success is consistent with previous results (levels G and F). The frequency maximum of practice/effort lies in the medium range of difficulty, while attributions to ability/skill do not systematically vary with the difficulty levels.

It is also noteworthy that success at this task is most frequently explained by the four causal factors assumed by Heider (1958) and Weiner et al. (1971) to be the predominant ones for explaining the outcomes of achievement-related activities (ability, effort, task difficulty, and luck).

Affects. For each level of difficulty, the affect differences between the social norm conditions were examined. Of these comparisons, six proved to be significant ($p < .05$). The significant differences appeared for satisfaction/contentment and relief/security. Satisfaction/contentment is evoked more often in the low social norm condition than in the other two conditions. On the other hand, relief/security is reported more often in the high social norm condition than in the low social norm condition.

In Figure 6-2, the affective frequencies are presented, combining the social norm conditions (the percentage frequencies of the affects total 100 percent at each level of difficulty). The distribution of the response frequencies deviates significantly from an equidistribution at each level of difficulty ($p < .05$). Figure 6-2 reveals that feelings of pride (together with happiness), which, according to Atkinson (1957, 1964), give rise to achievement strivings, are the most infrequently reported affect. In addition, pride and happiness do not vary according to the difficulty levels. The affects of expectancy confirmation and indifference are most frequently evoked when anticipated success is consistent with previous results and the subjective probability is very high (level G); with decreasing consistency or sub-

Figure 6-2. Percentage Frequency of Affects for Seven Levels of Difficulty.

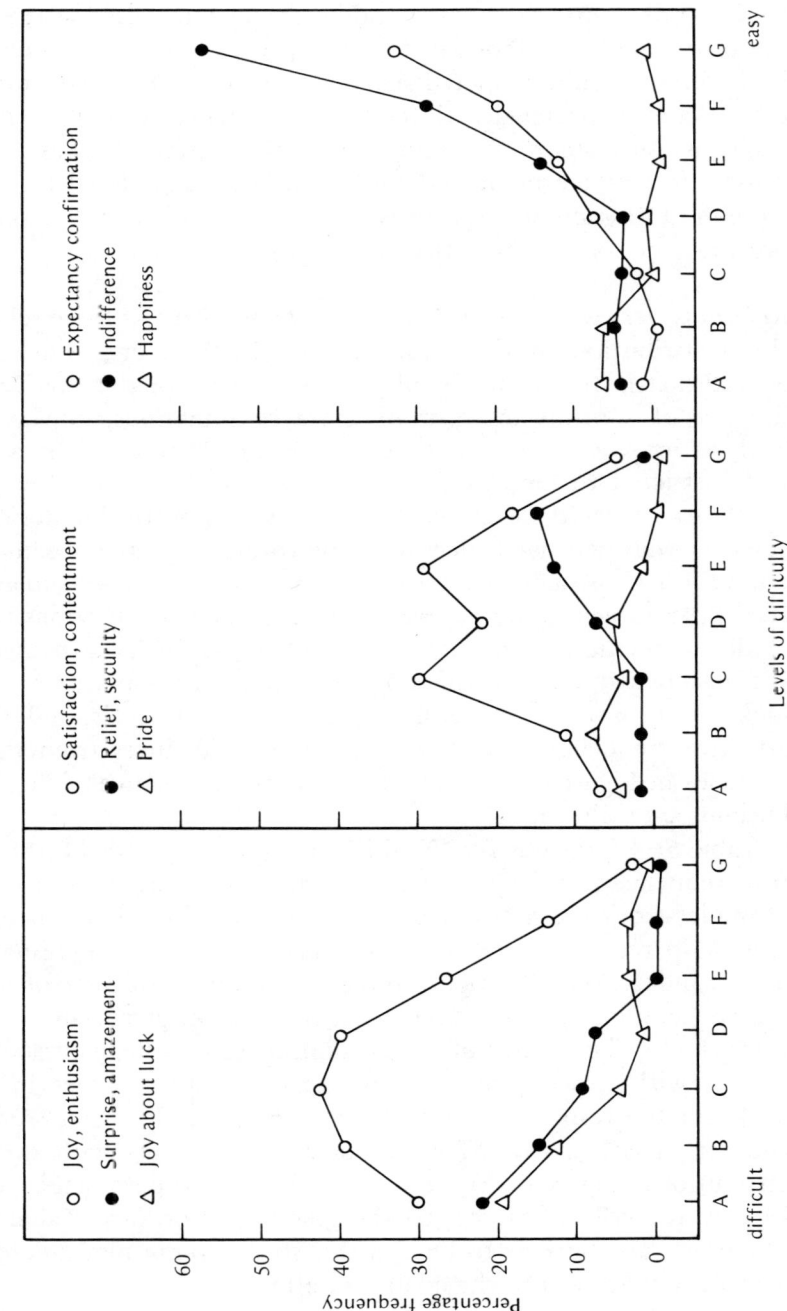

jective probability the corresponding frequencies also decrease. On the other hand, joy about luck and surprise/amazement are reported most often when anticipated success is not consistent with previous results and expectancies (level A); with increasing consistency or subjective probability the frequency of these affects lessens. Finally, satisfaction/contentment and joy/enthusiasm are related in a more curvilinear fashion to the consistency of the anticipated result with previous ones or the subjective probability.

Relations between Attributions and Affect. To test these relations, the 4 attributions were combined with the 9 affects, resulting in a 36-cell matrix for each difficulty level. Because of the relative small number of subjects in most of these combinations, however, the analysis in general proved to be inadequate. Therefore, the analysis was restricted to luck as the most frequent attribution (see Table 6–2). At difficulty levels A, B, and C was a sufficient number of subjects who perceived success as due to luck and at the same time reported a classifiable affective response: at level A 49 subjects, at level B 45 subjects, and at level C 26 subjects. If attributions to luck mediate specific affects, then two findings are to be expected: (1) the affective frequencies of subjects who perceive success as due to luck should not vary according to the difficulty levels, and (2) the affective frequencies of these subjects should differ from the frequencies in Figure 6–2, where all subjects, irrespective of their attributions, are included.

Table 6–4 indicates for the difficulty levels A, B, and C the affective frequencies of subjects who perceive success as due to luck. For example, from the 49 subjects at level A who attribute success to luck, 35 percent reported joy/enthusiasm, 22 percent surprise/amazement, and so on. The figure reveals that the frequency of affects varies according to the difficulty levels. That is, given same attributions (luck), the quality of affect is influenced by the consistency of success with expectations. Furthermore, the percentages in Table 6–4 and the respective ones in Figure 6–2 barely differ from one another. That is, the affects reported by subjects with different attributions (Figure 6–2) are very similar to those reported by subjects who attribute success to the specific factor luck (Table 6–4). Therefore, attributions to luck in this study do not play a determining role with respect to the quality of affect.

Table 6-4. Percentages of Affects at Three Difficulty Levels Reported by Subjects Who Attribute Success to Luck.

Difficulty level	Joy/ enthusiasm	Surprise/ amazement	Joy about luck	Satisfaction/ contentment
A	35	22	19	6
B	35	15	18	9
C	50	11	4	27

CONCLUSIONS

Implications for Atkinson's Theory

According to achievement motivation theory (Atkinson 1957, 1964), the tendency to approach success is uniquely linked to the specific affect of pride. Anticipated pride is conceived to be the only incentive for engaging in achievement-related activities. The findings in this experiment show, however, that many affects can occur in a fictitious achievement situation, with pride (together with happiness) being most rarely evoked. This suggests that in the framework of Atkinson's theory not only pride, but also other, perhaps more important, incentive-emotions should be accounted for (see also Weiner, Russell, and Lerman 1978, 1979).

The relation proposed by Atkinson between subjective probability of success and the incentive of success suggests that pride will be evoked particularly often at tasks very low in subjective probability. The findings reported here do not confirm this. This suggests that Atkinson's assumption of an inverse linear relation between subjective probability of success and the strength of anticipated pride (incentive) is not universally valid.

The affects evoked most frequently in this study at tasks very low in subjective probability are joy/enthusiasm, joy about luck, and surprise/amazement. The frequencies of the latter two affects are most close to an inverse and linear function of the subjective probability that Atkinson assumes for the intensity of the affect pride. Assuming that the frequencies of these two affects indicate their strength, then at this kind of task an inverse and linear relation between expectancy and the strength of surprise/amazement or joy about luck seems more plausible.

Attributions to Luck and Feelings of Surprise

Weiner, Russell, and Lerman (1978, 1979) recently investigated the role of attributions in the formation of affects. The authors discovered close links between both. For example, success ascribed to ability typically was associated with feelings of confidence and competence. Similarly, success perceived as due to other's effort was linked to gratitude. Weiner, Russell, and Lerman conclude from their data "that affects often (but not necessarily always) are directly tied to the causes" ascribed to an outcome (Weiner, Russell, and Lerman 1978: 82). Furthermore, they state that "perhaps the clearest finding in our data is the unique emotional reaction (surprise, astonished, wonderment) given a luck ascription for success" (p. 75). Weiner, Russell, and Lerman therefore conceive surprise, among others, as an attribution-dependent affect.

However, the data in this study are not consistent with these findings. The frequency of the emotions surprise/amazement does not differ between subjects who attribute success at levels A, B, and C to luck and subjects who perceive success at these levels as due to other factors. Surprise and amazement are, rather, linked to the consistency of success with one's own previous results or the subjective probability of success (see Table 6–4). Furthermore, in the view of many authors surprise and amazement are fundamental emotions (see, for example, Izard 1977) that occur as early as infancy (see, for example, Piaget 1952), at a time when the child seems not to be capable of generating causal explanations. Accordingly, surprise is considered to be functionally linked to cognitive development. It leads to attentional processes upon which cognitive development depends (Charlesworth 1969).

Consistent with this reasoning and the findings of this experiment, it seems more plausible to the present writers to conceive surprise, amazement, or wonderment not as attribution-dependent emotions. Rather, these affects seem to be of functional significance to the search for an explanation and to attribution. We assume that an outcome of an action is first subjected to a relatively simple assessment based on the expectations of the occurrence of that outcome. If the discrepancy between expected and actual outcome is very high, then the immediately and automatically evoked reactions to this discrepancy are surprise or amazement as *primary* affects. These emotions have cue function. They stimulate further cognitive activity, especially the search for an explanation for the discrepant outcome. The result of this activity is a subjectively more or less valid causal explanation. Outcomes that are inconsistent with expectations are often (but not always) attributed to luck as in the ring-toss game used here or the tasks used by Feather (1969) and Meyer (1973).

Discrepant outcomes at other tasks may lead to other attributions than luck. For example, an unexpected high score at an exam test (evoking surprise) may lead to a revision of the initial assessment of one's own ability or may be attributed to help received from others. This then may lead to *secondary*, attribution-mediated affects. According to Weiner, Russell, and Lerman (1978, 1979), success ascribed to ability leads to feelings of confidence or competence. Success perceived as due to help of others may result in gratitude. The close links between ascriptions to luck and the emotion of surprise, found by Weiner et al., do not contradict the position advocated here. But, according to this position, these links do not indicate that surprise is mediated by attributions to luck. The links rather result from the fact that ascriptions to luck and feelings of surprise or amazement are both linked to a third factor: the discrepancy between expected and actual outcome. Outcomes highly discrepant from expectations *first* lead to surprise or amazement; these outcomes are often, but only *subsequently* ascribed to luck.

In sum, attributions clearly often mediate affects as pointed out by Weiner, Russell, and Lerman (1978, 1979) (attribution → emotion). But, on the other hand, specific affects like surprise, amazement, or wonderment are of functional significance for the attribution process (emotion → attribution). A closer examination of the cue function of these specific emotions perhaps may lead to an answer for the neglected question in attribution theory: "When do people engage in causal explanations?"

7 SELF-ESTEEM AND ATTRIBUTION
Individual Differences in the Causal Explanation of Success and Failure

Wolfgang Stroebe

Experiences of acceptance-rejection and competence–incompetence, that is, interpersonal and task-related success or failure are major determinants of a person's self-esteem (Coopersmith 1967; Epstein 1973). It is also true, however, that the degree of a person's self-esteem determines to some extent whether a given interpersonal or task-related event is experienced as a success or a failure (that is, "as due to one's competence or incompetence... and not determined by chance or dependent on other factors which lie beyond the individual's personal control" (Meyer 1973: 30). The dependence of attributions on self-esteem is the subject of this chapter, the aim of which is to develop an approach that could account for the attribution of success or failure in the area of interpersonal relations as well as in achievement contexts.

Most researchers (such as Secord and Backman 1965; Coopersmith 1967) have considered self-concept and self-esteem as components of an attitude, namely, the attitude towards one's self. The self-concept represents the cognitive component of this attitude, that is, the beliefs a person holds about himself (the attributes and traits that he would use for self-description—for example "intelligent," "tall"). Self-esteem is the affective component: the positive or nega-

---

The author wishes to thank Th. Herrmann and W.-U. Meyer for helpful comments on an earlier draft of this chapter.

tive evaluations of these attributes and traits. Although being intelligent is presumably evaluated positively by most people, being tall is subject to differential evaluation. Physical size may contribute positively to the self-esteem of a man but negatively to that of a woman.

By self-assessment we mean the evaluation of one's self on a specific dimension, such as intelligence or appearance. Self-esteem can be considered the result of all these self-assessments. Since there is no reason to assume that theories of impression formation do not apply to the impression one forms of oneself, the self-esteem of a particular person at a particular point in time can be defined as an average of the evaluations of all these self-assessments, whereby each is weighted according to its importance or significance to the individual (Anderson 1965).

Thus, the more important a particular dimension of self-assessment is for a person, the closer should be the relation between his assessment on this dimension and his global self-esteem. As O'Brien and Epstein (1975) have shown, self-esteem is mainly determined by experiences of competence or incompetence in the area of achievement, and of acceptance or rejection by others in the area of interpersonal relations (at least among the students studied). Since we further assume that the self-assessment of one's traits or abilities affects one's expectations of the quality of one's relevant outcomes, a close relation between global self-esteem and the expectations of outcomes in the areas of achievement and interpersonal relations is likely to exist.

Such expectations have a significant effect on one's interpretations of the outcomes of one's actions. In the area of task-related behavior, Feather and his colleagues (Feather 1969; Feather and Simon 1971a, b; 1973; Simon and Feather 1973) have demonstrated that the interpretation of an outcome as due to chance or ability depends on the level of correspondence between expected and actual achievement. If the outcome corresponds closely to one's expectations, it is attributed internally to ability and knowledge (positive outcome) or lack of ability or knowledge (negative outcome). On the other hand, if the outcome is discrepant from these expectations, it is attributed more to the external factor of chance.

A person's expectations regarding the likely outcome of an action are often derived from experiences that he has had with similar tasks in the past. However, if the person has had no experience with the specific type of task he is confronted with, his expectations will be based on the general assessment of his relevant abilities. Given the close relation that we assume to exist between global assessment of abilities and global self-esteem, the interpretation of success and failure under these circumstances should be influenced by one's self-esteem. This assumption does not apply, however, to situations in which certain obvious causes present themselves from the outset as explanations for potential outcomes of actions. For example, our assumption is presumably not valid if a task is perceived as *extremely* easy or *extremely* difficult at the outset, if the individual for some reason has no intention to try hard, or if the task is experienced as a game of chance.

In the *area of interpersonal relations*, experiences of success or failure typically occur when a person believes that, in the course of an interaction, he has made a positive or negative impression on the other person. The question here is how one draws the "corresponding inference" (Jones and Davis 1965) that the friendly or unfriendly behavior of the other person reflects his true feelings and should not be attributed to other external causes. We assume here too, that attributions are influenced by global self-esteem and therefore by a person's self-assessment.

This chapter will examine whether the relation between these components of one's attitude toward one's self, on the one hand, and one's expectations as well as interpretations of the outcomes of one's actions, on the other hand, can be accounted for in terms of a self-consistency hypothesis.

SELF-ESTEEM AND THE CAUSAL EXPLANATION OF SUCCESS AND FAILURE IN THE AREA OF ACHIEVEMENT

Both Feather (1969) and Fitch (1970) examined how global self-esteem affects the interpretation of success and failure, using achievement tasks. The task in Feather's study consisted of ten anagram problems. The subjects were told that they must solve five or more problems to pass the test. The anagrams were chosen in such a way that about half the subjects were expected to pass. After completing the anagrams, the subjects were asked to indicate the extent to which the result was attributable to ability (internal) or chance (external). Global self-esteem was measured with the "Feelings of Inadequacy Scale" (Janis and Field 1959). Feather also asked his subjects before starting the task to indicate their specific expectation of success. The predicted differences in attribution were found only for specific expectation of success, and not for global self-esteem. Subjects who had a high expectation of success attributed success more internally and failure more externally than did subjects who had lower expectation of success. The correlation between global self-esteem and specific expectation of success was small and did not reach significance.

The reason for this failure to find a correlation between global self-esteem and both attribution and specific expectation of success becomes clear when one looks at the individual items of the Janis and Field scale. The scale is designed primarily to examine interpersonal relations and includes only a few items on the assessment of one's own achievement. Although a certain amount of consistency presumably exists between the different aspects of self-assessment, one could hardly expect the Janis and Field scale to make highly accurate predictions of specific expectation of success in the achievement context. A study conducted in Marburg also produced only a weak correlation ($r = .13$) between specific expectations of success and global self-esteem, as measured on the Janis and Field scale. On the other hand, global assessment of one's own abilities, measured with a newly developed test, correlated significantly ($r = .36$) with specific expectation of success. Nevertheless, this latter correlation is still disappointingly weak.

In the study conducted by Fitch (1970), subjects were asked to estimate the number of dots displayed for short intervals on slides. Success or failure was induced by giving subjects false feedback on their performance. Global self-esteem was measured a few weeks before the study began, by means of the "Tennessee Self-Concept Scale" (Fitts 1964). No data were collected on specific expectations of success. After receiving the false feedback, subjects were asked to indicate the extent to which ability, effort, luck, and their momentary physical condition had contributed to the outcome of their performance. In the statistical analysis, attributions of ability and effort were combined to give a measure of internal attribution, in order to assess the dependence of these internal attributions on global self-esteem. Although the interaction between self-esteem and the interpretation of success or failure was significant, an additional analysis of the simple effects revealed that the predicted differences in attribution were found only in the case of failure. The negative result was attributed more internally by a subject with low self-esteem than by a subject with high self-esteem.

In further studies of causal explanation of success and failure, Feather (Feather and Simon 1971a, b; 1973) examined only specific expectations of success, and not global self-esteem. The relation found earlier (Feather 1969) between specific expectation of success and attribution of success or failure was consistently replicated.

Similar studies were conducted by Weiner et al. (for example, Weiner and Kukla 1970; Weiner and Potepan 1970) and Meyer (1973). In these studies, however, attribution was investigated in relation to achievement motivation and not self-esteem. Nevertheless, if one regards high achievement motivation and high self-esteem as comparable, and likewise fear of failure and low self-esteem, then our predictions are identical to the predictions derived from our self-consistency approach. Meyer (1975, 1976) makes this connection explicit by accounting for differences in attributions of persons motivated by hope of success and those motivated by fear of failure in terms of differences in self-concept of ability.

However, by in addition predicting attributions to effort, task difficulty, and luck, Weiner et al. (1971) and Meyer (1976) make more far-reaching statements than would be feasible on the basis of our self-consistency approach. From the latter, one can only predict that outcomes consistent with expectations will be attributed to ability or lack of ability, and that the ability dimension cannot be used to explain outcomes that are inconsistent with expectations. In fact, it is precisely these more comprehensive predictions that are harder to confirm. Meyer summarized the research findings to date as follows: "An examination of pertinent studies on differences in causal explanation of achievement outcomes between those motivated by hope of success and those motivated by fear of failure revealed that people motivated by success attributed successes more to high personal ability than did those motivated by failure. No such consistent differences could be established for other causal factors" (1976: 102).

Meyer's finding is not surprising, since causal explanation using effort or task difficulty may be expected to depend to a large extent on the characteristics of the task, an aspect that has been systematically taken into account only in recent research (Meyer 1976).

In summary, a number of questions remain unanswered. Although the assumption that ability or lack of ability is more likely to be used to explain outcomes of actions that are consistent with expectations is well documented empirically (at least for tasks that were presumably experienced as achievement tasks of medium difficulty), the connection we assume to exist between these expectations of achievement and self-esteem has hardly been tested to date. Furthermore, it is surprising, in view of the correspondence between the predictions of self-consistency theory and the attribution-theory approach to achievement motivation (Weiner et al. 1971; Meyer 1973), that no study appears to exist that tests the dependence of the attribution of success and failure on achievement motivation as well as on global self-esteem and specific expectations of success.

SELF-ESTEEM AND CAUSAL EXPLANATION OF SUCCESS AND FAILURE IN THE AREA OF INTERPERSONAL RELATIONS

In the area of interpersonal relations, even less research has been done on the link between self-esteem and the causal attribution of success and failure than in task-related behavior. Success in the area of interpersonal relations means that we successfully produce a positive attitude in another person in the course of an interaction. A failure is the production of a negative attitude in another person. It is the aim of this section to clarify how a person recognizes another person's attitude toward him.

We are probably fairly certain of how our spouses or close friends feel about us. This certainty may be partially explained by the long acquaintance and partially by the fact that informal interactions make it easier to know the other person's true feelings. We are presumably less sure of the feelings of a new colleague or fleeting acquaintance. The formal interactions that are typical of the early stages of interpersonal relations make it difficult to draw inferences as to the motives of the interactors. This difficulty derives primarily from the norms of politeness, which exert strong external pressure on behavior. These norms oblige an actor, regardless of his true feelings, to pretend external causes for any actions toward others that might have negative evaluative implications, but to pretend internal causes for any actions with positive evaluative implications. Therefore, in cases of behavior having negative implications, a person will point to situational constraints and other external causes, in other words, to causes that lie outside his own control and responsibility. On the other hand, in cases of behavior with positive evaluative implications, he will deny such external causes and claim full responsibility.

Consider an example from everyday life: If one is invited to dinner by someone one has just met and finds dull, one will hardly be prepared to accept the invitation. However, in turning it down, one is unlikely to give the true reasons, but rather to plead overwork, urgent deadlines, bad health, or the like. One will thus try to reduce the negative evaluative implications of the refusal by giving external reasons. On the other hand, if one meets a colleague at a conference abroad who mentions that he will be visiting one's home country in the foreseeable future, politeness requires that one invite him to visit or even to spend the night. In this situation one will try to use a particularly warm tone in order to show that one really means it. Not necessarily because one does, but because it would be impolite to do anything else.

How does one draw inferences about other's motives in situations such as these? According to Jones and Davis (1965), such inferences depend primarily on the *freedom of choice* attributed to the actor and on the *probability* the perceiver attaches to the various motives as causes of the behavior in question. In situations in which the actor's freedom of choice is perceived as severely restricted, a target's inference regarding an actor's attitudes will be a joint product of two factors: the evaluative implications of the behavior, and the expectations of the target person as to the "true" attitudes of the actor (Jones and Harris 1967; Jones et al. 1971).

Jones and coworkers (Jones and Harris 1967; Jones et al. 1971) use a simple paradigm for their studies. Their subjects were given a speech, taking some fairly extreme position on an issue, and were informed, either that the speaker had absolute freedom to take any position on the issue or that the speaker had been instructed to take a given position on that issue. They demonstrated that even if the perceivers were informed that the speaker had been instructed to take a given position, their attributions of his "true" attitude were still affected by the position taken in the speech. However, while in the "free choice" condition, attributions were fully determined by the position taken in the speech, attributions in the "no choice" condition appeared to be a joint result of the position taken in the speech and the perceivers' "prior expectations" regarding the speaker's attitude. Thus, if the perceivers expected the speaker privately to hold a favorable attitude and he in fact gave a favorable speech, it did not matter for the perceiver's attributions whether the speech was given under "choice" or "no choice" instructions. The speaker was always perceived as holding an extremely favorable attitude. If, on the other hand, the speaker took an unfavorable position, contrary to the private beliefs he was expected to hold, attributions were markedly affected by the instructions under which the speaker was allegedly acting. If he was under "free choice" instruction, the perceivers apparently dismissed their prior expectations and attributed an unfavorable attitude correspondent with the direction of the speech. If, on the other hand, the speaker acted under "no choice" instructions, the perceivers were apparently in a conflict whether to rely on the speech or on their prior expectations. They resolved this conflict by attributing a moderately unfavorable attitude.

Extrapolating from these results, a target's inference in situations in which actors are under normative pressure to behave politely should depend on his "prior expectations," which are likely to derive from past experiences in similar situations. If people do use their past experiences in drawing inferences about the meaning of other's behavior and if self-esteem summarizes the evaluative aspects of this past experience, individuals with low self-esteem must, then, differ consistently from individuals with high self-esteem in the inferences they draw about others' feelings toward them. More specifically, the prediction follows that the higher an individual's self-esteem, the more likely he is to attribute any negative behavior (such as a refused dinner invitation) to external causes (such as previous engagements) rather than unwillingness, and to attribute any positive behavior (such as an invitation to visit) to internal causes (such as sympathy) rather than politeness. In other words, a person interprets another's behavior toward him as consistent with his self-concept.

A study by Stroebe, Eagly, and Stroebe (1977) tested these predictions. Subjects of chronically high or low self-esteem as measured with the Janis and Field (1959) "Feelings of Inadequacy Scale" were led to believe that another subject would evaluate them on the basis of a personality questionnaire they had filled out. In fact, they received either a positive or a negative standard evaluation. They were told that the other subject would act either under "sincere" or under "role-playing" instructions. Under "sincere" instructions the other person would be asked to give an honest evaluation. Under "role-playing" instructions, on the other hand, some of the subjects would be instructed by the experimenter to write a positive evaluation while others would be instructed to write a negative evaluation. It was the subject's task to decide, from reading the evaluation, under which instructions it had been written. Thus, the subjects were exposed to either a favorable or an unfavorable behavior and had to decide whether the behavior was due to an external or an internal cause (role-playing versus sincere). As predicted, subjects with low self-esteem felt that the negative evaluation was more sincere and the positive more role-playing, whereas subjects with high self-esteem came to the opposite conclusion. This prediction was supported by a highly significant self-esteem $\times$ evaluation positivity interaction ($F = 11.00$, $df = 1/52$, $p < .01$). (See Figure 7-1.)

As an indirect test of whether this interaction on attribution was mediated by the perceived inconsistency between "prior expectations" and actual evaluations, subjects were to judge the correctness of the evaluation received. Unfortunately, the results were not quite clear-cut. Although consistent evaluations, as expected, were judged as more correct than inconsistent ones, the interaction fell just short of significance. However, this could be due to the weakness of the correctness item as a measure of perceived discrepancy between "prior expectations" and the evaluation. Informal evidence from the postexperimental interview supported this view. Subjects who had judged an evaluation as correct but attributed it to role-playing instructions frequently commented that the evaluation was correct as far as it went, but that it was one-sided and failed to mention many of their good points (in the case of negative evaluations) or their bad points (in the case of positive evaluations).

Thus, the attributions obtained in this experiment confirm our general hypothesis, and the correctness judgments appear not to be inconsistent with an interpretation in terms of consistency between self-concept or "prior expectations" and the evaluations functioning as a determinant of attribution. When faced with situations in which other's behavior could be attributed to several probable causes, people appear to select the one cause that would make the behavior most consistent with their self-concept.

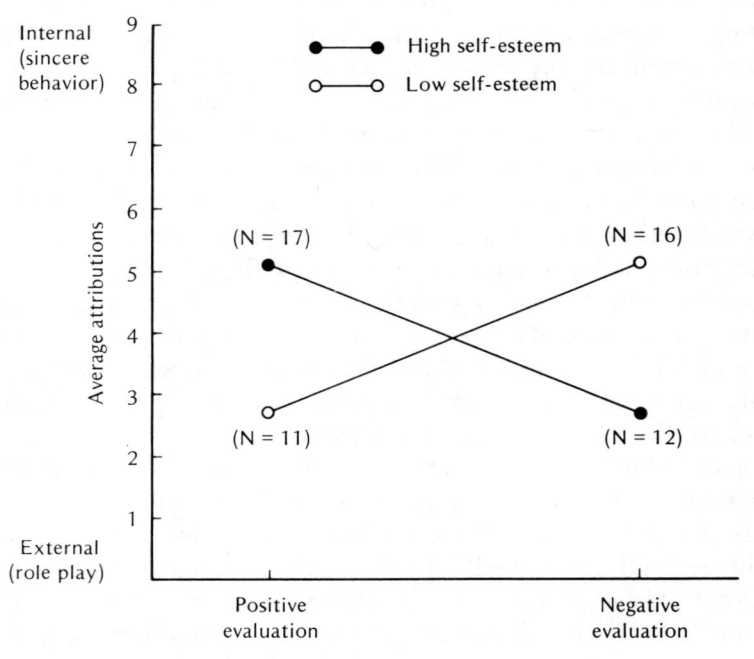

Figure 7-1. Attribution of Positive and Negative Evaluations to "Role Play" or "Sincere Behavior" by Subjects with High and Low Self-Esteem. (After Stroebe et al. 1977, pp. 265–274.)

SELF-CONCEPT AND SOCIAL REALITY

It is certainly a reasonable strategy in many cases partially to base one's attributions of success or failure in the areas of achievement and interpersonal relationships on one's self-assessment. Such an approach does not necessarily lead to a distorted perception of social reality. If, for example, student X, who has rarely been successful with the opposite sex and therefore considers himself unattractive, invites a co-ed to the movies and she refuses on account of another date, then presumably X is not totally wrong if he interprets the "other date" as a white lie. Or if a very good student unexpectedly performs poorly in an exam, then he is probably correct if he does not attribute this grade to the internal factor of lack of ability. However, if positive and negative outcomes of actions were always interpreted consistently with one's self-esteem, a correction of unrealistic self-assessments would be impossible, as would be changes in stabilized assessments. It seems likely, therefore, that after a person has had an accumulation of experiences that are discrepant from his self-concept, he will reach a point where he no longer adapts the experiences to his self-concept, but will change the self-concept to match the experiences.

Epstein (1973) called the self-concept a theory that one has unwittingly constructed about oneself, one's traits, and one's abilities. One could develop this idea further and consider experiences of success or failure as empirical tests of this self-theory, which can lead to a confirmation or falsification of the theory. As in the case of scientific theories, however, one will not discard one's self-theory on the basis of a single inconsistent finding, but will rather look for "confounding factors" in the situation that could possibly account for the unexpected outcome of an action. Only after an accumulation of inconsistent experiences will one consider discarding the theory. However, as with a scientific theory, one would probably hold on to a given self-theory until one has developed a new theory of "greater empirical content" that can not only account for all previous experiences but also the more recent inconsistent ones.

However, a lack of curiosity or fear of failure often appears to prevent stringent tests of one's self-theory. A consequence of this, particularly with low self-esteem individuals, is that false assessments may never be corrected. Furthermore, the expectation of failure can causally contribute to inducing failure. As Jones and Panitch demonstrated, "An individual who misperceives another person's feelings may create by his own actions the affective conditions he believed to exist in the first place" (1971: 357). When subjects in their experiment were led to believe that another person rejected them, they managed to evoke negative feelings in the other person through their own behavior in the experimental situation.

Attributions often affect future behavior. They can thereby become self-fulfilling hypotheses that cause the outcomes they predict. This would have particularly negative effects on individuals with low self-esteem. It is to be hoped, however, that one usually succeeds in maintaining a balance between the tendency to interpret experiences consistently with the self-concept and the necessity of changing one's self-assessment in accordance with new experiences. Only when these tendencies are balanced does our self-concept provide a realistic frame of reference for the interpretation of the never-ending flood of new experiences.

III ATTRIBUTION AND AFFECT

The role played by attributions in the emergence of affects is the subject of the chapter by Ernst H. Liebhart. The author's observations tie in with the so-called Valins effect, according to which perceptions of autonomic changes—correct or incorrect as they may be—have the same effects on emotions as the effects stemming from these changes themselves as postulated by Schachter's theory of emotions. With the inclusion of attributions, Liebhart develops a model for explaining the Valins effect, tests it against available experimental literature, and integrates findings that have up to now seemed contradictory.

ATTRIBUTION AND AFFECT

8 PERCEIVED AUTONOMIC CHANGES AS DETERMINANTS OF EMOTIONAL BEHAVIOR

Ernst H. Liebhart

Schachter's (1964) theory of emotion postulates that emotional behavior is determined by the interaction of autonomic changes—particularly autonomic arousal—with a cognitive factor, that is, the causal attributions, accepted by an individual, of these changes. With respect to the influence of causal judgments, the predictions derived from this theory have been confirmed by many experimental findings (see for example summaries by Dienstbier, Hillman, Lehnhoff, Hillman, and Valkenaar 1975; Liebhart 1974; Tannenbaum and Zillmann 1975; Nisbett and Valins 1971)—in spite of a few failures (Bootzin, Herman, and Nicassio 1976; Calvert-Boyanowsky and Leventhal 1975; Heffler and Lisman 1978; Rogers and Deckner 1975). On the other hand, with respect to the emotional effect of autonomic changes, the results are far less consistent and conclusive (see Erdmann and Janke 1977; Gerdes 1979; Schachter and Singer 1962; Schachter and Wheeler 1962; Tannenbaum and Zillmann 1975).

Valins (1966, 1967, 1970, 1974) modified Schachter's theory by assuming that autonomic changes are subject to the same operations of information-processing as other salient events and that they elicit and direct emotional reactions only through the information they convey—that is, neither unconsciously nor in any way specifically related to the autonomic response systems aroused. Hence, autonomic changes per se may not be important determinants or components of emotional behavior. In a sense, this approach radicalizes Schachter's theory, but it also avoids some of its difficulties. For example, Schachter's assumption of general arousal and his neglect of specific relations between autonomic patterns and experienced qualities of emotion—which are difficult to maintain in view of, for example, Lacey's findings (1967) on intrastressor stereotypy—are restricted to interoceptive feedback. Further, the fact that perception of autonomic reactions correlates but slightly—although usually significantly—with those reactions (see Borkovec 1976; Erdmann and Janke 1977; Mandler 1975; Mandler and Kremen 1958; Schaefer, Tregerthan, and Colgan 1976; Wilson and Lawson 1978) helps us understand the differential emotional impact of actually similar autonomic changes if we take Valins' hypothesis into account. Some experiments conducted in the framework of Schachter's theory of emotion (such as Erdmann and Janke 1977; Konecni 1975) suggest that real physiological changes affect emotional reactions only to the extent to which they are recognized. On the other hand, as we shall see later, emotional reactions occur quite independently of autonomic changes. It is true, however, that actual but unperceived changes in heart rate induced through a novel and ingenious technique (manipulation of cardiac pacemakers) were found to affect performance on cognitive tasks (Cacioppo 1979).

It follows from Valins' (1966) theorizing that the perception of autonomic changes, whether correct or not, should have the same effects on emotional behavior as would be expected to result from actual autonomic changes on the basis of Schachter's theory of emotion. The technique of producing such reality-independent (not necessarily false) perceptions, so-called false autonomic feedback, therefore becomes strategically important in testing Valins' hypothesis. In fact, experiments that employed false autonomic feedback (hereafter referred to simply as feedback) showed that perceptions of autonomic changes—independently of real changes—control a multitude of behaviors that may be related to the concept of emotion. Such feedback effects (referred to hereafter as Valins effects) were found in such different areas as interpersonal attraction, affiliation, attitude change, avoidance behavior, aggression, pain perception, extinction of autonomic responses, and task performance. (The reduction of avoidance behavior by means of feedback will be termed cognitive desensitization.)

The present chapter will develop a model to explain the Valins effect and will relate the model to the entire published research findings in this area. Particular attention will be paid to the reconciliation of seemingly contradictory results.

OUTLINE OF THE MODEL

The model interprets the Valins effect as a result of three successive intervening processes: explanation search, attribution, and attention to the perceived causes of fictitious autonomic changes. It is assumed, first, that the feedback conveys information the recipient cannot satisfactorily explain by means of immediately available knowledge about the context. In other words, the feedback information (such as large variations in the heart rate) and the context of the feedback (successively presented slides showing women similar in attractiveness) present an incongruous pattern. The initially low subjective probability of a causal linkage between the fictitious reaction and the context should activate evaluative needs: incongruity leads to explanation search. Next, we assume that the context of the fictitious autonomic reaction is scanned until aspects are found that "explain" the feedback information (sufficiently attractive features of the women, the sight of which allegedly increased the heart rate). If the causal linkage between an aspect of the context and the feedback attains a sufficiently high subjective probability, the search for an explanation should be terminated and the fictitious autonomic reaction should be attributed to that aspect. Finally for their part, attributions can influence verbal, motor, and autonomic behavior, provided that attention is paid to the "causal factors" at the time of the target behavior.

If this model is correct, four[a] conditions are necessary for the Valins effect to occur: (1) motivation for explanation search, (2) accessibility of context information, (3) plausibility of a causal relation, and (4) salience of the perceived causal factor. These conditions will be discussed in this order below.

---

a. Two of these conditions (2 + 3) refer to the attribution process; therefore, three hypothetical processes correspond to four necessary conditions.

MOTIVATION FOR EXPLANATION SEARCH

In this section, we will first review evidence for the occurrence of explanation search in the processing of feedback information. Then we will examine two factors that, according to Berlyne's theory of exploratory behavior (1965, 1974; Lanzetta 1971) determine the tendency to look for an explanation, viz., the subjective uncertainty about the causes of the fictitious autonomic reaction (explanatory uncertainty, hereafter referred to simply as uncertainty) and the subjective importance of uncertainty reduction.

Evidence for the Search Process

Schachter (1964) assumed that autonomic changes whose causes are not immediately clear arouse evaluative needs. This is consistent with Berlyne's general view that subjective uncertainty creates a drive state that is reduced by relevant information. A number of facts—self-reports by the experimental subjects, persistence phenomena, indicators of attention, and consequences of thwarted explanation search—point to the presumed search process (albeit with differing degrees of clarity).

First, the subjects spontaneously constructed far-fetched causal relations when no obvious "causes" could be identified. They reported having looked at the stimulus objects more closely with simultaneous feedback of change than without such feedback (Valins 1966).

Second, the changes of the attitude toward stimulus objects caused by the feedback persisted even when the subjects were informed about the experimental deception (the fictitious nature of the feedback information) (Valins 1974). Apparently the feedback promotes the discovery of stimulus features that lend themselves to explanation and, once discovered, these may remain salient even if the feedback is recognized to be false (thereby rendering the explanandum nonexistent).[b] Results of a recent experiment (Borkovec et al. 1979) point to a similar mechanism: Effects of increase feedback were strongly attenuated when subjects were told beforehand

---

b. In-depth discussions of this and comparable persistence phenoma are to be found in Nisbett and Valins 1971 and in Ross, Lepper, and Hubbard 1975. It should be noted that Holmes (1977) failed to replicate the Valins (1974) results.

that their reactions were common and to be expected, whereas attenuation was smaller when the same information was given after feedback presentation. Apparently, although in both conditions the information provided should have equally detracted from the feedback's subjective importance, the latter manipulation was not performed until the explanation search had already led to the detection of "causal" features.

Finally, it was observed that the subjects chose longer observation times and recalled more details when they received incongruous feedback than when they received no feedback. This points to an increase in directed attention due to evaluative needs (Girodo 1973; Liebhart 1977; Kanfer, Karoly, and Newman 1974; Misovich and Charis 1974). Apparently the observation period was used to extract information about the causes of the feedback (Misovich and Sosik 1975). The tendency to obtain actively from the environment information about one's own emotional reactions increased with the discrepancy between actual and expected feedback and with the variability of the fictitious autonomic indicator (Behar 1967; Gerard 1963; Gerard and Rabbie 1961). Viewing time was uninfluenced by the consistency of feedback and initial attitude when the consistency manipulation was rather weak (when there was no truly counterattitudinal feedback); additional data concerning evaluation of stimulus persons, however, show that even with slight inconsistency subjects became highly critical of the person they were falsely said to prefer—provided that this preference was expected to have future consequences—and, thus, apparently refuted the implications of the feedback. Anticipation of consequences led to longer viewing times; this lends support to the notion of different levels of inferential processes that may perhaps interact with stronger manipulations of inconsistency (Taylor 1975). Several experiments showed that feedback (versus lack of feedback) or the feedback of autonomic changes (versus stability) led to short-term cardiac deceleration (Bloemkolk, Defares, van Enckevort, and van Gelderen 1971; Borkovec 1973a; Detweiler and Zanna 1976; Liebhart 1977); this points to an increase in attention paid to the environment (environmental intake, Lacey 1967).

Last, feedback effects occurred only if context elements fit for explaining the fictitious reaction were accessible. Impediments to explanation search may under certain circumstances lead to behavioral disorders. For example, subjects who experienced a moderate insult but received feedback of very high arousal that they could not explain displayed symptoms of "neurasthenia" (exhaustion and restlessness, Berkowitz, Lepinski, and Angulo 1969; Berkowitz and Turner 1974). As might be expected on the basis of emotion reattribution research, feedback was ineffective when subjects were given an emotionally irrelevant explanation of their fictitious arousal (Gerdes 1979; compare Schachter and Singer's 1962 epinephrine-informed condition). Very ambiguous stimuli (electronically distorted passages of a speech) were perceptually distorted—even if the subject tried to reproduce them correctly—in such a way that they became suitable for explaining the feedback (Wilkins 1971).

Summarizing, it is assumed that feedback operates through what Kerber and Coles (1978) termed its directive influence, that is, indirectly by leading subjects to reevaluate specific attributes of the context. At present there is no unequivocal evidence for a direct feedback influence on emotion although Kerber and Coles (1978) claim to have shown this so-called informational influence when subjects inferred others' stimulus ratings. Their conclusion must be regarded as tentative because they did not measure reevaluation of specific context features and, moreover, inference of others' emotions is beyond the scope of the present review.

Explanatory Uncertainty

In order to trigger the explanation search and thereby possibly to influence behavior toward a target object, feedback must create subjective uncertainty; that is, it must deviate from the expectancies an individual holds concerning his autonomic reaction to the object. For example, the more the feedback deviated from the subject's initial appraisal of the target object the greater the change in attitude it effected (Kanfer et al. 1974). On the other hand, feedback of increased heart rate accompanying the presentation of slides depicting snakes did not affect subjects who had expected just that autonomic reaction to the stimuli (Rosen, Rosen, and Reid 1972). Similarly, no interpretable effects resulted when increasing heart rate was fed back during performance of a graded approach test with a phobic object (Borkovec 1973a). It is useful to determine in advance the level of arousal expected by the subjects in given situations or in front of certain stimulus objects (Bramel, Bell, and Margulis 1965). Student subjects may even consider a rose bush an instigator of sexual arousal (Brehm and Behar 1966).

If explanatory uncertainty is a crucial determinant of feedback effects, we may extend Valins' (1966) original hypothesis by including not only autonomic changes but autonomic reactions of all kinds, even unchanged activity (quiescence) of an autonomic system. In fact, explanation search was found to be as intense after feedback of minimal heart rate change as after feedback of maximal change (Misovich and Charis 1974; Misovich and Sosik 1975). Similarly, whether fictitious arousal increase or decrease has a stronger effect on information search and emotional behavior should not depend on feedback contents but on the degrees of subjective uncertainty induced through the feedback in a given situation.

Actually the findings on the effects of feedback parameters (such as increase versus decrease; change versus quiescence) are contradictory. If positive or neutral stimulus objects were presented, the Valins effect was consistently replicated with feedback of increased (versus constant) arousal (Barefoot and Straub 1971; Bloemkolk et al. 1971; Botto, Galbraith, and Stern 1974; Decaria, Proctor, and Malloy 1974; Golding and Lichtenstein 1970; Goldstein, Fink, and Mettee 1972; Kanfer et al. 1974; Kerber and Coles 1978; Misovich 1974; Piccione and Veitch 1979; Reisman, Insko, and Valins 1970; Stern, Botto, and Herrick 1972; Taylor 1975; Valins 1966, 1967, 1974; Woll and McFall 1979). On the other hand, feedback of decreased (versus constant) arousal produced less marked, nonsignificant, or opposite results (Botto et al. 1974; Decaria et al. 1974; Stern et al. 1972; Valins 1966, 1967). It appears possible to explain this discrepancy taking into account two factors that should influence explanatory uncertainty: ambiguity and salience of the feedback. Stern et al. (1972) found that it was more difficult to detect a decrease in fictitious arousal than an increase;[c] a decrease was often taken for an increase. Apparently, the subsequent regression to the base level was bewildering; the actual decrease (at the time the stimulus object was presented) notwithstanding, the impression of the (subsequent) increase was more salient perceptually. If fictitious decrease is more ambiguous and less salient than is increase, the former should produce less explanatory uncertainty than the latter. This applies only to naturalistic, not to reportorial, feedback—that is,

c. The fact that changes of feedback must be detectable in the first place in order to motivate information search might appear trivial. In fact, however, one study did employ feedback of heart rate decrease by 15 beats per minute within 3 minutes (Borkovec, Wall, and Stone 1974).

only when the subjects are continuously exposed to some indicator of their activation, but not when they are explicitly informed about the direction of the fictitious autonomic changes (see for example Hendrick and Giesen 1976).

On the other hand, it was found that the extremity of stimulus ratings was lowered no less following feedback of quiescence than it was enhanced following feedback of increase—provided that these rating changes were determined through comparison with appropriate control conditions (a condition with "irrelevant" sounds instead of auditive feedback, for example) (Bloemkolk et al. 1971; Taylor 1975; Stern et al. 1972; Thornton and Hagan 1976). In view of the usually strong manipulation of feedback (fictitious heart rate changes by 20 or 30 beats per minute) accompanying presentation of but moderately arousing pictorial stimuli (which usually cause a real heart rate change of less than 5 beats per minute—see Hare 1972), it is plausible that feedback of both arousal increase and quiescence produced incongruity to sufficient and almost equal degrees. The fact that fictitious decrease but not quiescence were less effective than increase may be due to differential ambiguity and salience of the feedback. Increase versus quiescence were in most experiments manipulated within subjects (for economic reasons), while increase versus decrease were varied between subjects (for reasons of credibility).[d] The former manipulation should reduce the ambiguity of the quiescence feedback (and increase its salience), whereas the latter should not have a similar impact on the perception of the decrease feedback.

In summary, we may conclude that subjective uncertainty is apparently a necessary condition of the Valins effect. Divergent results are compatible with the model if ambiguity and salience of the feedback are taken into account as moderator variables.

Subjective Importance of Uncertainty Reduction

The intensity of explanation search depends not only on the level of subjective uncertainty concerning the causes of a fictitious auto-

---

d. The only experiment employing a within-subjects manipulation of increase versus decrease feedback was published by Detweiler and Zanna (1976) but did not produce a Valins effect for other reasons. But the impact of increase versus constant feedback does not depend on the use of within-subjects designs, as was shown in several studies (Carver and Blaney 1977a, 1977b; Fenigstein and Carver 1978; Scheier, Carver, and Gibbons 1979).

nomic reaction but also on the respective subjective importance of the reduction of this uncertainty (see Lanzetta 1971).[e]

Feedback Parameters. Feedback of arousal decrease should present less of a "problem" (an "effect" in terms of Kelley's 1967 attribution theory) for the recipient than information about arousal increase; lack of clarity concerning causation should be less disturbing in the first case than in the second. It may sometimes be vitally important to react appropriately (among other things, guided by knowledge about the causes) to an increase in arousal, whereas a similar urgency may hardly if ever exist with arousal reduction. The differential effectiveness of feedback of these two events may therefore be due to the low subjective importance of uncertainty reduction in cases of fictitious arousal decrease. One would similarly expect that feedback of quiescence—in a sense a nonevent—should have less of an effect than change feedback. (With regard to the attributional asymmetry of the occurrence versus the nonoccurrence of events, see Ross 1977.) It is not clear why this is not the case.[f] Finally, information about autonomic reactions produces less intense explanation search if it presumably refers to the reactions of another person than when it refers to one's own reactions, particularly when the other is allegedly very different from the subject (Kanfer et al. 1974). In this case the assumption of differential subjective importance of uncertainty reduction is particularly plausible.[g]

Different feedback modalities, such as naturalistic versus reportorial, and different autonomic systems to which the feedback allegedly refers should likewise influence the subjective importance of uncertainty reduction. The data available at present, however, do not permit reliable conclusions to be drawn on that matter.

e. To avoid misunderstandings: Salience of feedback refers to the extent to which attention is paid to the feedback; subjective importance of uncertainty reduction refers to the perceived relevance of the reduction for the prediction and control of important events.

f. It is possible that the expected difference is superimposed by an artifact with the opposite effect: the feedback of indifference might create greater uncertainty than the feedback of change, since the participants in the experiment possibly expect changes rather than indifference in the experimental situation, in which attention focuses on their autonomic reactions.

g. The finding of Golding et al. (1970) that a Valins effect also occurs when the subjects are informed in advance of the experimental deception (see Hendrick and Giesen 1976) requires an improved replication; presently, it is not quite conclusive since we do not know to what extent the subjects mistrusted this information and possibly let themselves be "persuaded" by the procedure.

Context Factors. At least three categories of context factors may be expected to influence the subjective importance of the reduction of feedback-induced uncertainty: actual autonomic changes, own previous behavior, and attention-directing instructions.

With respect to the first point, it is plausible that uncertainty reduction is less important with very high levels of actual arousal. Very intense interoceptive feedback may render external feedback and the uncertainty it induces subjectively irrelevant. This is particularly plausible with aversive stimuli and very anxious subjects (see reviews of cognitive desensitization studies by Borkovec 1973b; Davison and Wilson 1973). Actually—in accordance with the results of the often-cited experiments by Valins and Ray (1967)—the avoidance behavior of subjects with relatively little anxiety was reduced by feedback of quiescence accompanying the presentation of phobic stimuli, whereas, in line with the unsuccessful attempts at cognitive desensitization (Gaupp, Stern, and Galbraith 1972; Kent, Wilson, and Nelson 1972; Rosen et al. 1972; Sushinsky and Bootzin 1970), no effect was obtained with very anxious subjects. (With regard to the interaction between feedback and level of fear, see Conger et al. 1976 and Defares, van Enckevort, van Gelderen, and Schendelaar 1969). Similarly, feedback of quiescence apparently led to improved performance only in subjects with low test anxiety (Koenig 1973). However, there is also evidence that feedback effects are independent of the fear level (Gerard and Rabbie 1961), and even that they are positively related to "emotionality" (Valins 1967)—a construct which, in view of its operationalization, is strongly reminiscent of trait anxiety. When actual arousal (epinephrine versus no epinephrine) and feedback (arousal versus no information) were manipulated orthogonally, both factors contributed significantly to self-reported anxiety preceding dental surgery; the lack of an appreciable interaction between them hints at the independence of feedback effects from actual arousal level (Gerdes 1979).

The discrepancy described has a parallel in reattribution research. Although some results suggest that a high level of activation facilitates attribution of arousal to a fictitious "cause" (Loftis and Ross 1974), in another experiment it was precisely intense fear that precluded such reattribution (Nisbett and Schachter 1966). Comparisons between the levels of fear aroused in these experiments suggest a curvilinear relation: the readiness to process external information about one's own internal state (about its nature and its causes)—

and, thus, the effectiveness of both feedback and reattribution manipulations—increases (versus decreases) with increasing actual arousal at relatively low (versus high) levels of arousal. Nevertheless, the nonoccurrence of the Valins effect should not be prematurely attributed to high arousal; effective feedback processes can also be developed for highly fearful subjects (Cohen, Meyer-Osterkamp, and Grusche 1974). As is argued repeatedly in this chapter, most of the published failures to replicate may be interpreted without assumptions about level of arousal as consequences of ignoring theoretically derivable preconditions of feedback effects.

A case in point is a condition of the experiment by Goldstein et al. (1972) in which male subjects were, by surprise, shown slides of nude males. Ratings of how "offensive" a subject found the experiment were independent of the feedback (increase versus quiescence), but they correlated with actual heart rate changes. In an "inoffensive" condition (slides of nude females), on the other hand, the Valins effect was replicated. The authors assume that the former condition was so arousing that external feedback became subjectively irrelevant. An examination of their data casts doubt on this interpretation: (1) Mean heart rate change in the "offensive" condition was only 1.4 beats per minute greater than in the "inoffensive" condition; (2) mean offensiveness ratings were well below the neutral point of the scale in the former condition, too; (3) the relation between actual heart rate and rated offensiveness was observed only with constant, but not with increased, feedback. I will discuss more plausible interpretations of the results of this experiment in another context.

Attentional processes, too, may moderate the influence of actual arousal on the occurrence of the Valins effect. For example, when subjects actually were not aroused, bogus information about the highly arousing (versus nonarousing) properties of the stimuli led to less enhanced (versus less reduced) arousal ratings when a high degree of self-attention was induced through the presence of a mirror than when attention was not manipulated (Scheier et al. 1979). Probably, self-focus increases the salience of veridical internal information. There is suggestive evidence that chronic focus on the covert aspects of the self as measured by the private self-consciousness scale also attenuates the effect of feedback when the latter is at variance with actual arousal (ibid.). Autonomic perception (see Woll and McFall 1979), internality (as defined in obesity research), and hypochondriasis might have a similar impact. Results obtained by Gerdes (1979) tentatively suggest that women are more aware of their actual arousal than are men.

With respect to the second point, the subjective importance of uncertainty reduction and, thus, the effectiveness of feedback may be reduced or eliminated if a person already has salient information about his internal state through recall of own previous behavior (such as failure at a behavioral approach test with a phobic object).[h] Similarly, reattribution manipulations appear to be ineffective when subjects have extensive experience with the real determinants of their reactions (Singerman, Borkovec, and Baron 1976). Nevertheless, the omission of pretests of avoidance behavior—which should render previous experience with, and behavior toward, a phobic object more salient—does not lead to feedback effects on avoidance behavior either (Kent et al. 1972; Sushinsky 1969). Borkovec and Glasgow (1973) manipulated this variable (inclusion versus omission of a pretest) but found no significant interaction with feedback.[i] The failure of cognitive desensitization should be due to reasons other than exposure to behavioral pretests. It has not been demonstrated to date that salient information about one's own previous behavior restricts the range of feedback effects. A related point concerns the subjects' previous experience with the stimulus category involved. Inferences from others' fictitious autonomic reaction regarding others' stimulus evaluations—for which own previously established preferences are irrelevant—were stronger than inferences in which own reactions and/or own evaluations were involved. Also, bogus information was less credible when it referred to own, as compared to others', autonomic reactions (Kerber and Coles 1978).

Third, verbal instructions may also influence the subjective importance of uncertainty reduction. In one experiment (Liebhart 1977b) feedback was more effective if subjects were instructed to guess the "causes" of their fictitious autonomic reactions (attribution instruction) than when they were simply requested to attend to the visual stimuli and the feedback (attention instruction). In addition, the valence of the perceived causes in the attribution condition was more strongly influenced by the feedback; that is, with altogether aversive

---

h. Cf. Bem's (1972) discussion of the subjective importance of pre-experimental attitudes in the framework of self-perception theory (simulation of forced compliance findings).

i. This is true when statistical methods (like analysis of variance) appropriate to the Solomon four-group design are used instead of the redundant multiple t-tests applied by the authors.

stimuli the causal attribution of the feedback to negative (versus neutral and positive) stimulus aspects increased more through feedback of arousal increase (versus quiescence, respectively) in this condition than in the attention condition. Apparently, the attribution instruction induced the subjects to focus on those aspects that seemed relevant for the explanation of their fictitious reactions. We would also expect that an emphasis—as through a high-demand post-test of avoidance behavior—on the therapeutic character (as against the research orientation) of an experimental procedure should enhance explanation-seeking and behavioral effectiveness of feedback. To date, most of the findings do not support this conjecture (Borkovec 1973a; Borkovec and Glasgow 1973; Cohen et al. 1974; compare Conger et al. 1976); this may, however, be due to the fact that the instructions did not direct subjects' attention specifically to the task of causally explaining the feedback.

Recently it was found that, apart from the information it provides, feedback also heightens self-awareness when compared to an extraneous-sounds control condition (Fenigstein and Carver 1978). Proceeding from this finding, Fenigstein and Carver attempt an alternative interpretation of the Valins effect: If explanation search is the appropriate response to the perception of bodily changes, it may be facilitated by the feedback because self-directed attention is known to increase conformity to standards of appropriate behavior. This somewhat roundabout theory, albeit intriguing, is bedevilled by the problem that the need to explain one's arousal (Schachter 1964) may not be construed as a standard of appropriate behavior.

ACCESSIBILITY OF CONTEXT INFORMATION

In addition to the motivation to search for an explanation, the Valins effect requires the opportunity to seek information, that is, absence of impediments to the search process, and the availability of explanatory context features.

Opportunity to Seek Information

First of all, the subject must have enough time to inspect the context. Barefoot and Straub (1971) obtained a Valins effect when subjects looked at a slide for 25 seconds, but not when they looked at it for 10 seconds. The time required depends on how readily explanatory stimulus features are available in the context (the stimulus object in question). For example, 15 seconds per stimulus object were usually insufficient in studies of cognitive desensitization, although Hirschman (1975) obtained clear feedback effects with 5 seconds per stimulus. Presumably, too, complex stimuli may not be recalled in sufficient detail to permit explanation search after exposure. For this reason, feedback is less effective if it occurs after or shortly before the end of the presentation of the stimulus object (see Barefoot and Straub 1971)—unless the "causal" characteristics were already salient during the presentation (Berkowitz et al. 1969; Bramel et al. 1965). Borkovec et al. (1974) even observed a delayed feedback effect; presumably the difficult task (giving a lecture in spite of strong speech anxiety) forced the subjects to postpone the search for an explanation.

The opportunity to search for an explanation is extremely restrained when, for example, fictitious arousal decrease is signaled by the termination of a stimulus presentation and immediate presentation of the next slide or when the presumed target objects are not presented at all but are replaced by tachistoscopically projected blank slides—purportedly representations of phobic objects. It is hardly surprising that feedback had no effect when such techniques were used (Wilson 1973). Similar experiments yielding positive results are not conclusive because in one case (Brown 1973) feedback was confounded by self-control due to the yoking procedure employed, and in other cases (Lick 1975; Marcia, Rubin, and Efran 1969) because of the strong placebo properties of the feedback treatment.

In addition to external factors, internal conditions can also prevent subjects from detecting explanatory context features. Arousing contrast stimuli (such as electric shocks) that alternate with the target objects can prevent important stimulus characteristics from being perceived or coping behavior (overt or covert) from being enacted. Thus, in one experiment with snake-phobic subjects avoidance behavior was reduced only when nonaversive contrast slides were shown instead of slides that signaled shock (Cohen et al. 1974). Emotional arousal generally restricts the range of cues used in problem solving (Bacon 1974; Easterbrook 1959), and with increasing stress the number of dimensions and concepts used in processing social information diminishes, too (Krohne and Schroder 1972).

Availability of Explanatory Context Stimuli

Usually, explanations of autonomic reactions are sought for in the overt context—primarily in the focal stimulus object and secondarily in additional elements of the situation. The success of the search depends largely on the complexity of the context. With aversive stimuli, explanation search poses special problems. Finally, covert (response-produced) stimuli may also be used to explain the feedback information.

Context Complexity. The Valins effect requires that a factor that "explains" the alleged autonomic reaction be "detected" in an initially nonsalient aspect of the context. The probability that such a characteristic will be found, that the "attributional flexibility" of the context (Davison, Tsujimoto, and Glaros 1973), should increase with the complexity of the context, that is, with the number and heterogeneity of its aspects as well as its ambiguity (see Berlyne 1965, 1971).[j] The "aspects" relevant for the complexity need not be easily designated or delineated. For example, it was observed that feedback had less average influence on the ratings of specific parts of the body of naked stimulus persons than on the ratings of the persons themselves (Valins 1967; Woll and McFall 1979). Presumably, in accounting for the causes of their autonomic reactions, people also take into consideration a stimulus object's more abstract characteristics and higher order structures that may be difficult to identify.

Although the influence of complexity has not been systematically studied in feedback research, the published data permit some pertinent observations. The fact that the variance of the ratings of pictorial stimuli, which had, on the average, approximately neutral valence for a particular sample, did not increase as expected after feedback of arousal increase (Bloemkolk et al. 1971) could be due to the selection of stimuli: the experiment used pictures with a minimal variance of attractiveness ratings—and, thus, presumably of minimal complexity, too. Similarly, the use of pictorial stimuli with a low association value (Decaria et al. 1974) should also attenuate feedback effects. On the other hand, strong feedback effects were found with extremely ambiguous stimuli (White and Wilkins 1973; Wilkins

---

j. Context complexity should not be confused with incongruity of a context-feedback pattern discussed previously.

1971; Reisman et al. 1970). Selection of pretested stimuli high in complexity—in this case strong evaluative heterogeneity of the stimulus elements (pictures with gruesome details in a rather neutral context)—enabled the demonstration of feedback effects with aversive stimuli and fictitious indifference that had otherwise usually failed (Liebhart 1977b). It is also not surprising that feedback of arousal had a greater impact on the attractiveness of women than of high-performance automobiles (Misovich 1974); presumably one would attribute greater complexity to the former than to the latter. The degree of ambiguity of a stimulus should vary greatly between situations and subjects; sometimes almost anything may be interpreted as a cause of sexual arousal (Brehm and Behar 1966). Of particular interest is the possibility that negative aspects of the context reduce its subjective complexity. The following section deals with this problem.

Aversive stimuli. It was shown that the valence of positive stimuli can be reliably increased and decreased through feedback. A striking asymmetry, however, exists in the case of aversive stimuli. On the one hand, their valence became still more negative when strong arousal was fed back simultaneously to their presentation (Bloemkolk et al. 1971; Carver and Blaney 1977a, 1977b; Hirschman 1975; Hirschman and Hawk 1978; Kent et al. 1972; Piccione and Veitch 1979; Thornton and Hagan 1976; Valins and Ray 1967; not replicated by Sushinsky and Bootzin 1970). Increase in extremity was approximately equal in this condition for both positive and negative stimuli (Misovich and Charis 1974). The extinction of the galvanic skin response (GSR) was also delayed when feedback of strong arousal followed the conditional stimulus (CS) (Koenig and Del Castillo 1969; Koenig and Henriksen 1974)—even when the subjects were informed about the removal of the unconditional stimulus (UCS). On the other hand, though, attempts to increase the valence of aversive stimuli were largely unsuccessful (see Davison and Wilson 1973 for summary; more recently, for example, Gerdes 1979).

These facts are probably best interpreted by reference to the interference hypothesis, which was developed to explain negativity biases in judgment (Kanouse and Hanson 1972): Negative attributes of a stimulus object interfere with the enjoyment of its positive aspects, but the latter do not, conversely, reduce the impact of the former.[k]

k. Consider the scholastic axiom "Bonum ex integra cause, malum e quocumque defectu."

If we look we will find in any attractive woman a less pleasant characteristic to explain our (alleged) indifference. On the other hand, at the sight of a frightening snake, one would hardly attribute (fictitious) quiescence to the pretty drawing of the animal's nicely patterned skin. Interference should be stronger the more negative are the object as a whole or some of its aspects, for example, the more intensely the object is feared. This helps explain why cognitive desensitization was effective only with low-fear subjects.

Perhaps this difficulty can be overcome if the context also contains positive elements as plausible "causes" of autonomic quiescence, and if the interference by the negative with the positive aspects is reduced. The latter requirement can possibly be met by including positive elements that, for their part, interfere with the experience of noxious features. For example, anxious subjects might be exposed to models whose behavior toward the feared object reduces its perceived noxiousness (see Bandura, Blanchard, and Ritter 1969). In this case the subjects would attribute fictitious arousal decrease and subsequent quiescence to newly discovered aspects of the object or the modeled behavior. In fact, appropriate feedback raised the perception of the quieting character of a communication about control behavior designed to cope with a feared object and thereby decreased anxious arousal (Harris and Jellison 1971; Hendrick, Giesen, and Borden 1975). A further possibility is the use of attribution instructions to direct subjects' attention to nonaversive stimulus elements and, thus, to lessen the unpleasantness of adverse aspects. It is true that, as usual, with attention instructions the valence of aversive stimuli decreased further following fictitious arousal increase but remained unchanged following fictitious quiescence. With attribution instructions, however, feedback of quiescence did not enhance the valence of the stimuli appreciably less than increase feedback lowered it (Liebhart 1977b). Thus, attribution instructions rendered quiescence feedback as effective with aversive stimuli as it normally is with positively valued stimuli. Further analyses showed that only when attribution instructions were given did subjects attribute causality for autonomic quiescence to nonaversive stimulus features; conversely, however, attention instructions were sufficient to effect attribution of fictitious arousal to aversive stimulus details. Both possibilities—presentation of cues to coping behavior and direction of attention through instructions—are consistent with the observation that interference does not occur when the positive and negative attributes of an object are "separable"

(Kanouse and Hanson 1972)—that is, when a person can control his interaction with the object in such a way that its aversive aspects become harmless.

Response-Produced Stimuli

When the stimulus objects fail to encompass features that may plausibly "explain" a particular feedback information—as is the case with phobic objects and feedback of indifference—no change in stimulus evaluations is to be expected. Nevertheless, subjects can be induced to attribute their fictitious autonomic reactions to their— overt or covert—voluntary behavior toward the objects or their internal representations instead. As will be shown shortly procedures that presumably lead to attribution to response-produced stimuli can influence the probability of occurrence of the behavior pattern in question. Whereas feedback of quiescence during presentation of aversive stimuli usually has no effect, instructions, for example, to vividly imagine touching the phobic objects and the concurrent presentation of progressive decrease feedback resulted in a significant decrease of avoidance behavior even with very fearful subjects (Cohen et al. 1974).

Response attribution becomes particularly important if the stimuli controlling undesirable behavior (say, disorders of task performance) are difficult to identify and if the evaluation of these stimuli can therefore hardly be influenced through external feedback. For example, feedback of quiescence (versus high arousal) during problem solving led to better (or worse) performance and corresponding changes in anxiety (Koenig 1973). I assume that in this case the fictitious autonomic changes were attributed to the stimuli produced by a subject's own attempts at problem solving. This is even more plausible when decrease feedback is provided over several training sessions (Gatchel, Hatch, Maynard, Turns, and Taunton-Blackwood 1979; Gatchel, Hatch, Watson, Smith, and Gaas 1977), although the researchers failed to measure the hypothesized intervening attributions. Similarly, feedback of arousal increase (versus decrease) during preparation and delivery of a speech enhanced (versus reduced) anxiety and speech disturbances; feedback effects combined additively with the spontaneous decline of anxiety during the subsequent speech (Borkovec et al. 1974, 1979). On the other hand, when a person has no opportunity of showing some sort of salient behavior whatsoever at the time of the feedback (see Wilson 1973; compare earlier discussion), or if the response-produced stimuli are not plausible causes of the fictitious autonomic reactions (Borkovec and Glasgow 1973), mere feedback of changes over time is ineffective—presumably because these changes cannot be attributed to relevant stimuli. The concepts of attribution of quiescence to response-produced stimuli and ascription of coping skills to the self appear to be virtually identical interpretive devices when feedback accompanies task-relevant behavior.

Apparently, covert behavior can interact with feedback information, so predictions made on the basis of the overt stimulus configuration may not always be substantiated. For example, Giesen and Hendrick (1974) expected more attitude change when the fictitious arousal was low during a waiting period but rose during subsequent presentation of a persuasive communication, than when it was constantly high. (Only in the former condition is the overt confrontation with attitude-relevant contents a plausible cause of the change in feedback). In fact, however, no difference was found. This may be due to the fact that the subjects knew the topic of the communication in advance and presumably harbored strongly affective thoughts concerning that topic while waiting. Accordingly, subjects in the latter condition, too, could explain their constantly high fictitious arousal by reference to attitudinally relevant cognitions. A subsequent study showed that the coincidence of the increase feedback with the onset of the confrontation with the attitude object enhanced the extremity of the attitude. Coincidence with the mode of confrontation (stimulation to think about the object by announcing the topic versus persuasive communication) on the other hand, was only effective when irrelevant stimulation occurred simultaneously: the distraction was presumably stronger during covert confrontation (Liebhart 1979).

PLAUSIBILITY OF THE ATTRIBUTION

Whether or not a person finds a "plausible" explanation of an autonomic reaction should depend not only on the motivation to search for an explanation and on the availability of potentially explanatory information, but also on the degree to which stimulus context and cognitive structure conform to the plausibility criteria as postulated in attribution theory. These criteria can be described by the concepts of covariation (Kelley 1967) and causal schema (Kelley 1972).[1]

Covariation of Cause and Effect

Attribution theory predicts that an autonomic reaction will be attributed to a context feature if the two are perceived to covary and if the latter appears to precede the former. The covariation can occur on different dimensions: with persons, with stimulus objects, with points in time, and with modalities of confrontation with the stimulus object (Kelley 1967). A very specific correspondence exists between the perceived causes of fictitious autonomic reactions and the dimensions of the covariation (Hansen and Lowe 1976). Negative results may be due to neglect of these principles of covariation and temporal sequence.

Presumably, covariation is perceived only if the feedback that arouses explanatory needs and the context aspect intended by the experimenter to "explain" the feedback information vary on the same dimension. Therefore, information about the modal reaction of reference group members (about variation between persons) has little subjective explanatory power if it was the temporal variability of the feedback that caused explanatory uncertainty (see Gerard 1963). It is possible that covariation of fictitious autonomic reactions with context features other than those intended by the experimenter is perceived, particularly if stimulus event and feedback occur together only once (Heider's minimum data pattern 1958: 155). Most of the unforeseen attributions that occur in this way do not affect the dependent variables and probably do not cause any changes in behavior whatsoever; they only weaken or hide the predicted effect. This probably applies to one of the conditions of the experiment conducted by Goldstein et al. (1972) mentioned previously. Male

---

1. A host of factors may interfere with processing in conformance to these rational criteria and lead to biased attributions. For example, we tend to overattribute causality to entities that absorb our attention. Feedback may enhance the salience of the self and, thus, raise the degree of self-attribution (Fenigstein and Carver 1978). Information conveyed by, and self-focusing influence of, the feedback should combine additively to determine attribution. However, this hypothesis has not yet been explored in the realm of emotional behavior and will not be considered here.

subjects were suddenly confronted with slides of naked men after they had been viewing slides of naked women. The fact that they did not attribute their fictitious high arousal to the supposed "offensiveness" of the experiment does not contradict the attributional model of feedback effects, as the authors contend; there were enough other plausible "causes"—albeit irrelevant, so far as the dependent variables are concerned; surprise, attractiveness of the men, concern about the possibility of having homosexual tendencies (see Bramel 1967), etc. Similarly, the effect of high arousal feedback on attitude change following a communication was reduced when the latter contained dramatic elements that were not intrinsically associated with the attitude object but that offered an attitudinally irrelevant explanation of the fictitious autonomic reaction (Bramel et al. 1965). Rosen et al. (1972) found that snake phobics attributed feedback of quiescence accompanying presentation of snake slides not to the feared object but to the fact of having seen slides instead of live animals—that is, to a therapeutically irrelevant modality of the confrontation. From a therapeutic point of view, nonsymbolic stimulus presentation may therefore be preferable (see Borkovec 1973a; Borkovec and Glasgow 1973).

As far as temporal sequence of stimulus presentation and feedback is concerned, there is at present a dearth of studies on naive assumptions about latency and duration of autonomic reactions as determined by stimulus characteristics and reaction systems. Nevertheless, it was found that fictitious arousal may be attributed to an event occurring as long as four minutes earlier (Harris and Jellison 1971). It is, however, difficult to imagine that—and it cannot be decided on the basis of the dependent variables measured whether—feedback effects are mediated by attribution processes when the fictitious autonomic change begins 20 seconds before stimulus presentation (Hirschman 1975). Problems in interpretation also arise when the "causes" to which subjects should—according to the experimenter—attribute their autonomic reactions are only very globally manipulated responses, such as behavior on a graded approach test (Borkovec 1973a) or covert processes such as the judgment that an experiment was "offensive" (Goldstein et al. 1972).

Causal Schemata

By causal schemata we mean implicit beliefs, held by naive subjects, about causal relations between specific definite phenomena (Kelley 1972).[m] It is assumed that, when an attribution problem becomes salient, judges derive causal hypotheses—each with a specific subjective probability—from the problem- and situation-specific schemata available to them. These hypotheses are thought to direct the information search and to compensate for incomplete actual covariation data, if necessary. Their prior probabilities may be revised if additional information is forthcoming. An attribution is defined as a causal hypothesis associated with a sufficently high posterior probability.[n]

In view of the relative paucity of covariation information typically provided in feedback experiments, attributions can hardly be expected if the causal hypotheses have very low prior probabilities. It is true that the feedback information must violate salient expectancies in order to produce explanatory needs, but it must not contradict all plausible hypotheses that might occur to a person in the course of explanation search. For example, phobic objects probably do not exhibit characteristics that could be regarded as possible causes of autonomic quiescence. In fact, no covariation manipulation has yet persuaded subjects to attribute fictitious quiescence to such objects. Similarly, the covariation of increasing task difficulty with feedback of quiescence (Borkovec 1973a) is more likely to create confusion than plausible causal hypotheses. The fact that the Valins effect did not occur in the experiment conducted by Detweiler and Zanna (1976, presentation of names of nations with simultaneous change feedback) may be due to the lack of relevant schemata in the student subjects. Different subjective probabilities of causal links between a context element and various levels of fictitious autonomic changes can lead to seemingly paradoxical results. For ex-

---

m. The concept of causal schema is probably the most important recent development in attribution theory. It is closely akin to several concepts that refer to implicit generalizations, such as social schemata, prototypes, naive theories, implicational principles, scripts, and the representativeness principle.

n. Attribution theory makes no explicit predictions about the integration of schematic and covariation information. According to the basic postulate of rational, quasi-scientific intuitive information-processing, however, the manner of combination should follow the laws of probability logic, that is, Bayes' theorem. In fact, however, judges appear to apply simpler additive integration rules (see Wyer 1976, for example).

ample, the finding that after moderately strong provocation medium fictitious arousal led to stronger aggression than did high arousal (Berkowitz et al. 1969; Berkowitz and Turner 1974) may be due to the higher plausibility of a causal link of moderate provocation with medium than with high arousal; the psychodynamic assumptions of the authors (denial of excessive anger) are, then, superfluous.[o]

"Naive" judges may not have clear and consistent schemata for every autonomic reaction. For example, schemata of the causal relation between visual stimuli and changes in the heart rate are better developed for acceleration than deceleration. This was shown in a study in which the consistency of attributions of fictitious autonomic reactions, rating of confidence concerning the attributions, and reaction time were used as indicators of the definiteness of causal schemata (Liebhart 1976). Possibly, people also have simply no opinion about whether pleasant or unpleasant stimuli are causally related to arousal decrease and that they are not given pertinent cues in the experiment either. In fact, the results of experiments with decrease feedback are somewhat contradictory, as mentioned previously. Schemata of the relation between heart rate acceleration and confrontation with snakes appear to increase in definiteness with chronic anxiety (Rosen et al. 1972). This is consistent with the ascending branch of the curvilinear relationship, discussed earlier, between (actual) arousal and effectiveness of feedback procedures. Presumably, causal schmata are the more definite, the more salient and subjectively important the phenomena concerned were in the past.

Causal schemata involving autonomic reactions have not been systematically studied; rather, they have sometimes been manipulated or controlled incidentally and without theoretical foundation. For example, subjects were told that certain stimuli would arouse anxiety (Decaria et al. 1974) or that arousal increase upon exposure to Rorschach cards was diagnostic of specific neurotic disorders (Reisman et al. 1970). Rosen et al. (1972) selected subjects on the basis of their belief that viewing snakes caused heart rate increase. (Obviously, these schema may not facilitate attribution of quiescence to snakes.) Unfortunately, we know very little about the "naive psycho-

---

o. Of course, such ex post interpretations point to the necessity of independently determining causal schemata as marginal conditions of attribution theory predictions; this is often overlooked — very much in the same way as in dissonance research.

physiology" of uninfluenced subjects, particularly about implicit beliefs concerning situational and internal determinants of, and interrelationships between, autonomic reactions (see Landy and Stern 1971).

In several experiments subjects were not only informed about variations in the activity of a specific autonomic system but different labels were assigned to the fictitious autonomic changes, too, labels such as joy, anger, heterosexual and homosexual or anxious arousal, even attitude reaction (implicit evaluative response, as it were) (Berkowitz et al. 1969; Berkowitz and Turner 1974; Bramel 1962; Bramel et al. 1965; Brehm and Behar 1966; Detweiler and Zanna 1976; Geen and Pigg 1973; Geen, Rakosky, and Pigg 1972; Giesen and Hendrick 1974; Hansen and Lowe 1976; Harris and Jellison 1971; Hendrick and Giesen 1976; Hendrick et al. 1975; Holmes and Frost 1976). To date, the use of such labels has not been guided by any explicit theory and their effect is not proven. Of course, a verbal label of fictitious arousal (like "anger") and the perception of a context element (say, presence of a frustrator) as "cause" of the arousal need not be functionally equivalent (Berkowitz and Turner 1974). Presumably, such labels operate in a similar manner as do schema-derived hypotheses in that they direct information search toward particular categories of (for example, annoying) context features and, thus, increase the subjective probability of causal links of the feedback with these features. In some of the experiments mentioned feedback informs mainly about the direction of fictitious reactions (say, positive versus negative "attitude"), while the aspect of autonomic activation becomes insignificant (most pronounced in the study by Hansen and Lowe 1976). These procedures are similar to the non-"physiological" techniques of deceiving subjects about their previous attitudinal reactions as used, for example, in the framework of the self-perception theory (Ross, Insko, and Ross 1971). They are but tangentially relevant for the present discussion.

BEHAVIORAL IMPACT OF ATTRIBUTION

In spite of the key significance of attributional concepts for explaining the Valins effect, attributions were measured in only five experiments. One researcher failed to analyze the relations between attributions and the remaining dependent variables (self-report of emotional state and a behavioroid measure) (Gerdes 1979). In two other experiments it was observed that relatively global attributions of fictitious arousal (for example, to a persuasive communication) do not mediate feedback-induced attitude change (Giesen and Hendrick 1974; Hendrick et al. 1975). On the other hand, results were as predicted when highly specific attributions to single aspects of the attitude object were measured (Liebhart 1977b, 1979). For example, with aversive stimuli and feedback of arousal increase, decrease in valence correlated only with the attribution to negative object details, while with fictitious quiescence increase in valence correlated only with attribution to neutral and positive aspects. Apparently, lists of the salient aspects should be prepared on the basis of pretests as was done in the last two aforementioned experiments. Presumably, the results would be more impressive when these lists were drawn up idiographically for each participant in the main study rather than normatively by averaging across a comparable pilot sample. In addition, we assume that statements by subjects about the causes of their behavior will correspond to the attributions expected on a theoretical basis to the extent that the determinants of behavior—real or fictitious—are available (sensu Tversky and Kahneman 1973) at the time of judgment.

The fact that attributions have rarely been measured in attributionally flavored emotion research may—apart from occasional dissociation of the linkage between theory and research—be due to the widespread observation that subjects' reports about the causes of their behavior are often futile and misleading. In accordance with the findings on the "unconsciousness" of numerous cognitive activities (Mandler 1975), no introspective access to the inference processes predicted by attribution theory appears to exist either (Nisbett and Wilson 1977). This may be expected to render development and tests of process models instead of "as if models" (Kelley 1972: 21) in attribution research still more difficult, as no methods for measuring causal attributions independently of verbal report are presently available. Attribution should therefore be considered as a hypothetical construct, at least in the realm of emotion research (see Kelley 1971). Such an approach is justified as long as attribution theory accounts for the available data better than do alternative theories.

Self-ratings of emotional state cannot replace measures of attribution. It is true that such ratings of mood have often been used as indicators of emotional behavior, and it was even assumed that they are "closer in meaning to . . . the experience of emotion" than are stimulus ratings (Harris and Katkin 1975). However, when feedback precedes such ratings, they presumably do not represent anything more than "shallow verbal definitions" of the fictive autonomic reactions (Valins 1966) — that is, simple descriptions that require no further processing of the feedback information; at most, they may therefore, be used as checks on the effectiveness of the feedback manipulation (see, for example, Scheier et al. 1979). Accordingly, significant feedback effects on self-report of emotional reactions almost always occurred, even if the remaining dependent variables were not affected (examples are reported by Cohen et al. 1974; Holmes and Frost 1976; Kent et al. 1972; Krisher, Darley, and Darley 1973; Rosen et al. 1972). In phobic subjects feedback can also induce the cognition "that stimulus has not affected me internally" (Valins and Ray 1967: 345), but this is not equivalent to a causal explanation of fictitious quiescence and, therefore, need not lead to any further behavioral consequences.

If we view attributions as hypothetical mediating responses we are faced with the difficulty that attribution theory can explain noncognitive behavior only by means of heterogeneous supplementary assumptions alien to the theory proper (Bem 1972). This general and thorny problem will not be discussed here. Instead, the present focus will be on one hypothetical condition of the behavioral effectiveness of attributions in the realm of emotions, viz., on the salience[p] of the causal factors (real or fictitious) at the time of target behavior. Whether or not this condition is met should depend on the type of the perceived causes. Adapting Kelley's (1967) fourfold classification of such causes we may distinguish between attributions to (1) global object categories, (2) specific stimulus objects, (3) subject categories, (4) variable context aspects.

Attribution to global *object categories* — and, thereby, to dimensions along which these categories differ — should occur when distinctiveness information, in particular, information about covariation of feedback with categories of stimuli objects, is provided. For example,

[p]. To the extent that this reasoning is correct, it is plausible that feedback effects on verbalized attribution and on nonverbal behavior are, in part, under control of different factors. Availability ("the ease with which the relevant mental operations of retrieval, construction, or association can be carried out" Tversky and Kahneman 1973: 129) is not the same as salience (the extent of disproportional attention — as compared to the entire context — paid to the stimulus in question). In addition, these two requirements must be realized at different points in time.

in attempts at cognitive desensitization, feedback typically varies between phobic stimuli and aversive contrast stimuli. Presumably, however, a person confronted with a phobic object will consider perceived dangers and possibilities of avoidance or coping rather than whether another object is still more frightening. In this situation, therefore, he or she will not attend to features that differentiate between the noxious objects. This may be one of the factors contributing to the relative ineffectiveness of cognitive desensitization. On the other hand, if the situation suggests comparisons between stimulus objects and if such comparisons are instrumental for the target behavior — as is the case, for example, with ratings or choice problems — numerous studies have shown that distinctiveness information affects behavior. The comparison stimuli need not be actually presented but may be purely fictitious; the mere belief that autonomic reactions covary with stimulus categories is sufficient for a Valins effect to occur (Scheier et al. 1979).

Attribution to specific *stimulus aspects* may be expected to occur if a person is induced to pay particular attention to the stimulus object while searching for an explanation and if the object encompasses aspects apt to explain the feedback. The salient aspects of the object correspond to different modalities of the confrontation as conceptualized by Kelley (1967). Attribution to specific stimulus aspects — due to low perceived consistency of autonomic reactions between modalities — is probably the most frequent intervening mechanism in feedback effects. The effects of fictitious autonomic changes on ratings of single stimulus elements (Valins 1967) and on attributions to different stimulus details presented to or imagined by the subject (Liebhart 1977b, 1979) are consistent with this interpretation. Piccione and Veitch (1979), for example, had feedback maximally covary with another's fictitious attitudinal responses (similar versus dissimilar to subject's attitudes) and obtained a strong feedback effect on interpersonal attraction. Experiments on cognitive desensitization have mostly used objects that did not encompass elements suitable for explaining autonomic quiescence; however, change in behavior toward very attention-absorbing objects should depend on whether it is possible to detect calming aspects inherent in the objects themselves. For similar reasons it is plausible, for example, that the attribution of own arousal to a frustrating other will elicit aggressive behavior only toward this other but not toward a neutral third person (Berkowitz and Turner 1974).

Attribution to *subject categories*—and, thus, to dispositions along which these categories differ—is to be expected with consensus information, especially information about covariation of feedback with subject categories. Usually, it does not affect behavior. It is plausible that confrontation with a stimulus object directs attention to features of this object and not to traits differentiating between subjects. If, for example, subjects are led to believe that their fear of certain objects is much above average (consensus information), feedback is ineffective; but if they are deceived into believing that their anxious arousal is far greater than they themselves had expected (consistency information concerning modality), the perception of threatening aspects of the objects is enhanced through increase feedback (Bramel et al. 1965; compare Behar 1967). Consensus information is effective, however, when the target behavior implies self-concern or in some way suggests interpersonal comparisons and, thus, directs attention to those perceived dispositions to which the fictitious autonomic reactions were attributed. Presumably, such was the case in a few experiments that demonstrated feedback effects on task performance, test anxiety, and GSR-extinction (Koenig 1973; Koenig and Henriksen 1974) as well as on susceptibility to persuasion— whenever the instructions emphasized the subjective nature of the opinions in question (Harris and Jellison 1971; Hendrick et al. 1975). When such instructions were missing, attitudes were unaffected (Bramel et al. 1965; Walsh, Meister, and Kleinke 1977). Interestingly, when speech-anxious subjects were given increase feedback during preparation and performance of a speech and received prior high-consensus information concerning their fictitious autonomic reactions, the feedback effect was attenuated but anxiety was even less than without any feedback (Borkovec et al. 1979); probably, the consensus information reassured the subjects with regard to their autonomic reactions.

Attribution to variable *context aspects* is to be expected with information about the consistency over time of autonomic reactions. Variable context aspects, for example, may be arguments presented in the course of a persuasive communication; simultaneous slow rise in fictitious arousal enhances the communication's effectiveness (Hendrick and Giesen 1976). Usually, however, feedback covaries with voluntary behavior; the resulting attribution to one's own responses should increase or lower, depending on the direction of the fictitious changes, the probability that similar behavior will occur. In fact, procedures that presumably cause response attribution of fictitious quiescence reduced avoidance behavior but did not affect stimulus ratings and autonomic reactions (Borkovec et al. 1974; Cohen et al. 1974). I suspect that a perceived cause of autonomic reactions (such as thinking about successful coping behavior) differs in salience depending on the kind of target behaviors, (such as approach to the real object versus rating of this object) to be performed.

I do not maintain that attentional processes are the sole determinants of feedback effects on behavioral measures. The strength of such effects should diminish to the extent that the behavior in question is under the control of external contingencies (see Gerdes 1979). Even subjective measures like expressions of an attitude were uninfluenced by feedback when subjects expected to have to act upon their attitudes (Taylor 1975).

CONCLUDING OBSERVATIONS

Alternative Interpretations of Feedback Effects

It is often assumed that the Valins effect is mediated by real autonomic changes rather than by information search and attribution (see the review by Harris and Katkin 1975). It appears plausible, for example, that arousal of explanatory needs is accompanied by autonomic arousal and that—according to Schachter's (1964) theory—the latter, for its part, may increase emotional behavior. (Schachter himself considered only the cognitive aspect of the evaluative need he postulated.) Nevertheless, studies in the framework of Schachter's theory showed that the perception of arousal symptoms is a more important and consistent determinant of emotional behavior than is actual arousal. Among the feedback experiments there are fourteen in which no impact on autonomic reactions was found (Borkovec et al. 1974, 1979; Cohen et al. 1974; Decaria et al. 1974; Gerard 1963; Gerdes 1979; Hendrick et al. 1975; Hirschman, Clark, and Hawk 1977; Holmes and Frost 1976; Rosen et al. 1972; Thornton and Hagan 1976; Valins 1966, 1970; Walsh et al. 1977). It is unlikely that insufficient methods of measurement were employed in all of these studies. In twelve other experiments, the feedback caused autonomic changes, although in different directions. Further, five of these studies yielded no significant relations between feedback-induced autonomic changes and verbal or motor behavior (Goldstein et al. 1972; Hirschman 1975; Kerber and Coles 1978; Liebhart 1977b; Woll and McFall 1979). This contradicts the hypothesis of autonomic mediation. In five cases, no data on such relations were reported (Bloemkolk et al. 1971; Borkovec 1973a; Borkovec and Glasgow 1973; Hirschman and Hawk 1978; Stern et al. 1972). Feedback-induced information search was independent of autonomic reactions, too (Misovich and Charis 1974). In addition, subjects classified as high in chronic autonomic perception were no more susceptible to feedback than were subjects classified as low (Woll and McFall 1979). In two studies correlations between behavioral and autonomic changes were found.

In one of these experiments (Detweiler and Zanna 1976), feedback of heart rate (versus no feedback) did not affect attitudes toward nations (whose names were simultaneously presented) but produced cardiac deceleration which, for its part, correlated with the increase of the stimulus valences. The failure to obtain a Valins effect is not surprising since reading nation names is unlikely to be considered by students as a sufficient cause of autonomic arousal. The authors interpret the relation between changes in heart rate and changes in attitude in terms of Schachter's theory of emotion. This is questionable, however, since, according to this theory, too, attitude change likewise requires that the subjects can plausibly explain their autonomic reaction by reference to the attitude object. Rather, cardiac deceleration may be viewed as an indicator of effortful attention, required in the instructions, to the feedback changes that were smaller than in similar experiments and not very easy to recognize (Detweiler and Zanna 1976: 110). The degree of this effort should determine the strength of reinforcement obtained through final recognition of the feedback variations and, thereby, affect the valence of the attitude objects presented concurrently.

In the second experiment (Gaupp et al. 1972), too, cardiac deceleration was found to be a function of feedback (false feedback versus biofeedback and allegedly irrelevant auditory stimuli) and to correlate with the reduction of avoidance behavior. Behavior change was independent of feedback content but dependent on the factor of treatment (versus no treatment). The authors interpret these results in terms of differential conditioning: The aversion-relief model assumes that phobic objects become safety signals if—unlike the contrast stimuli—they are not accompanied by painful shocks. This interpretation is probably untenable as the ineffectiveness of manipulation of the interstimulus intervals (Conger et al. 1976) is at variance with the classical conditioning assumption. The cardiac deceleration probably had two independent components: one caused by increased attention in the feedback condition, the other by fear reduction during extinction in all treatment groups.

Clearly, these two studies do not prove autonomic mediation of feedback effects on verbal or motor behavior. Behavior change did not occur as a function of feedback proper (see also Goldstein et al. 1972: exp. 2) but of theoretically irrelevant aspects of the procedure (independent of the specific feedback information) and presumably mediated by noncognitive processes.

Stern et al. (1972) attempted to explain the Valins effect in terms of mere attention processes. They found that the instruction to focus on extraneous sounds (allegedly not heart-related) led to a similar degree of change in behavior toward visual stimuli as did information labeling the sounds as heart rate feedback (similarly Clark 1976; Hawk 1975; Hirschman et al. 1977; see, however, Kanfer et al. 1974). The attention hypothesis is consistent with data indicating an orientation reaction in feedback conditions. It is not clear, however—and this may be the main problem with this interpetation—why focusing on extraneous sounds should enhance, for example, the attractiveness of women viewed simultaneously. It is possible, however, that judges do not correctly attribute feedback-induced explanation search to the incongruity of certain stimulus patterns but mistakenly infer more extreme valence of the object on which they are focusing at that moment. Then, the explanandum of the attribution would not be the fictitious autonomic change but—as in self-perception theory (Bem 1972)—the subject's own concern with the object. This possibility is consistent with the discrepancies discussed previously between types of feedback with different subjective importance.

Validity of the Model

There are several reasons that speak in favor of the validity of the model presented. First, it is consistent with well-supported theories, particularly with attribution theory and Berlyne's theory of epistemologic behavior. Second, it permits a uniform explanation of almost all pertinent results. Specifically, it accounts for seemingly contradictory findings and also for failures to replicate. The model is not merely fit to the data ex post; the bulk of published studies tested various less comprehensive versions of the model. Finally, alternative explanations currently available apply to single findings but not to their entirety.

Weaknesses of empirical support may particularly be seen in the fact that some critical variables have not yet been experimentally manipulated. For this reason some of our conclusions are based on comparisons between experiments with inevitable confounding of some variables. In addition, some important parameters (like causal schemata) and intervening processes of the model (like information search and attribution) have rarely been identified or measured.

Cognitive Desensitization

Studies in this area usually violated more than one of the postulated requirements of feedback effects. It therefore is not clear which processes or procedural aspects caused the failure of most of these therapeutic approaches. The most likely candidates are (1) actual arousal, which may reduce the subjective importance of uncertainty resolution or restrict the range of the cues processed; (2) lack of context features (characteristics of stimulus objects and of response-produced stimuli) to which fictitious quiescence or arousal decrease might be attributed; (3) interference of aversive stimulus aspects with the explanatory power of nonaversive aspects; and (4) attribution to "causes" that are not salient at the time of the critical behavior. The difficulty of recognizing arousal decrease and insufficient opportunity for information search may also have contributed to failure. Given this state of affairs, delay of therapeutic applications is suggested until more is known about the significance of the factors mentioned. The desensitization effect, however, should not be prematurely considered as an artifact since it was replicated even when the methodological flaws of the classical studies by Valins and Ray (1967) were remedied (Conger et al. 1976; Defares et al. 1969; compare Cohen et al. 1974).

Equivalence of Real and Fictitious Autonomic Changes

Many laboratory experiments appear to support Valins' basic assumption that "nonveridical representations of physiological changes should have the same effect as veridical ones" (1966: 401). Conflicting results and failures to replicate may be attributed to one or more violations of the model's requirements. Nevertheless, that assumption should not be considered as proven in every respect. We may feel uneasy if states induced by arousal feedback are simply and without closer examination equated with actual arousal (Horowitz 1972) or even when their consequences are predicted from a drive-reduction model (Harris and Jellison 1971). Apart from the unproven possibility that autonomic arousal "functions as an essentially unconscious mechanism intrinsic to emotional experience" (Goldstein et al. 1972: 51), it is doubtful whether the readings of a galvanometer are equivalent to the interoceptive cues produced by arousal in natural situations. Perhaps, internal stimuli are not always as "weak, ambiguous, or uninterpretable" (Bem 1972: 2) as suggested by experiments that drastically restrict the range of behaviors available to the subjects. For example, the information provided by readings on two dials labeled "sexual arousal" and "shock arousal" sufficed to significantly affect subjects' choice between viewing slides of attractive women and delivering electrical shocks to confederates (Geen and Pigg 1973; Geen et al. 1972). However, this does not preclude that sexual and aggressive behavior in more naturalistic situations is controlled by more variegated and complex internal cues that can hardly be simulated by external feedback. To date there are no approaches to clarify that issue.

The equivalence of fictitious and actual arousal is doubtful for yet another, paradoxical reason: Taken together, evidence is stronger for the emotional effects of the former than for those of the latter; the substitute is more effective than the original. Although this may be due to the difficulty of experimentally manipulating actual arousal, the question arises as to the origins of the link between perceived arousal and emotional behavior—particularly in view of the utterly unprecise perception of autonomic changes. Possibly, very intense autonomic reactions are perceived more precisely than those of low to medium intensity studied thus far; schemata representing that link might be acquired during states of extreme arousal and, subsequently, direct the processing of information about autonomic reactions including milder ones. Meanwhile, these considerations are still speculative and alternative possibilities are conceivable.

Doubtless, these unanswered questions are empirical in nature and may not be resolved by definitional fiat. "Emotion" should not be viewed as an entity but as a construct amenable to different operational definitions. Rejection of particular operational indices—and of the relations obtained for these—on a priori grounds hardly contributes to clarification. For example, statements that stimulus ratings accompanied by low actual arousal "have nothing to do with experienced emotion" (Goldstein et al. 1972: 50) or that "none of the feedback studies to date have actually dealt with the nature and meaning of emotion" (Harris and Katkin 1975: 913) provide less information about reality than about the authors' labeling preferences. Instead, the relevance of various dependent variables should be determined on the basis of their interrelations and of the strength of the effects associated with them—regardless of whether or not one decides to label the behaviors in question as "emotional."

IV METHODOLOGICAL PROBLEMS AND THE SOCIAL CONTEXT OF ATTRIBUTION

The last part of this book deals with methodological problems of measuring attributions and investigates the place that attribution theory has in the broader context of the social sciences. The chapter by Streufert and Streufert reports on two experiments that discuss in detail the measurement of attributions. The first of these examines the effects on attributive judgments when different types of scales are used. The second pursues the further question of how much concordance there is between the experimenter's assumptions of dimensionality and the subject's perception of which dimension causal factors belong to. On the basis of their findings, Streufert and Streufert make methodological suggestions for future experiments in the field of attribution. In his commentary on the Streuferts' work, Heckhausen points out possible alternative interpretations of the data in the studies. The subsequent contribution by Gergen and Gergen attempts to define the place of attribution in the context of social explanation and tries in a disciplinary approach to determine the contribution of attribution theory to the social sciences. In so doing, the Gergens spur the hope for a discriminating and reasoned revision of work on attribution, for which the authors cite impulses from related disciplines as well. Mentioning essential ideas involved, the Gergens include ethnomethodological contributions of sociorationalism, the recent debate within psychology about the awareness of mental processes, and certain positions of analytic philosophy having to do with speech. These lead the authors to examine how socially malleable attributive behavior and its dimensions are. In addition to noting the questionable objectivity of attributions and the difficulty of assessing them reliably, the Gergens emphasize the fruitfulness of further differentiations in the classification system of explanations, which they compile in a draft design for an ethnography of explanation. Heckhausen's critical commentary on this chapter focuses particularly on the Gergens' assertion that all explanations and understanding depend on social agreement (negotiation); he further touches on the distinction the authors make between causes and reasons.

9 ATTRIBUTION, DIMENSIONALITY, AND MEASUREMENT
How You Measure Is What You Get

Siegfried Streufert and
Susan C. Streufert

During recent years, psychologists have been widely concerned with artifacts and other problems of experimentation. We initially learned that it was necessary to avoid or to control for acquiescent response set and social desirability (see Bass 1956; Cronbach 1946, 1950; Couch and Keniston 1960). Later we found that we needed to concern ourselves with experimenter bias, demand characteristics, and a host of other experimental artifacts (see Aronson and Carlsmith 1968; Fromkin and Streufert 1976). Yet, while we have been concerned with avoiding bias that is due to experimental design, the wording of questionnaires, and so forth, we (that is, most nonquantitative psychologists) have paid relatively little attention to the scales that we employ in measuring the treatment effects in a large proportion of the experiments with human subjects. This seems to hold true particularly for measurement in social and motivational psychology: while researchers in personality theory are quite concerned with reliability *and* validity of measurement, social psychologists often tend to assume validity if the scale was designed to measure some particular behavior of interest. However, research by Spence, Helmreich, and Stapp (1975) has shown that even interspersing a different kind of measure (subjective TAT responding) between stimulus and scale response can seriously alter the responses obtained from subjects in social psychological measurement. If responses on social psychological scales shift very easily, then one can hardly assume that the measured treatment effects are valid representations of behavior that is relevant to some overall theory.

Furthermore, different researchers often employ diverse scales in search of the same theoretical phenomenon, even though Anderson (1970), Brogden (1972), and others have warned that the development of theory and scale should be intimately related. Lack of concern with scales and their effects can, for example, result in potential misinterpretations of nonreplication: A researcher who does not obtain a previously reported result tends to suggest that the phenomenon itself is unstable, even though his inability to obtain the same results might have been due to employing somewhat different scales or measuring differences by comparing other scale points than these previously compared. Similar problems may arise when a researcher involved in programmatic research changes one variable (for example, in conjoint experimentation techniques) to check on its effects in an obtained relation among a group of variables, but simultaneously alters the scale or scales that were previously utilized. Any obtained discrepancy is typically assigned to the effects of the modified variable, not to the effects of scale alteration.

But discrepancies occur for yet other reasons as well. In many cases researchers measure effects on variables that stand as "representative" for certain theoretical concepts that they may or may not in fact represent. Further, concepts that appear as opposite poles on one dimension to the experimenter may in fact be viewed by his subjects as points on quite different dimensions. For that matter, the representation of semantic or conceptual multidimensional space by a psychological experimenter may or may not have very much to do with the representation of that space by another experimenter and even less with the "naive" conceptual space of the subject(s). If the experimenter only "seduces" his subjects to utilize the psychologist's dimensional space in responding to an experimental scale or task, then he may or may not get meaningful data (depending on the subject's ability to respond to the unfamiliar dimensionality); and if he does get "meaningful" results, the observed effects could be spurious, could be relevant to only the particular experimental setting and might have no further relevance. Further, the experimental results may be a far cry from the "real" behavior that an applied psychologist may want to measure in the "real world." In many cases, psychologists seem not to be aware of these and related problems.

However, there certainly are situations where the introduction of dimensional space and dimensional content by the experimenter (space and content that has nothing to do with previous conceptualization of related stimuli by the subject) has applied value: specifically in those situations where people are typically influenced by outside sources in their judgment and where personal experience that would have established conceptual dimensionality in the specific domain is limited. These, however, are special cases and should be recognized and investigated as such. It would be misleading to view such situations as representative of the "typical" reality in which we are so often interested.

These are some, but by no means all, of the problems that are often encountered by (but frequently unknown to or ignored by) experimenters. In this chapter we report some research we have completed on the degree to which such problems can and do interfere with measurement in the area of attributions. Certainly we cannot deal with the effects of *all* measurement problems in the space of one chapter based on two experiments. Consequently, we shall be rather selective. We shall approach two sets of problems in two types of experiments and maintain only some degree of overlap between the two approaches. If serious problems should be demonstrated on the basis of this research, then further efforts will be needed to provide more precise information about how and where measurement problems occur and where they can be avoided. If, on the other hand, no problems turn up in this set of experiments, then the issue can be laid to rest.

In a first experiment, we shall focus on the effects of different kinds of scales in the measurement of attributions: forced-choice versus non-forced scales and bipolar versus percentage scales. In addition, we will include a factor of time and a factor dealing with dimensionality. In the second experiment, we shall maintain a dimensionality factor and the forced- versus non-forced-choice scale. In addition, we shall measure the degree to which subjects respond in accordance with the experimenter's dimensionality assumptions under conditions of increasing success or increasing failure.

Another distinction between the first and the second experiment is the "established" character of the research area. For the first experiment, we have selected a research area (responsibility for an accident) within the attribution framework that has provided contradictory and confusing results, where methods have been less than ideal, and where no "established" focus has developed. This first experiment is relevant to the area of attributions of responsibility for accidents (as exemplified in the Walster versus Shaver controversy). Our second experiment deals with an area of theory and research that has produced *reliable data*: the work of Weiner (1974) with the internal–external and stable–unstable dimensions in attributions to luck, ability, task characteristics, and effort under conditions in which subjects experience or observe success or failure. We deal with both approaches in this chapter because this procedure should (1) provide the opportunity to test for different potential problems in the measurement of attribution, and (2) should allow us to compare an area with reliable results with an area where results are contradictory.

We are dealing here with measurement problems in attribution psychology. The research we did was specifically focused on that area, but the implications might be wider. We would be surprised if equivalent issues did not exist in other research areas as well.

EXPERIMENT 1: ATTRIBUTIONS OF RESPONSIBILITY AND CAUSALITY

In her work on defensive attribution, Walster (1966) measured subjects' responses to a description of an accident on non-forced-choice 4-point and 15-point scales. Shaver (1970) was unable to replicate her results. Aside from changing instructions to the subjects, Shaver also used different scales (encompassing 4 and 26 points). Relevant research also has been reported by Shaw and others, and again their scales are different: Shaw and associates (McMartin and Shaw 1971; Shaw and Skolnick 1971) used 11-point scales. Others have used a digital choice followed by a 5-point scale (Shaw and Sulzer 1964).

However, scale length is only one problem in attribution measurement. Potentially, it is even the least important problem in as much as Miller (1956) has shown that responses to various scales longer than the "magic number 7" are correlated anyway. More important, and of specific concern in this chapter, may be the divergent *types* of scales that can be and have been used to collect dependent variable data. The data collected by Walster, by Shaver, and by Shaw and associates were collected on non-forced-choice scales that are frequently employed in social and motivational psychology. However, forced-choice techniques have been used as well. For example, as reported in Streufert and Streufert (1969) we employed forced-choice percentage measures transformed for analysis into arcsine values. Other researchers interested in the measurement of attribution have used yet different techniques, varying from experimenter interpretations of written protocols via digital choices to 100-point scales, some of which were forced, others non-forced; some were bipolar and others were percentage scales.

Generally, the researchers utilizing these various scales have assumed that the attributions they were measuring reflected a single dimension: being responsible versus not being responsible. But if that is true, how can opposite results be generated—for example, those of Walster versus those of Shaver? Streufert and Nogami (1973) have shown that subjects (can) distinguish between attributions of causality and attributions of responsibility, a distinction that falls in line with the earlier versus the later stages of the development of attribution as discussed by Heider (1958; see also Piaget 1932). If subjects make such a distinction, then they might view causality as the opposite pole to responsibility on one dimension (for example, one might assume that if someone can be linked to an event he must be either causal or responsible for the event, but not both). Another possibility, however, is that subjects might view causality and responsibility, with their respective opposite poles reflecting the absence of causality or responsibility, as two orthogonal or oblique independent dimensions. As the "naive" experimenter, one could make either assumption and structure one's experiment accordingly. We will here investigate how one such rather arbitrary assumption (causality and responsibility as opposite poles on one dimension) will affect data in comparison to data collected on non-forced-choice scales where subjects were able to utilize their own dimensionality.

The previously discussed data of Streufert and Nogami (1973), indicating that responsibility and causality are not one and the same concept, were collected in the same experimental simulation in which Streufert and Streufert (1969) measured attributions of causality—that is, a task in which groups interact and attributions are made to groups, not to individuals. The causality/responsibility distinction and the flexibility of the setting (Streufert, Kliger, Castore, and Driver 1967) led to the choice of the same technique for the present experiment. We shall ask (1) what scale types produce what response levels and response changes over time, and (2) to what degree do different scales result in subjects distinguishing (or not distinguishing) between two concepts of attribution that recent research has shown to be distinct entities, and not necessarily unidimensional. Whereas the first question is akin to "reliability" of dependent variable measurement, the second is more akin to concerns with "validity."

Method

The research reported here employs basically the same design that has been utilized in past attribution research by Streufert and associates (for example, Streufert and Nogami 1973, Streufert and Streufert 1969). The method of data collection was, however, modified to permit the experimenters to obtain data on various kinds of attribution scales.

Subjects and Task

Forty-eight undergraduate volunteers at a midwestern American state university participated as subjects in the Tactical and Negotiations Game, an experimental simulation technique. (Experimental simulations as research techniques are discussed in detail in the handbook chapter on laboratory research by Fromkin and Streufert 1976). The arriving groups of subjects were randomly divided into four-member teams. Team members were instructed to act as equal rank commanders with responsibility for economic, intelligence, and military functions of the experimental simulation. The task is described by Streufert, Kliger, Castore, and Driver (1967) and has been used in considerable previous research. The teams were told that they were playing against another team and that the experimenters would serve as judges (assisted by a computer). Subjects were free to make any kind or number of decisions possible within the constraints of available resources. They were told that the experimenters would determine the "wins" and "losses" based on the decisions made by the two opposing teams. Such "consequences of decisions made by all groups of subjects" would be fed back to the subjects. In fact, the groups of subjects were playing the game against a predetermined program. All information fed back to the teams was controlled so that all teams received the same messages (in different random order) no matter what their specific decisions had been.

Treatments

Time and Information. All four-member teams participated in the game for six consecutive 30-minute periods. Time was the only treatment variable. To avoid an end effect, teams were not told which period would be their last. During each period, each team received ten typed messages in equally spaced time intervals. The order of messages for each period was randomized. Messages were neutral in information (based on prerating by parallel populations); that is, they communicated neither success nor failure to the subjects. The messages used here were the same as those used in previous neutral information manipulations of Streufert and associates. Subjects responded to the messages as groups and indicated on a 7-point scale running from success to failure whether each message communicated either success or failure. All mean ratings were in the range between 3.5 and 4.5 on the 7-point scale—that is, around the scale midpoints.

The Concepts of Causality and Responsibility. Each of the 30-minute playing periods was followed by an intermission. During these intermissions, subjects responded to a number of scales, among them a measure of the degree to which either success or failure was experienced during the last playing period, a measure for attribution of responsibility and a measure for attribution of causality. Subjects responded to the scales as individuals. Success/failure ratings were again in the neutral range and did not change over time. Subjects were instructed to attribute *causality* for the current situation, as it had developed during the immediately preceding playing period, to those persons, or groups (targets) that had acted so that the current situation had come about. (The reader will note that we are here dealing with *experimenter-induced*, not with naive, dimensions.) Subjects were also told to assign causality for the initiation of an event, no matter whether the groups had intended the outcome or not. Subjects were instructed to attribute *responsibility* to a group or person if it/he had intended an outcome or had acted negligently to produce an event or had allowed it to occur if the event was foreseeable, whether or not the event had been directly initiated by that group.

To give a more detailed explanation of the meaning of causality and responsibility subjects were told:

> People make decisions all the time. At times these decisions result in the intended outcome, at times they don't. At times the outcome is unexpected, i.e., the person who made the decision could never have known that such an outcome would have occurred. Of course, any action in which we engage may result in an unlikely outcome. However, it is clearly impossible to think of all potential possibilities. If a decision produced an effect which was *intended or* clearly should have been *anticipated*, then the decisionmaker *caused* the outcome *and* is *responsible* for it. If he could not have been expected to reasonably anticipate the outcome of a decision, then he has *caused* the effect *but is not responsible* for it. An example might make the difference more clear. Let us say that Mr. Jones is washing the window in his fifth floor apartment. As he presses with the sponge against the window, the glass falls out, drops to the pavement, and injures a passer-by. If Mr. Jones knew that the window was defective, he is clearly responsible for the accident. If, on the other hand, the landlord had just assured him that the window had been repaired and was now safe, then he has *caused* the accident but is not *responsible* for it.

These definitions do not necessarily place responsibility and causality on opposite poles of one dimension, but allow for this possibility: someone can be responsible without being causal and vice versa.

The Measurement of Causality and Responsibility: The Four Scales. Subjects were asked to attribute causality and responsibility for "the current situation"—the events during the last half-hour playing period—to their own team, and to the opposing team. The data were collected on separate scales. Because of the greater interest value of attributions to subjects' own team (see Streufert and Streufert 1969), the data from that category were used for the analysis reported in this chapter.

In a 2×2 design, each of the subjects in each four-member team received a different attribution scale (unknown to the other subjects). Two of the scales were non-forced, two were forced; two of the scales were bipolar scales and two of the scales were percentage scales. The subject of each group receiving the non-forced bipolar scale was asked to indicate the causality he attributed to his team (or the responsibility on a separate scale) on an 11-point bipolar scale, with the end points marked: My four-member group is "extremely causal" (or responsible) versus "not at all causal" (or responsible). Eleven scale points were selected in order to enable us to match the scale to percentage decimal units running from 0 to 100. The second subject in each group was instructed to indicate responsibility (or causality) in percentage values in a space provided for that value. Percent values were to be given in units of 10 (equivalent to 11 scale points). Subjects in this group again responded separately to responsibility and causality scales. Both of these conditions were nonforced; that is, the subject was allowed to consider responsibility and causality separately as potentially orthogonal concepts.

The remaining two conditions employed forced-choice manipulations; that is, subjects could view each of the events during a playing period as due to either causal action (unforeseeability of outcome) or due to responsible action (foreseeability indicating either negligence or intent). Forced-choice responding therefore requires the placement of responsibility and causality as opposite concepts on a single-dimensional scale. The third subject received a bipolar scale similar to the one received by the first subject but was told to divide the scale between "responsible" and "causal." The endpoints of the scale were so marked. Subjects were told that if their group had been as responsible as it had been causal, the division should be in the middle of the scale. If the group had been three times as causal as responsible, then the dividing line should be at a point one-fourth away from responsible and three-fourths of the scale away from causal, and so forth. The fourth subject in every team was given a similar task as the third, except that he again had to indicate percentage values. He was instructed to indicate the percentage that would state the degree to which his team was responsible for the events during the last playing period, and the percentage to which his team was causal. The two values had to add to 100 percent. Basic instructions to the two subjects on forced-choice scales were identical. Similarly, identical instructions were given to the two subjects responding on bipolar scales.

Overall instructions on causality and responsibility were identical in all four cases. Each subject responded to the scales at the end of each of the six playing periods. Although all subjects in any one of the four categories received the identical scale at the end of each of the playing periods, the order of presentation of causal versus responsible as the first or second scale was varied across subjects (except in the forced-choice cases, where the direction of the scale labeling was reversed for half of the subjects).

For purposes of data analysis, all scales were made equivalent; that is, a scale value on a bipolar scale running from 0 to 10 was multiplied by 10. Percentage values were left as provided by the subjects. It should be noted, however, that the forced-choice responses (except where multiplied by 10) were not modified, so that the combined response to causality and responsibility ratings on any forced-choice scale could never exceed the potential maximum scale value for either causality or responsibility alone on the bipolar scales. Consequently, the mean value for causality and responsibility attributions to any forced-choice scale would be half the scale length (0.5 or an entered value of 50).

Results and Discussion

The data were analyzed with separate analysis of variance (ANOVA) techniques of the specific type required for measures that are subject to a unity problem (a necessary by-product of forced-choice scales). The problem and its resolution via analysis procedures are discussed by Streufert and Streufert (1969, 1974). Factors in the ANOVA were forced-choice versus bipolar scales and time, periods of play in the simulation.

The data analysis indicated that attribution responses on bipolar scales exceeded those on percentage scales. Obtained significance on the time factor was due to a warm-up effect: Newman-Keuls analysis indicated that during the first playing period attributions to both causality and responsibility were generally lower than during later playing periods. This finding replicates the data reported by Streufert and Nogami (1973) showing that attribution responses need some time to stabilize. (Significant interaction effects indicated that responsibility attributions exceeded causality attributions on forced-choice scales: the inverse held on non-forced-choice scales. Causality attributions were more stable over time, whereas responsibility attributions showed an increase, particularly between playing periods 1 and 4. In general, increases in attributions of both causality and responsibility were observed on percentage scales over time. Finally, a significant four-way interaction among all factors in the analysis was obtained. Whereas responses on non-forced-choice scales remained relatively unchanged over time (after a shift from the warm-up to the following periods), forced-choice scales (of course, in the corresponding inverse patterns) showed increases in responsibility attributions between periods 1 and 4 and subsequent slight, but insignificant, decreases between periods 4 and 6. Causality attributions necessarily showed the inverse pattern. A closer look, however, shows that some *small* increase (again disregarding the shift between periods 1 and 2) occurred for the non-forced-choice causality attributions as well, but not for non-forced-choice responsibility attributions. These results are primarily due to the already mentioned upward shifting of percentage scales. In this analysis, percentage and bipolar scales produced (except as discussed) similar results for forced-choice causality ratings and forced-choice responsibility ratings. However, non-forced-choice percentage responsibility ratings stayed well below non-forced-choice bipolar responsibility ratings, and non-forced-choice percentage causality ratings remained even more strongly below the non-forced-choice bipolar causality ratings. In addition, the forced-choice bipolar responsibility and the forced-choice bipolar causality ratings did not demonstrate the warm-up effect obtained for all other measures between the first and second period of play. Particularly interesting, then, is the finding that percentage rating scales initially depressed non-forced-choice ratings of both responsibility and causality, and that forced choice produces greatly depressed attributions of causality as compared to attributions of responsibility. The results are presented in Figure 9-1.

Responsibility versus Causality

As we stated earlier, Streufert and Nogami (1973) demonstrated in the same experimental environment that causality and responsibility can be divergent concepts. In the research reported here, we have — for the forced-choice scales — placed responsibility and causality on opposite poles of single scales, implying a single dimension to the subject. This choice was made with intent: in many cases, experimenters attempt to impose their assumed dimensions on subjects, and, of course, subjects do respond to them. But are these responses in any way meaningful? If the subjects had accepted the experimenter's implied assumption that responsibility and causality are on opposite poles on a single dimension, then they should have

Figure 9–1. Effect of Scale Characteristics and the Time Factor on Attributions of Causality and Responsibility.

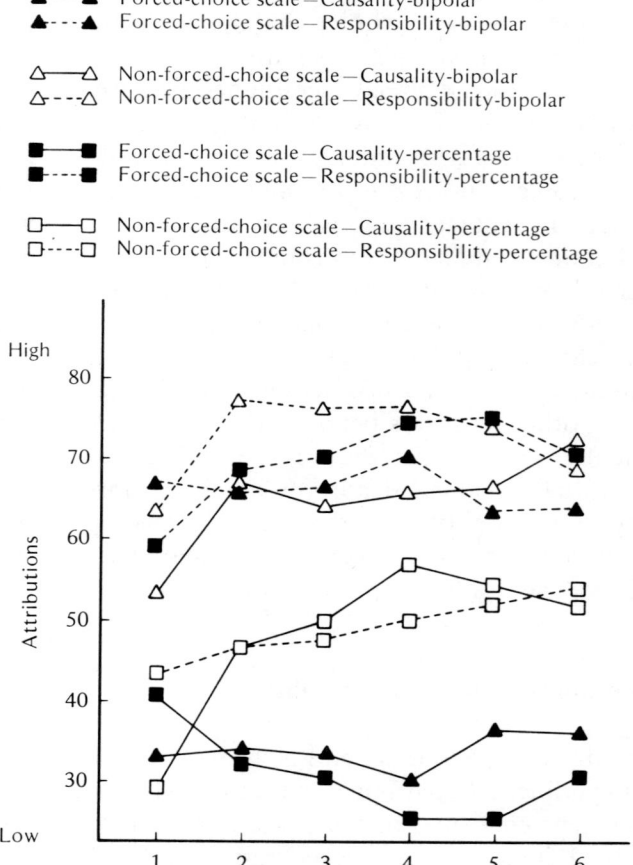

responded equivalently on forced-choice and non-forced-choice scales. They did not. As we reported, causality attributions exceeded responsibility attributions slightly on non-forced-choice scales. On forced-choice scales, however, attributions of responsibility exceeded those of causality. Apparently the salience of the responsibility was greater than that of action in creating this response.

These data show how important it is to study carefully the dimensionality that underlies the attributional judgment of subjects in psychological experiments. We do not mean to say that the experimenter must pick the specific dimensions that each individual subject might bring with him to the experimental situation. In many cases, this may not be necessary; often dimensionality can be induced appropriately through experimental instructions. Nonetheless, the subject must be able to gain a clear understanding of the induced dimension(s) and must be able to respond, and respond reliably, before the resulting data are meaningful. The degree to which the resulting data have external validity is, of course, yet another problem. As another paper points out (Streufert and Streufert 1978), the problems with the discrepant attributional data on attributions of responsibility by Shaver (1970) and by Walster (1966) may lie precisely in erroneous assumptions of dimensionality. Both experimenters assumed that their subjects were responding with responsibility attributions since the scales were so labeled. In fact, however, the instructions in one of the experiments may have made it impossible for most subjects to respond on a "moral" responsibility dimension and may have cued them to reinterpret that dimension as "causality." To summarize: Care should be taken that various dimensions, for example responsibility and causality, are not inappropriately provided to the subjects or cued by "misleading" instructions. Differential understanding of instructions and cues or inability to respond meaningfully to the experimenter's assumed dimensions could result in quite unreliable or meaningless data. We will return to this problem later when we discuss a second experiment. In that case, an example for a much better match between experimentally provided and the subjects' own response dimensions is provided.

Let us now turn to scale characteristics. We are concerned with two separate distinctions among scales: forced-choice versus non-forced-choice scales and percentage versus bipolar scales. Since much research in social and motivational psychology uses non-forced-choice bipolar scales, even though they are often of widely discrepant length, labeling, and so on, we will use that form of scale as the standard against which the other results from this experiment will be judged.

Forced versus Non-Forced-Choice Interval Scales

The results indicating that differences in forced- versus non-forced-choice scales show significant effects only in relation to the already discussed differences between responsibility and causality attributions.

Specifically, two interpretations of this result may be suggested. It may be necessary to "cue" subjects more intensively to the concepts utilized. In other words, the forced-choice method may have forced subjects to think more seriously about the degree to which they were indeed causal *and/or* responsible, so that their responses may have become more meaningful when obtained via forced-choice measures. (Similar questions can be raised on the question of dimensions and quadrants in the work of Weiner and associates later; we shall return to that issue.) Similar changes in results toward a more "meaningful" or "honest" response on scales was obtained by Spence, Helmreich, and Stapp (1975) by interspersing a TAT-type measure between stimulus and scale response. For the present data, the "cueing" may have been achieved by the forced-choice method of placing the "causal" and "responsible" concepts on the single dimension on which they conceptually belong, paralleling the definition of causal as unforeseeable action versus responsible as foreseeable (negligent or intentional) action. However, this interpretation appears unlikely, both in the light of the task and in the light of the recent data on separate dimensionality for causality and responsibility.

A second interpretation may be based on the "meaning" of scale responses per se. Fishbein and associates have repeatedly demonstrated that attitude scales, for example, are insufficient to predict "real" behavior. Relations between beliefs and attitudes and attitudes and intentions (a second dimension!) need to be taken into account before behavior can be predicted (see Fishbein 1963, 1965, 1967; Fishbein and Ajzen 1972). There is no reason to assume that *attribution* scales should be better than attitude scales. In this case, for example, the discrepancy between responsibility and causality attributions on forced-choice scales may have been due to separate dimensionality of the two concepts in the responses of subjects, necessitating the preferred treatment of one of the two as more salient under forced-choice conditions: since the participants in this task were actively involved in a situation that was very important to them and that appeared to carry much responsibility with it, the causality dimension may have been relegated to a secondary position. This would allow the subjects to assign it to whatever remained of the forced-choice scale after attributions of responsibility were made. Postexperimental interviews with subjects tended to support such a view, at least in part.

The use of separate (non-forced-choice) causality and responsibility scales, on the other hand, would have allowed for separate utilization of both dimensions. The discrepant data between forced-choice and non-forced-choice scales may tell us something about the "value" of the concepts to the subjects,[a] particularly in regard to any "reality" implications. Apparently, subjects are quite able to use a causality dimension but appear to consider it less important than the responsibility dimension. In terms of "external validity" then, forced-choice scales (with potentially arbitrarily selected concepts as opposing poles) may be quite useful for producing salience information, even though they may not provide us with a "true" indication of subjects' attributions. But for accurate estimates of subjects' "true" attributions, non-forced-choice scales, which match the "real" dimensionality the subjects are using, appear necessary (unless, of course, the forced-choice scales let the subject choose between concepts that are indeed located on opposite ends of a single dimension for him).

Bipolar Scales versus Percentage Scales

Psychological bipolar[b] scales tend to be very familiar to the researcher, but they are relatively unfamiliar to most subjects who have not been extensively exposed to psychological experimentation. It is uncertain, for example, how many subjects can really distinguish among

a. This procedure and its effects are not unlike those in multidimensional scaling tasks.
b. We are including under the rubric "bipolar" both scales with divergent concepts as endpoint descriptions as well as those running from a positive to a negative pole of a single description (for example, responsible–not responsible).

more than seven scale points and whether the employed opposite pole endpoints indeed made much sense to them. Further, our usual "equal interval" assumption of bipolar scales may often be little more than a *fata morgana*. On the other hand, subjects are quite familiar with dealing in percentages; percentage values occur with frequency in everyday life—from the weather forecast to the amount of carbohydrates and vitamins in the breakfast cereal. Can we expect subjects to respond similarly to percentage and bipolar measures?

To examine the differences produced by these scales, let us initially focus again on the non-forced-choice scales. Responsibility and causality attributions on percentage scales are much lower than equivalent attributions on bipolar scales, averaging 47 percent and 48 percent for causality and responsibility, respectively, as compared with 6.6 and 7.3 on a 0 to 10 bipolar scale. The discrepancies between the two sets of responses (non-forced-choice percentage versus non-forced-choice bipolar scales) are highly significant.[c] The trend of the curves over time is, however, rather similar. One might conclude that subjects are much more cautious on percentage scales, possibly because they are more familiar with what a "percent" means as compared to an unmarked scale point. Postexperimental interviews with subjects supported that view; apparently subjects felt no problems about marking the bipolar scale somewhere near to its end "because the middle of it did not have much meaning" to them.

Time Effects

Previous Tactical and Negotiations Game research of Streufert and associates has shown that a warm-up effect is obtained for the first period of play but dissipates after that period is completed.[d] This effect has been observed reliably both in responses on rating scales and in several behavioral measures (of decisionmaking, risk-taking, and aggression, for example). For this reason, data from the first (warm-up) period are usually disregarded in our research. For the present purpose, the first playing period was allowed to remain part

---

c. For analysis purposes, the scales were of course made equivalent by placing all of them on a 0–100 scale. In other words, a response of 40 percent would be entered as 40, an interval scale response of 4 also as 40.

d. This warm-up effect occurs both in the indirectly measured decisionmaking and in the directly measured scale responses.

of the data. The reason for this procedure is rather straightforward: most research in social psychology collects data from subjects only once, and that after minimal pretraining and little previous exposure to experimental settings. To take a closer view of scale responses in attribution research we may then ask ourselves two questions: How does responding differ at the onset of an experiment? And can subsequent meaningful alterations in responses over time be detected on various scales beyond any initial "warm-up" effects?

The first question has a rather clear answer: Where it is technically possible, attributions increase sharply between the first and the following playing periods. In other words, single measurement after limited exposure in this experimental setting may produce rather depressed attributions of causality and responsibility. In part this may be due to the task employed here, which is rather complex and may require some familiarity before one feels that one can clearly establish how "responsible" or "causal" one has been. However, in this experiment, in contrast to most experiments, subjects do receive two hours of pretraining. Furthermore, many other attribution experiments have at least some complexity. Some concern might then be expressed that one-shot data collection may not be representative of subjects' "real" attribution levels if they were more familiar with and more experienced in the task at hand. Of course, this may not be as much of a problem in pure theory oriented research as it may be in research that is to have external validity.

Significant changes in attribution levels beyond the second playing period were obtained only for percentage scales. This effect appeared even though forced-choice percentage causality attributions negate the rise in forced percent responsibility attributions (unity). Bipolar scales registered no such rise in attributions. The reason for this result may be due to the level of the two sets of attribution: subjects may indeed have felt that they were becoming more responsible and causal of current events as time went on (such data were obtained previously by Streufert and Streufert 1969 in a success/failure manipulation), but the unrealistically high initial response level on bipolar scales (ceiling effects) may have prevented subjects from indicating greater levels of responsibility and causality.

Conclusions

It should be stated again that this research was not designed to indicate the value of one type of scale over another; rather it was designed to test for potential differences among them. Since there is currently little theoretical basis for predicting scale reliability and validity, the data obtained here may be viewed as suggestive for theory.

We indicated an interest in the answers to two questions: What scale types produce what response levels and changes over time? And to what degree do different scales result in subjects distinguishing between associated concepts or dimensions? It appears that the use of different scales indeed produces different results: how you measure *does* determine what you get. While the standardly used non-forced-choice bipolar scales produce relatively high (possibly too high) attribution levels, percentage scales produce more attenuated attribution ratings, thereby allowing for improved measurement of potentially meaningful changes in attributions over time. Forced-choice scales result in quite different attributions than non-forced-choice scales. It appears as though forcing the subject to choose between two concepts measured may enter additional considerations, such as salience, into the response, possibly making the measure sensitive to external validity demands but potentially allowing distortions of attributions. Time seems to have a relatively common effect on all types of scales (with minor exceptions): initial measurement of attributions appears to be depressed as opposed to later measurement after subjects have become fully familiar with the task and its requirements. This finding has clear implications for limitations potentially inherent in the "one-shot" experiment.

The most interesting results, however, are probably those dealing with the dimensionality issue. Apparently it is necessary to select very carefully the experimental dimensionality to allow subjects to respond reliably and meaningfully.

EXPERIMENT 2: ATTRIBUTIONAL DIMENSIONS OF THE EXPERIMENTER AND THE SUBJECT

We have already mentioned the problem that can be encountered when an experimenter labels scales according to his specific theory.

One wonders whether the theory represents the (typical or induced) reality of subjects' perceptions.

The work of Weiner and associates (e.g., Weiner, Frieze, Kukla, Reed, Rest, and Rosenbaum 1971, 1972) provides a useful vehicle for the test of one such theory-measurement coordination. We have specifically chosen the Weiner paradigm because its previously demonstrated reliability seems to suggest that if appropriateness of measurement (as discussed previously) is possible, it should be found there.

Weiner et al. (1971) assume that attributions under conditions of success or of failure can be represented as at least two dimensions: representing stability versus instability and internality versus externality. The four quadrants divided by the orthogonal dimensions are called ability (internal, stable), task (external, stable), effort (internal, unstable), and luck (external, unstable). The system is represented in Figure 9-2.

As yet unpublished research by Meyer and associates (personal communication 1977) has demonstrated that subjects (on their own) indeed select the labels of the four quadrants to describe the causes for success and failure. But are these quadrants comparable? Do these labels actually represent the underlying dimensions to the subjects? For example, does an increase in internal attributions necessarily result in a decrease in external attributions? (Is there really an underlying internal-external dimension?) Do increases in attri-

Figure 9-2. Dimensionality of Attribution as per Weiner et al. (1971).

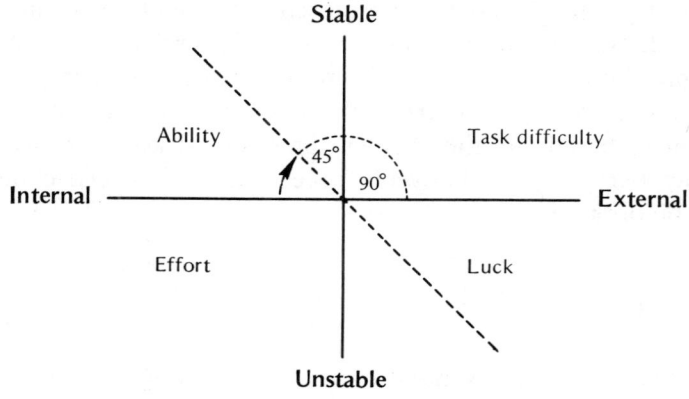

butions to ability and effort result in decreased attributions to task characteristics and luck? (Do the quadrant labels reflect the supposed underlying internal–external dimension?) Will the subjects, exposed to forced-choice scales, employ the concepts in the same way as they will on non-forced-choice scales? (Is the dimensionality meaningful to them?) Will they view a forced-choice scale representing a dimension (such as internal–external) as equivalent to their respective ratings of the associated quadrants (luck, ability, task, effort) on non-forced-choice scales? (Is there a common dimensional value for the four quadrant concepts?) Can one rotate the dimensions around the point of intersection of the axes and still get meaningful data (in terms of equivalence of forced- versus non-forced-choice attributions, for example)? When rotating the axes 45° to form an ability–luck dimension, would a decrease in ability attribution result in an equivalent increase in luck attribution on *both* forced- and non-forced-choice scales? (See the dotted line in Figure 9–2.) We intended to try to answer some of these questions in this experiment. For this analysis, the internal–external dimension of the Weiner system was selected; we will not deal with the stable–unstable dimension. Rotation analysis will focus on the ability–luck dimension; we will not deal with the alternative task–effort dimension.

The results should be particularly interesting in a comparison with the first experiment. In that experiment we had chosen a forced-choice dimension (causality–responsibility) that could be meaningfully conceptualized, but appeared nonetheless somewhat arbitrary. The Weiner dimensions seem much less arbitrary and are much more "established." If, as we have already implied, dimensional matching of subjects' typical perceptions or reliable induction of meaningful (usable) dimensions are possible, then the data relevant to the Weiner paradigm should produce much more reliable and comparable results than those reported from the first experiment. That is, in an experiment based on the Weiner dimensional assumptions, a considerably better match between forced- and non-forced-choice data should be obtained.

Method

The same experimental simulation technique was again used. Twenty-four subjects participated in the fashion described for experiment 1, except that half of them experienced increasing failure, while the other half experienced increasing success. Further, subjects received seven rather than ten informative messages per playing period. Failure was induced over six periods of play in the Tactical and Negotiations Game by providing subjects with one message out of seven communicating failure during the first period, two messages out of seven communicating failure during the second period, and so forth until subjects received six of seven messages communicating failure during the sixth and last period. Again subjects did not know which playing period would be their last. Information that did not communicate failure was held neutral in content. Manipulation checks (based on group responses) indicated that failure messages were perceived as failure and that neutral messages were perceived neither as failure nor as success. A further manipulation check obtained from individual subjects at the end of each playing period indicated that subjects saw failure as increasing in linear fashion with the manipulation over periods of play.

Success manipulations were parallel to the failure manipulations. Twelve subjects received one out of seven messages communicating success during the first period, and so on, until they received six out of seven success messages during the sixth period. The manipulation checks again indicated that success was perceived as induced.

By necessity, success and failure had to be confounded with time. Decreases in success are often perceived as failure, and decreases in failure as success. To avoid such a confusion, sequential induction of success and failure became necessary. To determine whether time was a factor in producing the results on the dependent variables, a control condition with neither failure nor success (similar to the condition described in experiment 1) was included in the design. Analysis of the data determined that the results reported here were not due to time effects.

Aside from measures employed for the purpose of manipulation checks, subjects responded to several seven-point scales at the end of each playing period. Subjects (individually) indicated how much of the situation, as it had been developing during the last playing period, could be ascribed to the ability of their team, to the task the team had to perform, to the effort the team had invested and to the (good or bad) luck the team had experienced. These were non-forced-choice scales with endpoints labeled "very much" and "none at all." Further, they were asked to indicate on a seven-point forced-choice scale to what degree the situation, as it had been developing during the last playing period, had been due to the ability of the team in contrast to the luck the team had experienced (the endpoints of the scale were marked with the word *ability* and the word *luck*). Finally, they were asked to indicate (on another forced-choice seven-point scale) the degree to which the situation, as it had been developing during the last playing period, was due to factors that were external to (not controlled by) the subjects and to what degree it was due to factors that were internal to (under control or influence of) the subjects. The endpoints of the scale were labeled "external, i.e., not under control of your group" and "internal, i.e., under control of your group."

The scales were scored so that all of them could be directly compared: on the forced-choice internal–external scale, the internal pole received a value of 7 and the external pole a value of 1. On the ability-luck scale, a high attribution to ability was scored 7, a high attribution to luck was scored 1. Attributions on non-forced-choice scales for ability and effort were scored with the value 7 for high attributions to those concepts and the value 1 for low attributions to those concepts. In contrast, high attributions to task and to luck were given the score 1, low attributions to those concepts were given the score 7. If equivalent, the attributions from the four concepts should be "superimposed" upon each other in a graphic representation.

Results and Discussion

Data analysis indicated that attributions to ability and effort generally increased (higher mean score) with success, whereas attributions to task and luck decreased (higher mean score) with increasing success. An exception to this finding was the last period of play, where some decrease from the previous maximum attribution was observed. Failure conditions, on the other hand, produced very small decreases in attributions to ability and effort and equivalent very small increases in attributions to task and luck. All in all, these results are not unusual in the light of research reported in the literature and seem to parallel in good part the results reported by Streufert and Streufert (1969). It is interesting to note, however, that attributions remained generally above the midpoint of the scales even in failure conditions. This effect is in part based on the finding that, on the average, attributions to ability and effort exceeded those to task and luck even when subjects were failing!

One purpose of this experiment was to check on the potential similarities and differences of subjects' responses on the forced-choice scale (single dimension) as compared with the responses on the non-forced-choice scales representing the concepts supposedly described by the dimension. If Weiner's point of view is correct that the four quadrants luck, ability, task, and effort represent the space described by an internal–external and a stable–unstable dimension, we would expect the following: the mean value of the four non-forced-choice scales (measuring attributions to ability, luck, task, and effort, respectively) as they were scored here should be equivalent to the corresponding value on the forced choice internal–external scale, unless measurement problems or theoretical error interfere. Further, if we rotate the axes on Figure 9–2 by 45°, maintaining the same point for the intersection of the coordinate system, we should obtain two new dimensions, running from ability to luck and from effort to task. The ability–luck dimension (represented on the forced-choice ability–luck scale) should produce equivalent results to the mean value of the attributions that subjects assigned to the separate non-forced ability and luck scales, unless measurement or scale meaning (since the same names were used, there is no implication for theoretical problems) problems interfere. Let us first take a look at the results on the ability–luck dimension (see Figure 9–3). As the graph shows, attributions to luck and ability from the single forced-choice scale and the mean of the two separate non-forced scales under failure conditions are strikingly similar. The results for the success condition are nearly as good, except for the one experimental condition where subjects were exposed to four out of seven success messages. Here the two means differ at the level of $p < .05$.

A further analysis compared the internal–external single forced-choice scale to the mean obtained over all four separate non-forced-choice scales, for ability, luck, task, and effort. As can be seen from Figure 9–4, no significant differences are obtained from a comparison of the points representing the various playing periods (success levels) in the success manipulation. The shapes of the curves are parallel. However, problems occur for the failure manipulation. Several of the points representing playing periods—that is, failure levels—on the two curves are significantly different from each other, and the

Figure 9-3. Effects of Increasing Success and Failure on Attributions of Luck versus Ability.

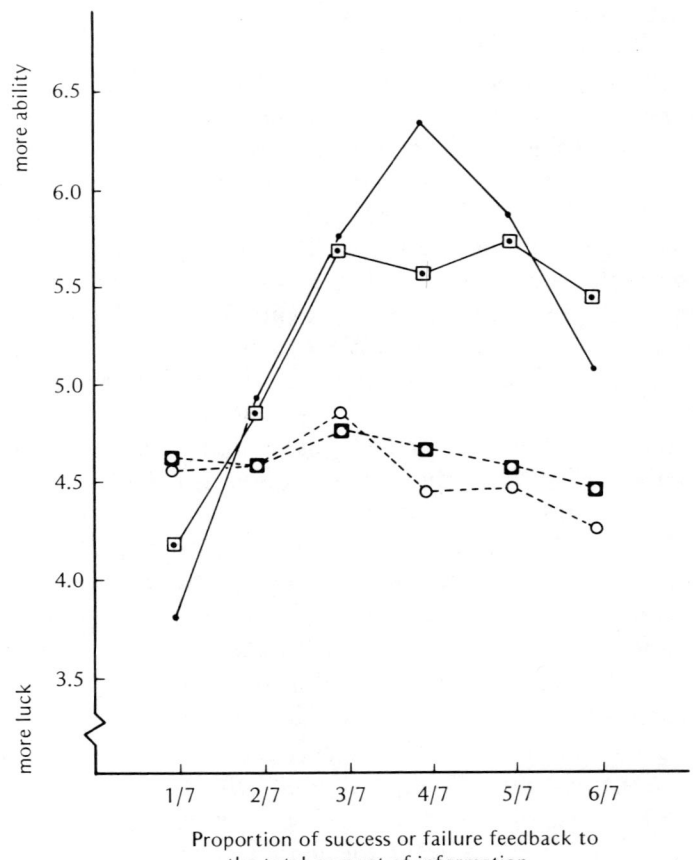

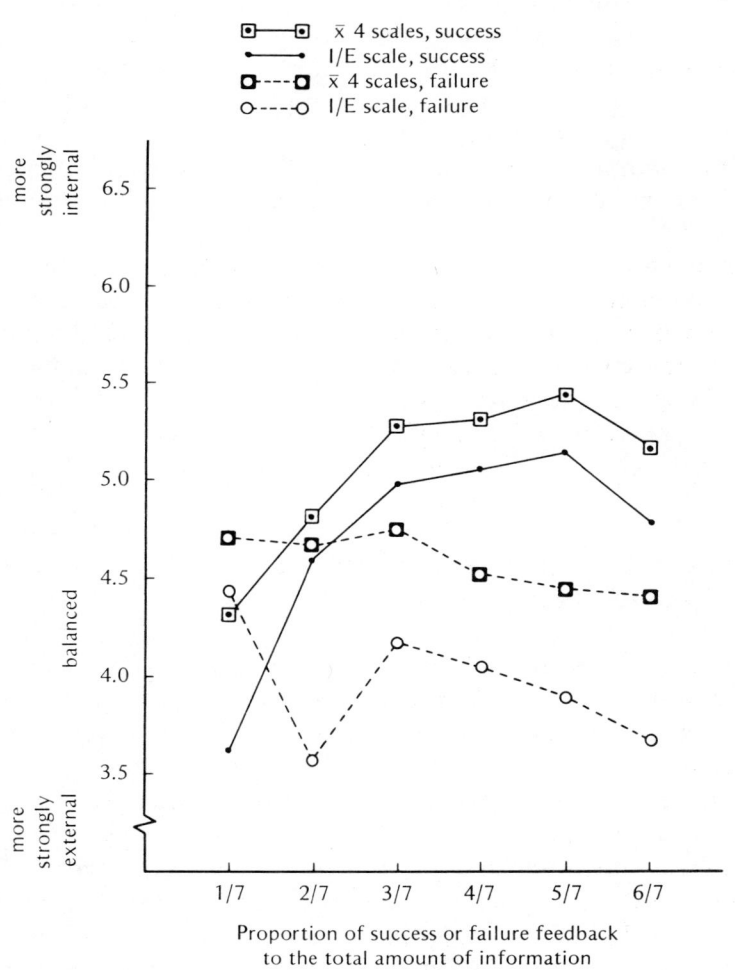

Figure 9-4. Seven-Point Forced-Choice Scale for the Internal–External Dimension Compared with Sum of the Scales for Task Difficulty, Effort, Ability, and Luck (Cases of Task Difficulty and Luck are Evaluated in Opposite Manner) Yielded by Experimentally Induced Conditions of Increasing Success or Failure.

curve shapes show discrepancies between conditions 1 and 7, 2 and 7, and 3 and 7. The drop in internal attributions on the forced-choice scale from period 1 to period 2 is significant beyond the .01 level. No such drop occurs for the averaged scales representing the four quadrant concepts. Although one could explain the higher attributions on averaged scales (as in experiment 1) to potentially unrealistic high responses on non-forced-choice scales, one cannot explain the change in curve forms as easily. It might be that the theoretical assumption that the quadrants represent an internal–external dimension does not hold under specific failure levels. Another potential explanation could be that measurement on a forced-choice scale was sensitive to some variation in subjects' attributions that was not captured by the non-forced-choice scales. Whether it is one of these or another phenomenon that produced this result, an explanation needs to be found.

In sum, with some exceptions, Weiner's assumptions are supported by this research. In most cases (possibly with an exception under failure conditions with the internal–external dimension), the subjects seem to conceive of the concepts employed in that research in the same way as the theoretical assumptions imply. As a result, the data are likely much more meaningful (and reliable) than the data in the area of research on attribution of causality and responsibility.

CONCLUSIONS BASED ON THE TWO EXPERIMENTS

An attempt has been made to answer a series of specific questions about the methodology of attribution research in particular, and perhaps of psychological research in some other areas as well. None of the questions we have raised and neither of the experiments we carried out are all-encompassing. We intended to employ only some specific manipulations as a first step toward the analysis of attributions measurement techniques. The hope was to discover whether variations in the way data are collected can produce variable results.

Two general problems have been approached in these experiments: (1) variations in scale characteristics and their effects under variations of time, success, and failure and (2) dimensionality assumptions and their effects. It was found that scale differences can result in data differences even though the experimenter may be attempting to measure the same attribution process. It appears that percentage scales produce reliably lower attribution levels than bipolar scales. Attribution responses on bipolar scales may be unreasonably high, resulting in potential ceiling effects that would hide increases in attributions under certain conditions. Further, percentage scales may be more meaningful to at least some subjects, allowing them to express fine gradations in their attributions more effectively than they could on bipolar scales.

Forced-choice scales apparently produce results that are quite equivalent to those of non-forced-choice scales, if no problems with the dimensionality of the attributions are encountered. Nonetheless, subjects will respond on forced-choice scales even if the dimensional assumptions represented by the poles would otherwise not be utilized by them. In that case, the choice of response (particularly in comparison to equivalent responses on separate non-forced-choice scales) might be informative as to the salience of the concepts (or dimensions) that are implied or represented by the endpoints of the forced-choice scale. In general, however, it appears that forced-choice scales offering only two choices are subject to error and consequently are less than ideal for the measurement of attributions.

It was shown that attribution responses need some amount of time to stabilize, so that responses, particularly on non-forced-choice scales, may be underestimating standard or average attributions at the beginning of long-term experiments. Similar underestimates would likely occur in experiments with one-shot measurement techniques. It was also shown again that internal attributions increase with success, and that internal attributions remain relatively stable with failure experience. Even under failure conditions the attributions to ability and effort (though lower than under success) exceed those to task and luck.

One probably cannot make a fixed recommendation to future experimenters on what kind of scale to use. The experimenter should base his decision on the kind of data he expects to obtain, and on the assumptions he can make about how subjects are utilizing the information they have to deal with. Nonetheless, being aware of the specific advantages, problems, and characteristics of each scale type can make the choice a better one.

The second general problem with which we have dealt is the effect of dimensionality. By comparing the results of the first and the second experiment, it becomes obvious that problems arise when the dimensionality employed by the subjects does not match the dimensionality assumed by the experimenter. In those conditions, unreliable results and consequent misinterpretations are likely to occur. In contrast, an experimental dimensional system that is meaningful to the subjects and is used by them pervasively throughout the experiment should produce reliable data, even if different scales are used to measure the effects of the independent variables. In other words, it is quite important that experimenters assure that the assumed or theoretical dimensionality that they employ is also meaningful to their subjects, no matter whether that dimensionality is "standard" in the attributions of the subjects outside of the experiment or whether the dimensionality was specifically "induced" for the attribution response.

COMMENTS ON THE CHAPTER BY STREUFERT AND STREUFERT

Heinz Heckhausen

To look into some problems of attribution measurement, as the Streuferts have done, is a highly commendable undertaking. There is an obvious discrepancy between the importance of conclusions drawn from attribution data and the crudeness in the measuring of such data. The Streuferts make four main points taking account of their metric and dimensional analysis based on the use of different types of scales, bipolar versus percentage and forced-choice versus non-forced-choice ones:

1. Bipolar scales produce higher levels of attribution than do percentage scales. This does not cause trouble as long as one refrains from translating scale values of one type into the other type.

2. With repeated scaling of attributions there is a "time effect"; that is, the level of scale values rises. The Streuferts ascribe such a time effect to the subject's getting familiar with the task or to some kind of cognitive stabilization. This might be. However, there is an explanation that is much more upsetting to the attribution researcher. "How you measure" is not only "what you get." How you measure—or, more precisely, how often you measure—does change the behavior of your experimental subject. It is obvious that the repeated request for overt attribution, after failing or succeeding at one task after the other, may alter a subject's outlook, sharpen the salience of initially preferred causal factors, and modify ensuing behavior corre-

spondingly. Patten and White (1977) have published evidence that the act of overt causal attributions is an ego-involving operation that leads to differential improvement and persistence under continuous failure feedback. (Patten and White's article is a critical replication of Meyer's original 1973 study.)

Thus, an innocent time effect might turn out to be a Heisenberg type effect: Measurement changes successively what is to be measured. Repeated measurement over time, then, creates problems so that one may reverse the good advice the Streuferts give in favor of repeated measurement and against "one-shot" experiments; unless one would utilize repeated measurement on purpose as a treatment condition, a treatment that may successively amplify initial individual differences.

3. The crucial issue of individual differences in "metacognition" is finally raised. That is the question of how much overlap there is in the dimensionality of meaning laid down in the experimenter's scale and the subject's original understanding of the concepts in question. In their first experiment the Streuferts find a difference when estimations of responsibility and of causality are forced on one bipolar scale dimension as compared with separate estimation on two unipolar scales. They explain the relative excess of responsibility over causality in forced-choice scaling as a salience effect because subjects have to choose between two opposite concepts. Whether this explanation is correct or not (I am quite willing to accept such an explanation as a very plausible one), one has to conclude, in any case, that we get with both scale types different dimensionalities for the two concepts.

In the second experiment the Streuferts expected and found a better match of dimensionality using the internal versus external dimension, partitioned by the stability dimension as proposed in Weiner's 2×2 set of causal factors. The authors predicted and explained the better match with the "well-established" nature of the Weiner dimensions. However, compared to the concepts of responsibility versus causality, the Weiner dimensions cover a much broader semantic space with two pairs of clear-cut opposite poles. Therefore, it is not surprising that the Weiner dimensions are more resistant against scale-based distortions of dimensionality.

There is still a point to be concerned about. In the case of failure the data still show a relative mismatch between the forced-choice internal versus external scale and the sum of non-forced scales for the two internal and the two external factors (the latter with inverted scorings). Two reasons come to my mind which could have caused the mismatch (see Figure 9—4).

The first reason is the ambiguous nature of ability attribution in the case of failure. As we repeatedly noticed in our attribution research at Bochum, subjects can understand an ability attribution scale ranging from "not at all" to "very much" in two different ways: (1) as overall importance of ability factor for the given task (be it one's ability or one's lack of ability) and (2) as amount of possessed ability for that task. For instance, a low score could have opposite meanings: (1) Ability or lack of ability does not count much for failing in this task; (2) my ability is too low, therefore I failed at this task. Such an ambiguity may well wash out the true variation of ability attributions in the mean scores of a group of subjects.

The second reason concerns the definition of the internal versus external scale as "under control of" versus "not controlled by" subjects. Such a definition presupposes that subjects feel that the internal factor of ability is under their control, which, obviously, contradicts everybody's conviction. Effort, but not ability, is under one's control. Implicitly, the authors have contaminated the internal versus external dimension with the dimension of intentionality. I feel this could be another potential source for the mismatch between the two types of scales.

A final word about the 2 × 2 Weiner dimensions. The more they have been established as a fourfold attribution table in achievement motivation research, the more questionable they have become, and this for several reasons. First, ability and effort are often perceived the other way around along the stability dimension. Ability can be a variable cause as in learning, and effort a stable cause as in traitlike notions of industriousness or laziness, as Weiner himself meanwhile states (Weiner 1974). Second, there is obviously a third dimension, namely intentionality. Internal factors, such as volitional effort, and even external ones, such as available power resources, are under intentional control of the actor (see Rosenbaum 1972). Third, bodily state, such as fatigue, is a much more employed cause than luck. Bodily state is a variable and unintentional cause, but one may wonder whether it has to be classified as internal or as external.

4. The Streuferts have shortly raised the important question whether the four quadrants of the Weiner scheme are comparable.

Among the four causal factors there are two that are closely interrelated because they both delimit each other: ability and task difficulty. As it were, they are the two sides of the same coin. If somebody fails he may either say that the task was too difficult for him or that his ability was not sufficient; and if he succeeds, that the task was too easy for him or that his ability was sufficient. Logically speaking, ability statements and task statements are equivalent. An ability attribution implies a task attribution and vice versa. But is this also true psychologically speaking? Logic does not always preempt psycho-logic. In fact, people do not always use the one or the other statement interchangeably but prefer either an ability or a task attribution.

Under what conditions do people prefer ability attribution over task attributions? Besides a general self-enhancing tendency to ascribe success more to ability than task easiness (Miller 1976), the preference for ability, instead of task, attributions depends on the difficulty level of the task. If the task is perceived as a fair challenge to one's own ability one feels more responsible for the achieved outcome than if the task is either too easy or too difficult. Correspondingly, within an intermediate range of task difficulty one tends more to invoke ability as a cause of success and failure. Intermediate difficulty levels have the highest diagnosticity for inferring one's "true" ability. Moreover, and to complicate matters, within the intermediate difficulty range amount of expended effort has the greatest influence on whether the outcome will be successful or unsuccessful.

A last remark about task difficulty: This factor is frequently ill-referenced, or underreferenced, in attribution research and causes, therefore, some confusion. Essentially, three reference norms are possible: (1) task-inherent reference norms, which are independently definable from anybody's ability; (2) individual-referenced difficulty, which is the difficulty of a task for the individual actor; (3) group-referenced difficulty, which is defined by the percentage of group members able to master a given task. The mentioned intermediate range of difficulty that arouses self-responsibility and a tendency for ability attributions presupposes a task difficulty in individual-referenced terms. If an experimenter induces task difficulties he must make sure that the subjects can build up an individual-referenced norm. Otherwise he would create ambiguity as to where his single subjects will locate their personal abilities within either a task-inherent or a group-related reference system of difficulty for the task presented. Defining one's ability in ipsative or in social comparison terms (in individual or social reference norms, respectively) does, incidentally, make a difference for some motivation parameters, as has been shown for goal setting and for effort regulation after unexpected success or failure (Heckhausen 1975).

ATTRIBUTION AND MEASUREMENT
In Response to Heckhausen

Siegfried Streufert and
Susan C. Streufert

The comments of Heckhausen on our chapter, particularly the proposals for alternate interpretations, are stimulating and useful. In part, there are data and facts that argue against these alternate views that deserve to be mentioned. Because of the limited space, we will deal only shortly with some of Heckhausen's comments. We will not deal with the latter part of his comments, which appear less relevant to our chapter.

Heckhausen argues that changes in attribution measurement may not be due to greater familiarity or cognitive stabilization of subjects in a new environment but rather to measurement repetition: a sharpening of salience of initially preferred causal factors. If this were so, then responses to scales in the simulation after the second period of play should differ (Heisenberg effect), depending on whether data were gathered or not gathered after the first playing period. In several manipulation checks for various runs of the simulation with various independent variables this effect did *not* occur. Consequently, the interpretation of Heckhausen—even though apparently feasible—is not applicable in this case, and what Heckhausen called our "good advice" appears to stand.

Further, Heckhausen criticizes the scale endpoint description of "internal (under control of your group)" because it contradicts "everybody's conviction" that ability is not under control of the subject. Indeed, applied to individuals with whom Heckhausen and associates tend to work, this is quite true. In the simulation, control (we have data to support this) is related to the *ingredients of the group's own actions*—those "things" which the *group* of subjects can bring to bear upon the situation, such as their combined efforts and capacities. In contrast, those things that they cannot have any direct influence upon, such as the task, the actions of other groups, and the chance (luck) factor, are viewed as "not under their control" and remain "external." The reader should probably be warned that this use of the term "control"—based on pretesting subjects in the simulation—may indeed be specific to this simulation, to simulations in general, or to group tasks. It probably is inappropriate for use with individuals in the kind of design used by Heckhausen.

The comments of Heckhausen again point out the diversity in the approach to dimensionality and measurement in the area of attribution and probably elsewhere. Heckhausen's attributions with regard to our analysis are different from our own, in part because of apparent differences in the conceptualization of dimensionality, in part because of the typically different methodologies employed in our respective research. It is these confusions with which our chapter attempted to deal in another vein. However, disagreements such as these, carried out in this form, appear particularly useful for increasing communication among diverse scientists.

10 CAUSAL ATTRIBUTION IN THE CONTEXT OF SOCIAL EXPLANATION

*Kenneth J. Gergen and
Mary M. Gergen*

The investigation of attribution processes has largely followed a pattern long familiar to social psychologists, a pattern that might roughly be characterized as self-consuming. That is, once the initial questions are posed and research is underway, the area can be almost indefinitely sustained by feeding upon itself. Approximately twenty years ago Fritz Heider (1958) challenged the field with the question of causal attribution in the perception of others. Stimulated by his analysis, research has vigorously attempted to isolate the effects of a broad range of relevant variables and to differentiate among various aspects of the resulting reaction. Thus, factors such as role demands (Jones, Davis, and Gergen 1962), ability (Lanzetta and Hannah 1969), hedonic outcome (Gergen and Jones 1964), effort (Weiner and Kukla 1970), actor's power (Thibaut and Riecken 1962), actor versus observer standpoint (Nisbett, Caputo, Legant, and Maracek 1973), foreseen consequences (Sogin and Pallak 1976) and so on have all received attention, both as they influence the attribution of causality and as they are associated with the assignment of responsibility and/or a variety of behavioral reactions. Those theoret-

---

Gratitude is expressed to the Fulbright-Hayes Committee for grant support to the senior author, and to Robert Pages, Laboratoire de Psychologie Sociale, Paris, France, for providing all necessary facilities. Siegfried Streufert also furnished valuable criticism of an earlier draft of the present chapter.

ical models that have emerged over the years (see Jones and Davis 1965; Jones and Nisbett 1971; Kelley 1973; Weiner et al. 1971) have ordered and integrated the results of such research, and in doing so have stimulated further attempts at clarification and extension. Systematic research and integrative theory have thus maintained a mutually sustaining relation. Our capacities for differentiation have become increasingly sharpened; our sensitivities to manifold potentials have become heightened. Yet the contours of the initial question have largely remained unchanged. Understanding seems largely to have proceeded in depth, with progressively less attention given to the broader intellectual context in which the questions are asked.

Of particular importance, the question of how it is we go about explaining behavior, and for what purposes, has begun to emerge in a variety of adjoining disciplines. It is our present contention that there are vital linkages to be articulated between the specific inquiry into causal attribution and the more general problem of social explanation. The exploration of these linkages may serve to expand the range of our concerns, the character of our inquiry, and the general implications of our results. It is our belief that when nurtured in the proper context, the study of attribution may be employed in fundamentally reshaping our understanding of social life, including the nature of social psychology itself.

Although an exigesis on the nature of social understanding is beyond the scope of this chapter, it is useful to explore significant lines of development in several neighboring disciplines. Specifically, the development of sociorationalism within sociology, research on self-understanding in psychology, and recent concerns in analytic philosophy are of special significance. In each case we may relate these concerns to traditional inquiry into causal attribution, and in doing so progressively elaborate the contours of a new and exciting range of challenges. One prefatory statement is required before embarking on this analysis. Specifically, we wish to bring to the forefront of our concern the parallel between the efforts of the common individual to explain the wide range of actions confronted in daily life, and the efforts of the scientist to explain the actions of the common individual. In the past there has been a marked tendency for the scientist to view the common individual as a "scientist in miniature," that is, as one whose mode of forming attributions is essentially similar to that of the scientist, but whose methods of verification are open to a greater range of bias (see Shaver 1975). In effect, the positivist perspective assumed to undergird the scientist's own activities has frequently entered into attributions made to his subjects of study (Gergen in press). In the present case we would like to draw special attention to the reverse of the traditional direction of influence. That is, it seems essential that we reflect upon our activities as scientists in light of our discoveries concerning ordinary attribution. We must be prepared to examine scientific forms of explanation, their advantages and shortcomings, within the context of our knowledge concerning social explanation more generally.

THE EMERGENCE OF SOCIORATIONALISM

Positivistically oriented analysis of social life has traditionally assumed that individuals of sound mind can progressively improve their understanding of social life through keen observation and careful thought. Thus, people are viewed as capable of making objective discriminations among various social actions and among varying psychological underpinnings. They can properly discriminate between friendliness and unfriendliness, activity and passivity, dominance and submissiveness, learning and forgetting, and so on; they may ultimately comprehend when an action is motivated by fear as opposed to love, by rationality as opposed to emotionality, by cognitive assimilation as opposed to accommodation, and so on. Within this perspective one may assume a dimension of veridicality such that perceptions of others' behavior or inferences regarding psychological activity may vary from accuracy to inaccuracy.

In contrast to the traditional positivist conception of social life, we may identify what can be termed a *sociorationalist* orientation. This perspective, which draws its primary intellectual sustenance from the philosophical writings of Kant, Hegel, and Husserl, along with the social inquiries of Marx and Schütz, essentially views the individual as operating in a reality that is primarily social in origin. This is not merely to say that social communication depends on agreement with respect to how various actions or behaviors are to be called. Rather the basic social inventory ("what there is") along with the significance of any particular event depends on a continuous process of social negotiation. Thus, whether an individual is friendly or unfriendly, is active or passive, honest or dishonest, whether he is motivated by optimism or pessimism, guilt or malevolent desire, feelings of responsibility or irresponsibility are primarily matters of interpretive agreement. They are not matters that can be adjudicated according to the "facts before us," but must ultimately depend on a series of often tentative social agreements.

For an amplification of this emerging position we must turn primarily to wide-ranging developments within sociology. One must begin in this case with the seminal influence of Howard S. Becker. Although it is vitally influenced by George Herbert Mead, himself typically identified with the positivist epistemology, Becker's work clearly contains the seeds of the sociorationalist perspective. His major concern with those unspoken agreements among members of a collectivity used for purposes of sustaining their own interests are of particular concern. Thus, argues Becker (1963), the concept of deviance is generated by one sector of society for its own advantage, and often to the disadvantage of others. Deviance is not an empirical reality, a palpable social event, so much as a conceptual construction used by a certain sector of the society to sustain or enhance its well-being. The perspective becomes further elaborated in Becker's (1963) analysis of drug experience. In this case it appears that the most important effects of hallucinogenic drugs may be socially mediated. What drug takers experience is not so much dependent on the intrinsic properties of the drugs themselves as on the conceptual or interpretive agreements prevailing within drug-using subcultures.

Similar concern with the seemingly arbitrary character of common understanding pervades the work of Harold Garfinkel (1967) and his colleagues in the *ethnomethodological* tradition. In this case the central focus is on the "methods" by which people render their actions, or the world about them, reasonable and accountable to others. The ethnomethodologist is curious about what others take as givens, or "the common facts of life," and through descriptive analysis attempts to elaborate their origins in social agreement. Thus, for example, Cicourel (1968) has demonstrated how within the system of juvenile justice, an elaborate system of agreements must be sustained by police, probation officials, and so on, in order to convert the immense complexity of an ever-shifting reality into ordered units called "offenses," "harmless behavior," "family units," and so on. Garfinkel (1967) has carried out a similar analysis of the manner in which officials determine what counts as "death by suicide." In each case what appear to be commonsense realities are shown to rest on seemingly arbitrary social convention.

Similar concerns are echoed in Erving Goffman's (1959, 1961, 1963) descriptive analyses of commonplace social activities. For Goffman, individuals punish deviation from normative patterns primarily because such deviations threaten the shared understandings prevailing in the culture. As he argues,

> The process of mutually sustaining a definition of the situation in face-to-face interaction is socially organized through rules of relevance and irrelevance. These rules for the management of engrossment appear to be an insubstantial element of social life, a matter of courtesy, manners, and etiquette. But it is to these flimsy rules, and not to the unshaking character of the external world, that we owe our unshaking sense of realities. To be at ease in a situation is to be properly subject to these rules, entranced by the meanings they generate, and stabilized; to be ill at ease means that one is ungrasped by immediate reality and that one loosens the grasp that others have of it. To be awkward or unkempt, to talk or move wrongly, is to be a dangerous giant, a destroyer of worlds. As every psychotic and comic ought to know, any accurately improper move can poke through the thin sleeve of immediate reality.

The fourth major contribution to the sociorationalist perspective is furnished by exploration in the sociology of knowledge. With differing emphases and interpretations, the classic works of Marx and Mannheim demonstrated how various bodies of "established knowledge" might depend on particular sociocultural circumstances. Sociology of knowledge, as it is said, is preeminently concerned with the fragile "web of meanings that allow the individual to navigate his way through the ordinary events and encounters of his life with others" (Berger, Berger, and Kellner 1973). Traditional analyses have thus centered on the needs of the culture for knowledge in specific forms, the role of institutions such as government or economy in shaping the course if not the outcome of inquiry, and the socioeconomic circumstances giving rise to particular intellectual positions. And, in a related vein, recent critics have attempted to show how a wide range of social theory, including structural–functional theory (Gouldner 1972), conflict theory (Plon 1973), and intergroup relations (Billig 1976), for example, may all depend for their attributed validity on common value and/or ideology.

Let us now link the sociorationalist perspective more directly to the study of causal attribution. First, there is little reason to believe that the attributional processes with which the field has been traditionally concerned are somehow fashioned by the genetic code, essentially built into the physiological system. That is, we do not appear to be studying determinant systems, specifying what the individual *must* do, but malleable systems that may allow the individual to move in a variety of directions. For example, the attribution of causality in the case of what we term "mental illness" has undergone marked transformation over the last fifty years, and even today the assignment of causal locus is a matter of considerable debate (see Szasz 1960). And, if Skinner's (1975) arguments were widely accepted, common reliance on internal attributions would all but disappear from society. This is not to say that genetics are irrelevant to attributional systems. Indeed, the available forms of attribution may be derived from the interaction of the biological system with essential features of the sociophysical environment. However, although certain forms of attribution (viz. internal versus external) may be favored by bioenvironmental interactions, there appear to be no biological requirement that we employ specific attributions on any particular occasion.

Given the apparent malleability of our attributional behavior, there is good reason to consider it within the sociorationalist perspective. That is, we may essentially be concerned with a system of explanation that enables the individual to "make sense of" both his own behavior and the actions of others. Because it is primarily dependent on a potentially fragile set of social agreements, the explanation of all social activity may be subject to continuous negotiation. From this perspective, our empirical research has succeeded, thus far, in tapping into various normative patterns of social explanation and in demonstrating a variety of contingencies sometimes affecting their employment. Models of causal attribution may thus be viewed as attempts to provide a systematic account of contemporary norms or mores of social explanation. Several significant implications immediately follow from this line of argument.

Flexibility of Behavioral Explanation

We may first anticipate considerable flexibility with respect to the way in which any given behavioral event is "explained," or the manner in which causal attributions are made. This flexibility may manifest itself both on the level of changing preferences in the attributional norms of society, and in the moment-to-moment negotiation taking place within any given relationship. Given the lack of attributional imperatives, the causal source of any given action may be viewed as subject to negotiation. One may explain a given action in virtually any manner so long as social support may be found (or anticipated) for the explanation. This is to say, for example, that whether one views a given act as internally or externally caused, whether one views the individual as responsible or not, is primarily a matter of social negotiation. Any interpretation can be made as long as agreement may be found. To be sure, whether or not one can obtain agreement may depend in large measure on the current norms or rules pertaining to attributional inference within the culture. However, if such rules are so loosely tied to observables as the sociorationalist perspective suggests, then with effort virtually any given action may yield a variety of equally plausible and convincing interpretations.

We may illustrate with the particular drama often attached to courtroom deliberations. Whether a crime is "intentional," "the result of circumstances beyond the individual's control," "carried out under duress," or "the result of an unfortunate childhood" seems almost entirely a matter of social negotiation. Given the rich array of experiences to which the individual has been exposed, the immense range of previous actions on his part, the inaccessibility of his thoughts or feelings, and the wide range of interpretations to which any given experience or action is subject, the question is not so much one of objectively establishing guilt or innocence, but of developing the most convincing account of the range of particulars brought to bear in the case. Thus, for example, kidnapped heiress Patty Hearst was neither innocent nor guilty on any objective grounds; whether she won her case was primarily dependent on whether her lawyer, F. Lee Bailey, could convince the jurors that her activities could be reasonably attributed to what was being called "brainwashing."

Inquiry into Function

To adopt the sociorationalist perspective is to raise questions regarding the function of causal attribution. It has traditionally been assumed that attributional processes function to increase our predictive capability (see Shaver's 1975 summary). That is, by determining whether a given act is intentional or unintentional, the result of a temporary emotional state or an underlying disposition, for example, enables us to estimate more accurately the future behavior of the individual. If Patty Hearst robbed a bank because her captors would shoot her if she did not, we may reasonably conclude that she would not do so if set free; however, if she intentionally engaged in the bank robbery, society might be safer if she were imprisoned. Yet, from the present perspective this traditional reasoning is rendered suspect. As we have seen, what conclusions we reach with respect to the causal wellsprings of a given action may be essentially unverifiable and ultimately dependent on a process of social negotiation. With effort, we may find support for the attribution of intentionality, temporary emotional upheaval, social pressure, or underlying disposition for most social actions.

Let us consider the most convincing of cases, robbing a bank under threat of death. Can we not say in this case that the act was unintentional? How can we hold someone responsible for robbing a bank under this threat and punish her for breaking a law? Perhaps we cannot, but we would submit that the fact that we cannot has nothing to do with locating the true or objective source of a person's actions in this case. That is, even when a gun is pointed in one's direction, one is not *required* to respond obediently; if the individual under duress were required to kill 1000 people or be killed, we might well be inclined to hold her responsible for her actions. The attribution of responsibility depends largely on normative agreement that robbing a bank may acceptably be attributed to threat of death, while slaughtering 1000 people cannot. The threat of death is not the objective cause in either case.

If we are unable to identify the causal source of social action, then we are left with the essential question of the function of causal attribution in social life. It is extremely important that we attend to this problem, for the manner in which it is answered has implications not only for the interpretations we make of our research findings, but for the more general importance we may attach to such research. To illustrate, it can be argued that social explanation functions primarily as a device for making oneself intelligible or justifying one's behavior within the structure of normative understanding. It may serve, as Goffman (1973) might say, as a means of furthering one's "moral career" in society. If we accept this view, it suggests that people do not go about continuously engaged in the process of attribution. Rather, they may do so primarily when either their actions or another's are called into question from the standpoint of the normative system. Attribution may be a sometime affair and typically resolved in ways that favor oneself. We do not wish to suggest that this is the only function of attribution, but much depends on what further functions we assign to such processes.

Explanation in the Social Sciences

If causal attribution is primarily a matter of social negotiation, then we must be prepared to ask a number of serious questions about the function of explanation within the social sciences themselves. Here we must be prepared to face the possibility that interpreting various actions in terms of motives, emotions, cognitive processes, or other mental events does not aid at all in the process of prediction. This argument was in fact made by Gilbert Ryle (1949) in philosophy, and more recently in sociology by Thomas Wilson (1970). Of course, explanation need not be predictive. As Steven Toulmin (1961) has pointed out, Darwin's theory of evolution is highly satisfactory as explanation, even though it may have very little predictive value. And, too, social theories may serve a variety of important purposes outside those of prediction and control (see Gergen 1977a). However, in this case we must also ask about the extent to which social science explanation also serves normative purposes. That is, as social scientists engaged in the specification of causal locus, we are at the same time inextricably embroiled in the process of redistributing blame and praise. This is wholly apparent in the case of mental illness, where scientific explanation over the last century has shifted the blame almost entirely from the patient to the society. More recent analyses even cast the patient in the role of cultural hero. Similar negotiation of causal locus has taken place in the case of delinquency, revolutionary activity, aggression, obesity, and the behavior of minority groups and of women.

THE AWARENESS OF MENTAL PROCESSES

We must now shift the focus of our analysis to a second line of thinking, one that has its roots within psychology. Nisbett and Wilson

(1977) have recently described what appears to be growing agreement among cognitive psychologists that most cognitive processing takes place at a level well below conscious awareness. As George Miller stated, "It is *result* of thinking, not the process of thinking, that appears spontaneously in consciousness" (1962: 56). Or, as Neisser put it, "the constructive processes [involved in encoding sensation] themselves never appear in consciousness, their products do" (1976: 301). And we find Mandler commenting, "The analysis of situations and appraisal of the environment . . . [presumably] goes on mainly at the nonconscious level" (1975: 53). Stimulated in part by these developments, and in part by recent social psychological findings, Nisbett and Wilson (1977) have undertaken an intensive review of research findings dealing with the cognition of the mental process. Based on this review and original research of their own, it appears that the tentative conclusions reached within cognitive psychology may be valid across an immense range of psychological processing, including problem solving, creativity, and comparative evaluations, dissonance reduction, and attitude change. In broader terms, it appears that asking someone what cognitive processes are responsible for his behavior is not asking a question to which he can give an objective answer, a response based on specifiable or palpable experience.

Let us now extend this line of argument. If self-examination does not generally yield valid answers to the question of "why" or "how" a given behavior came about, can such answers be provided in terms of the external environment? For example, if an individual says that he ran from a bear either because he was fearful (an emotional basis) or because he weighed all the evidence (a cognitive basis) and it was the only reasonable response, we have substantial reason to doubt his explanation. Based on evidence such as that cited before, there appears to be no way in which he could have looked inward and located a valid answer (either cognitive or emotional) to the question of why he ran from the bear. However, if in contrast he says that he ran because a bear was growling at him, it may be said that his reason is linked to a palpable reality and is thus a valid reply. In effect one might argue that whereas resorting to internal processes as an explanatory base is to engage in what might be viewed as social mythology, external sources of explanation are objectively verifiable.

Let us examine this account more closely. At the outset there is little reason to believe that we are genetically disposed to run at the sight of a growling bear. There are a multitude of other responses available to us, many of which we display on other occasions (at the zoo, in national parks, on a hunt). Thus, to explain our running in terms of the bear's ferocity is not in itself sufficient; bears do not automatically produce such responses. In order to produce the running response, some form of psychological construction is required. That is, we must interpret the bear's approach and its "meaning" for us. In effect, we do not respond directly to the bear's approach, but rather, to some internal interpretation of the bear and what it might do to us.

At this point the explanatory analysis reverts to subjectivity. As soon as we have shifted the locus of explanation from the external stimulus, the bear, to the internal representational schema (say, that the bear may kill me, and I don't want to die), we have stepped once again into the realm of subjective and arbitrary interpretation. If the individual does not generally have access to mental and emotional processing, then in what sense can we trust the response "I ran because the bear seemed dangerous, and I didn't want to be killed"? How does the individual *know* that he ran for this reason and not some other (say, because he felt any normal person would, or because his father told him he should run in such cases, or because the bear was a threat to his masculinity)? Further, on the phenomenological level, it seems doubtful that people entertain any such notions on such occasions. If a growling bear appears, they run first, and they may never stop to ask themselves "why" until much later—if at all.

It remains now to make firm the implicit linkage between this line of argument and the preceding discussion. As earlier ventured, the manner in which we attribute causality appears to reflect a system of normative social agreement. Our understanding of "why" we act as we do may primarily serve as a means of rendering action socially accountable, that is, acceptable or unacceptable according to our purposes. The present analysis serves to underscore the nonobjective character of these accounts. First, the individual cannot look inward and with any certainty determine when his actions are based on "intention," "premeditation," "emotional upheaval," "concern for others," "esteem needs," "achievement motivation," or whatever. Likewise, he cannot with any certainty look inward and determine why it is that he has responded to the environment as he has. This ignorance must essentially be paralleled by ignorance on the part of others, including the scientist. For others to attribute various mental, emotional, or intentional processes to the individual is to engage in the same variety of virtually groundless conjecture. Thus, the ultimate dependency of attributional accounts on social negotiation seems all the more convincing and extends from the individual's understanding of self to his understanding of others.

Does this mean that there is no form of causal accounting that may be said to have objective validity? No, not if we are willing to confine ourselves to the Humean definition of causality as essentially a statistical relation holding between independent events. Or as Harré and Secord put it, "Causation [in the Humean sense] is nothing but the regular sequence of one kind of event and another of the kind which usually follows" (1973: 31). This form of social explanation is best exemplified in psychology by Skinnerian behavior theory. The tracing of a systematic relation between particular environmental observables and certain behavioral actions itself provides "the explanation" of the behavior. In this form, if an individual smiles each time Charlie Chaplin throws a brick and does not smile when Chaplin does not throw a brick, we have essentially "explained" her smiling. And we have done so in a form that is objectively verifiable. Yet, in spite of its singular advantage, this form of explanation is most unsatisfactory. It essentially fails to satisfy our desire for an answer to the question "Why?" Typically we would say that the statement that the individual smiles each time she sees Charlie Chaplin throw a brick is "merely descriptive," and we would still be left with the question of "why" she does so. Is it because of latent sadistic motives, the clownlike motions of the brick-throwing, relief from tension, or what? For many people the question of explanation is not solved until one has penetrated the psyche of the individual. We do not find it congenial to live in a world of black boxes.

ANALYTIC PHILOSOPHY: REASONS AND CAUSES

We may now turn to a final line of relevant inquiry. From the logical positivist attempt to construct a model of proper scientific conduct has emerged a philosophic concern with language that has come to question the very grounds of its predecessors' attempts. This philosophic movement, frequently termed analytic, was principally intent on paring away the confusions built into ordinary language systems and reducing the complexity of such systems to a series of basic elements. Largely because of Wittgenstein's trenchant criticism of such efforts, the attempts to isolate essential components for scientific communication were abandoned. Yet the concern with ordinary language and its implications for human understanding was actively maintained. This latter concern ultimately led to investigations of central relevance to the social sciences. We must, according to philosophers Ryle, Anscombe, Austin, and others, distinguish between the movements of the body itself and common conceptions of the individual's action. The discrete movements themselves are of little consequence until they are translated into the molar terms of human communication. More specifically, it is argued, the vocabulary employed in "making sense of" the immense welter of discrete movements is a vocabulary of "reasons." If we observe a man in a series of successive bodily contortions, his actions are rendered wholly comprehensible when we learn that he is "trying to get a bit of exercise." Or as Peters (1958) has put it, if we ask a man to explain his actions and he responds that he is going to purchase tobacco, the statement of the goal (the reason) provides us with a satisfying sense of understanding. When the reason is made known, the series of otherwise meaningless actions is essentially "explained." Further, it is argued, a response in terms of reasons allows us to adapt or respond far more adequately to the actions than if we were provided the most precise and detailed account of the same actions in terms of the physical inputs acting upon the individual and/or the behavior itself. In effect, a separate domain of discourse seems required for the everyday understanding of human action, and this discourse primarily rests on a vocabulary of reason. This form of explanation may be contrasted with that employed by the natural scientists, which is said to be based on a vocabulary of cause.

This line of argument has been employed for a variety of purposes. For one, the attempt has been made to spell out the implications of this distinction for our basic conception of the human being. To say that John Jones is crossing the street in order to purchase tobacco is to suggest that Jones is a purposive individual who operates on a set of rules in order to achieve goals of which he is cognizant. This conception of human activity may be contrasted with the traditional psychological image of the individual as an organism whose actions are principally dependent on antecedent conditions. In keeping with the criteria supplied by ordinary human understanding, it is argued that the behaviorist orientation should be replaced with the conception of the human being as purposive and rule-following. It is this latter line of reasoning that Harré and Secord (1973) have extended in their outline for an *ethogenic* social psychology. From their perspective, social behavior is to be understood in terms of the rule-following models employed by individuals; in this sense the research psychologist may function much like an ethologist attempting to document the particular rule systems currently in practice within a culture.

It is this latter view of the psychologist's task that may be usefully linked to our earlier discussion of sociorationalism. From both perspectives, understanding of social action depends on the study of the individual within specific spatiotemporal circumstances, that is, located within a particular culture at a particular point in history. Setting aside the related debate over natural versus social science inquiry (Gergen 1973), it is now useful to adopt this ethnographic lens to reexamine the work of the analytic philosophers. That is, we may agree with Harré and Secord that it is useful to view much of the individual's activity as rule governed. But in keeping with our sociorationalist perspective, we may say that certain rules are commonly employed in our efforts to understand or explain social behavior. This distinction between causes and reasons, in this sense, is less interesting philosophically than it is a reflection of people's common rules of explaining their behavior or making it intelligible. The fact that we can be impressed with the phenomenological correctness of the distinction between reasons and causes indicates that contemporary rules of interpretation do employ this distinction. The analytic philosophers have succeeded, then, in providing valuable ethnographic data that must be taken into account if we are to understand contemporary systems of social explanation.

TOWARD AN ETHNOGRAPHY OF EXPLANATION

It is at this point that the implications of the present analysis are broadened considerably. It is initially apparent that we must ask about the extent to which traditional attribution research reflects the major explanatory rules existing within the culture. Thus far, the vast share of the experimental literature has distinguished only between internal versus external sources or loci of causality. However, as both

Kruglanski (1975) and Buss (1978) have argued, this one major bifurcation obscures a variety of very important distinctions found in our common patterns of explanation. What other distinctions are required is largely an open question, but at a minimum we should profit by taking into account the very useful distinction derived from the analysis of ordinary language, that is, the distinction between reasons and causes. As Buss (1978) has noted, the language of reasons is itself multifaceted, and therefore even this simple distinction is misleading. However, we may for the present single out one of the included facets for attention. In particular, we may center on the distinction between voluntary and involuntary sources of behavior. That is, a language of reasons often (but not always) rests on statements of voluntary intent, while causal explanations are largely viewed as involuntary.

Given the traditional social psychological distinction between internal and external sources of behavior and the philosophically based distinction between voluntary and involuntary sources of behavior, we may derive a fourfold set of explanatory categories. As Table 10-1 indicates, when asked why a given behavior occurs, the individual may respond by singling out an *internal (voluntary) reason* ("I am going across the street because I would like to buy some tobacco"), an *internal (involuntary) cause* ("My craving for heroin is driving me to get it all costs"), an *external (voluntary) reason* ("I'm going to Paul's house because he invited me to his party"), and an *external (involuntary) cause* ("I was late because I was trapped in the elevator that was stuck between two floors").

What does this fourfold division tell us? For one, it appears that the notion of human responsibility (blame, guilt, honor) is primarily attached to the voluntary-involuntary distinction, and not to the internal versus external distinction, as often supposed. Further, there may be differing functions associated with preferences for one versus the other type of distinction. The voluntary-involuntary distinction may be used for purposes of allocating blame and reward;

Table 10-1. Explanatory Categories: A Preliminary Schema.

	Reason (voluntary)	*Cause (involuntary)*
Internal	"I would like to ..."	"My craving ..."
External	"Paul asked me to ..."	"I was trapped ..."

the internal–external distinction may be used for far different purposes. One may favor internal explanations when there are questions of personal coherence, identity, or selfhood at stake whereas one may employ external loci of explanation to avoid disclosure or to direct attention away from self. These varying distinctions may also enable us to resolve various conflicts in the discipline. As Buss (1978) has argued, for example, observer–actor differences in attribution may largely be explained in terms of the differing loci of explanation that the observer is asked to employ. We further suggest that the controversy over situationalism in personality research may be resolved in a similar fashion. Situationists versus personality enthusiasts are primarily adopting differing loci of explanation for the same phenomena, and all behavior may be adequately explained (or rendered intelligible) from either perspective.

We are not at all proposing that this fourfold division exhausts the sources of explanation typically employed in Western culture. Far from it. We rather view this single elaboration as a preliminary challenge for a fuller ethnographic analysis of the range of explanatory possibilities. Should this challenge be accepted, it will mean moving away from strict laboratory methodology and into a comprehensive systematization of the language of everyday life. When we have carried out this necessary piece of ethnographic work, we can begin to ask a variety of extremely important questions virtually untouched by research to date. For example, can people actually move across the entire range of explanatory options with relative ease, as the previous analysis suggests? Closely related, what conditions favor certain explanatory options as opposed to others? What cross-cultural and transhistorical generality may be discovered in the range of options currently employed? If there is substantial generality across time and culture, as we suspect, how can we account for them? Further, could we derive various philosophical accounts of causality from such ordinary social usage; can we develop a social psychological analysis of philosophical systems? And, finally, what advantages and disadvantages do we encounter as social psychologists in our selection of explanatory loci?

In summary it would appear that in adopting a positivist model of cause and effect in our own research we have overly restricted the scope and implications of inquiry into attribution. In the attempt to isolate particular relations between variables, we have paid insufficient attention to the broad pattern and functions of social understanding in society. In adopting a sociorationalist perspective, and considering research into self-understanding along with contributions to analytic philosophy, we are furnished with a number of highly challenging possibilities. First, we find that accounts of social explanation may essentially be nonobjective. What we take to be a satisfactory explanation may depend entirely on normative preferences existing at the time and the manner in which these are negotiated within the given situation. Guilt and innocence for any given act may thus depend primarily on prevailing rules of negotiation. Second, because of the nonobjective character of such explanation we may find that individuals are capable of rapid shifts in perspective. Essentially, they may be able to facilely recast social explanation into a variety of differing but equally plausible forms. Analysis is thus demanded of the function of social explanation. Given a variety of plausible explanations in any given situation, how are decisions reached and to what end? Third, we find that we must expand our pursuits to include an ethnographic inquiry into the variety of existing explanatory modes. Increasing our understanding in breadth may allow us to deal with a range of new and exciting questions. Finally, we stand to gain (or lose?) much by turning our analysis of social explanation inward upon the discipline of social psychology itself. What functions do our explanations fulfill for us as scientists and for the society at large? What blindnesses are created in their use? For almost twenty years we have pursued the problem of causal attribution. We have learned much. But we are far from reaching the stage of tidying and refining. Rather, in our opinion, we may be poised at the brink of a new beginning.

COMMENTS ON THE CHAPTER BY GERGEN AND GERGEN

Heinz Heckhausen

The Gergens have pleaded eloquently in favor of a pervasive cross-cultural and transhistorical relativity of scientific facts and factors. They have gathered testimony from such diverse sources as socio-rationalism, ethnomethodology, analytic philosophy, and philosophy of science. They have made powerful points in reminding us that in the realm of social and behavioral sciences we do not dwell on unchangeable bedrocks of objectivity. Instead, understanding, explaining, and predicting is subject to continuous "negotiation." And the negotiated meanings, transient as they are, serve vested value interests and established social systems of the contemporaneous scene.

However, there remain questions: What is it that is ever-shifting? How much shifting is there? Are there directional trends in shifting, or is it arbitrary, as the Gergens contend? And what does "arbitrary" mean? In each respect, I feel, the authors keep overdoing well-taken points. Before I take up these questions I would like to react to their favorite metaphor (or is it a description?), namely, that meaning is continuously negotiated.

I can well understand that meaning is negotiated in courtroom deliberations or in other social transactions loaded with problems unresolved and uncertainties unreduced. But I would go further than that and contend that common understanding in present situations is, as it were, always based on "negotiations" already there without anybody ever knowing when, where, and how these negotiations might have come about. Human beings are always being enveloped by a huge web of shared meanings. Otherwise there would be no possibility for mutual understanding and for verbal communication to start with. This web of shared meanings—at least in its basic structure—can hardly have arisen as a result of some initial negotiation in remote historical darkness. It appears to rest on built-in mechanisms of man. Take the Kantian categories such as identity, space, time, and causality as the conditions for the possibility of all experience and understanding. Take the rules of logic in reasoning (Smedslund 1970, 1972). I am even inclined to subsume under the built-in universals, which need not be negotiated, the resulting units of Heider's naive analysis of action, such as "effective environmental force" versus "effective personal force" or "can" and "try" as a subdivision of effective personal force (Heider 1958). I include the basic dimensions of causal explanations of human behavior and its outcomes: internal versus external, stable versus unstable, intentional versus unintentional (and perhaps, and not identical with the last dimension, "controllable" versus "uncontrollable"). Furthermore, Harold Kelley's causal schemata (1972) might represent universals, too.

What, then, is shifting? There remains a lot. All content being processed, analyzed, and sorted into the cells and spaces of a universal matrix with laiddown dimensions of meaning. It is the sorting of the same pieces of information that undergoes transhistorical and ontogenetic change, that shows flux and relativity in individual and cultural difference. But is this sorting arbitrary? I do not think so. I see a directed change, an unfolding logic, both ontogenetically and transhistorically speaking. Is not there progress in utilizing, first, more dimensions for categorization and, second, more pieces of relevant information? In an ontogenetic perspective the studies in moral evaluation and, in an historical perspective, the transformations of the term of mental illness are cases in point.

Although there is still considerable debate in the assignment of causal locus of phenomena of mental illness, hardly anybody would, for instance, still prefer an attribution to demoniacal possession or to that strange fusion of internal and external causes whereby witchcraft was explained and persecuted in the sixteenth century by a woman's invitation to the devil to dwell in her body. Since Freud we take a lot of environmental factors into account and weigh them against genetic ones. If there is still considerable debate, the allocation of causes cannot still be said to be left with much room for arbitrariness and capricious negotiation. On the other hand, there is still enough room left for controversial explanations. For mental illness is still presenting problems that wait for solution. But who would deny that there is some slow progress of scientific knowledge, that our present assimilations of mental illness phenomena will have to accomodate more and new information and thus be navigated closer to so-called reality?

I think it is more adequate to view such epistemological problems within the framework of assimilation and accommodation processes of a Piaget-type interactive constructivism than to simply juxtapose "objective" or "true" causes to arbitrary or negotiated ones. No doubt, in the long run we come closer to "reality" or to "truth," but can we ever say what is "objective" in the sense of really real facts? If one perceives a bear, one is neither cognizant of the "external stimulus" nor of the "internal representational schema" (as the Gergens put it) but is cognizant of a bear. In the attempt to explain the perceiver's reaction to the bear, I do not see why we stay with so-called external stimulus within the realm of objective facts and why, relying on internal representational schema, we step into the realm of subjective and arbitrary interpretation. Why is a reference to an external stimulus not as subjective and arbitrary, or objective, as is a reference to an internal representational schema? In each case we rely on explanatory constructions. Looking for immediate evidence of what happens why, I agree with the Gergens that verbal reports on cognitions of mental processes present problematical access to what has been going on and what, however, can be a reliable source under certain circumstances, as Nisbett and Wilson (1977) have shown.

Anyway, scientific inquiry is the most powerful source that feeds back in the huge web of contemporary public opinion, belief systems, shared meanings, and social understanding. Thereby, something, but not all, is being changed. Content may change, accentuation shifts, sorting preferences vary, classification schemas become more expanded and differentiated—but the underlying structure of the huge web of common understanding does not change; that is, basic categories, logic, the main dimensions for ordering the vast array of perceived causes do not change.

Contrary to the Gergens, I would not state that we study malleable and not determinant systems. We do study determinate systems within which there is some malleability. There are limitations to society's malleability. For instance, the Gergens overdo the point when they contend "if Skinner's (1972) arguments were widely accepted, common reliance on internal attributions would all but disappear from society." This "if" is a utopian "if" because Skinner's arguments can and will never be widely accepted (see Heckhausen 1976). The reason for my contention is quite simple. Skinner's doctrine harbors one flaw, one inherent contradiction that prevents the doctrine from becoming credible and being acceptable for the public at large. The flaw is its lack of reflexivity; the effects of reinforcement contingencies hold for patients, students, and all the other people, but not for Fred Skinner himself. Or would Skinner ever be able (even if willing) to explain his brilliant prose, his incisive arguments as outcomes of prior reinforcement schedules? Who could have shaped up him?

The Gergens doubt that causal attribution increases our predictive capacity. I cannot see their argument. It is not necessary to know the "true" or "objective" causes of some event or of somebody's actions in order to predict future events and actions efficiently. It is usual business in research that highly restricted (or even falsified) theories have some predictive power. The explanations on which correct predictions are based may even be wrong. In motivation research the inclusion of causal attribution theory has improved our capacity for prediction, although one may doubt whether those cognitions the attribution theorists attribute to their subjects occur at all in their subjects.

In the last part of their chapter, the Gergens distinguish between causes and reasons and marshal testimony from analytic philosophy. I asked myself whether all this has not been said long ago in psychology when, in the thirties, Tolman outlined his psychological behaviorism in order to take full account of molar and purposive behavior. Do we still adopt the traditional psychological image that actions are wholly determined by various antecedent conditions, that a "positivist model of causes" is being adopted? This is really building a man of straw.

As their examples make clear, the Gergens equate reasons with a pull conception of motivation, and causes with a push conception. Reading these examples, I was surprised how much the Gergens trust in the overt phrasing of self-reports. I am not at all convinced by the fourfold division of motivation types. Each statement can easily be extended or rephrased in such a way that it changes its place in the classification scheme without changing its meaning. I guess the distinctions between causes and reasons and between internal and external have still to be spelled out.

The case of relativity is still up in the air if one wants answers to questions as to what, how much, and in what direction. The Gergens raise several important questions that deserve to be tackled now. For example: "Can people actually move across the entire range of explanatory options with relative ease?" "What cross-cultural and transhistorical generality may be discovered in the range of options currently employed?" "If there is substantial generality across time and culture, ... how can we account for them?" Among possible approaches, I would like to encourage the Gergens to turn to data of historical documentation. There are rich sedimentary data pools from which to probe and to test their assumptions, for instance through comparison of court files or pupil evaluations across decades and centuries. Let us see more evidence for relativity. It will be well received.

APPENDIX TO THE CONFERENCE
Dietmar Görlitz

This Afterword to our symposium is written from the perspective of an attentive, participating, and at the same time partial listener. The function of the following pages is to recapitulate the content and results of the contributions discussed in Bielefeld in June 1977. I assume the reader is familiar with the various chapters of this book, and I present this Appendix as an accompaniment to them, trying to elucidate the basic intentions of the individual authors with no referral to the relative sequence of their contributions in the discussions of the symposium and with even less pretense of appraising them (the respective commentaries already do this). Written by an observer, this elucidation is often more an interpretation of the author's intended meaning than a summary. Because of its space limitations, it is shorter than careful argumentation would deserve, and, not solely for stylistic reasons, it is meant to provide a more integrative, coherent framework than the conference meetings allowed. Here, too, lies the partiality of assuming that attribution theory finds itself engaged in a productive reformulation and expansion of its ten-

The appendix is based on the discussions and contributions at the Bielefeld symposium and has been left in its original form to preserve the line of argumentation. It does not reflect the fact that Wulf-Uwe Meyer and Bernard Weiner have substituted in this American version of the book more recent research for their original papers. Rather, the intention is to allow the reader to follow the development of the individual authors' positions over the last three years.

ets, which are part of a larger concept in which related basic dimensions become recognizable.

In Part I, "History and Scope of the Theory," the reader initially encounters attribution theory apart from that relation to everyday life that has attracted so much attention in past years of psychological work. The dedication to Fritz Heider, which opens this book, is much more biographical-historical; the presentation of the theory refers to basic patterns of science. Bernard Weiner's review of Fritz Heider's academic development lends to the history of Heider's *idea* a personal element, which Heider himself subsequently takes up as he gives a deeper insight into the individual and historical characteristics of his own contribution to psychology. In retrospect this review concerns the establishment of relations, the relations in the facts and in the concepts of the problem areas central to Heider's thinking. The consideration, beginning with Chapter 1, "Perception and Attribution," is clearly accentuated in questions concerning the subject of psychological research, especially the structure and valency of spheres of reality in object perception. What Heider reflects on and works out in more relevant terms here are things that have been of obvious interest to Gestalt psychology for a long time, such as how the world we are able to perceive is or must be structured in order to allow the collection of information (as perception) and the establishment of causal links (as attribution).

The difference between product (say, perception) and process (say, perceiving) is thereby noted more in passing. Underpinning the exposition of Heider's idea are two basic elements of the reality that human beings can experience: that the world is made up of parts that are ordered according to function and effectiveness (the idea of centers and subordinate parts), and, consequently, that the way in which we experience our world is nondirect, as in quite concrete examples of our daily social life and our everyday scientific routine. The mediator (the medium) and the effects as such each form a duality: the mediator with that which is mediated (thing), and the effects with that which is effecting (causes)—dualities that must reckon with illusions, alienation, and diminishing representativeness. The basic circumstances of order aimed at through this last thought are negatively valuated in the given culture.

In Chapter 3, looking back on the course of his own scientific thinking, Heider also makes order in the second relation referring to attribution, the balance concept so significant to research in this field. He tries to see common elements and connections, to let the continuity of his thinking become apparent beyond the possible discontinuities of the concept. A basic thought of the preceding contribution is taken further, for here, too, the structure of the reality we experience represents a requisite circumstance upon which the individual bases his efforts at creating order. Because it is the interaction of processes that is concerned and not merely the establishment of logical relations between concepts, the definition of proportionality followed by Heider himself remains dynamic and fixes no stable limits. Trying to create order would involve the formation of units, of unit relations. The clearest case of such unit formation is represented by balance. It is structurally or relationally composed of parts. Corresponding to balance within certain limitations (to cause-effect relations) is attribution, which at the same time—seen as a process—is a consequence of previous balance tendencies. This yields partially equivalent functions for both: first, the tailoring of parts in the cognitive field, and, for attribution, the additional task of culling information from the environment. As significant as it is, though, attribution nevertheless remains less important to the whole process of broader cognitive activities than its counterparts of perception and balance. Attribution is not everything. Heider would have us be more modest.

Attribution is then treated in the realm of concrete personal interaction by Harold Kelley's contribution, which carries the engaging title of "Magic Tricks." Showing how causal attributions can be manipulated, Kelley aims at revealing intended deception, "dishonest" interaction (here, for entertainment purposes); the chapter clarifies our understanding of how processes of attribution can be determined in advance. It appears possible, then, to make verifiable statements about everyday social interaction in which one person is deceitful and "pulls the wool" over another's eyes. That is the everyday part of Kelley's formulations, from which emerge the more threatening dimensions of deception and control. Kelley thus elucidates a second, more basic thought—that of the difference in the actor's and the observer's perspective resulting from their different positions in the attributional interaction. He states that it is necessary (and fruitful) to differentiate between the perceived causal sequence and the intended real causal sequence (as a theory about the graduation of perspective that can be perpetuated for either the observer or the actor). The concealment versus the discrepancy of these sequences forms an essential characteristic of magic tricks (a new *four-field table* classifies the relation to science on this point), expanded by a taxonomy of unusual cause–effect relations, which makes clear for a multitude of situations "when" attributions occur and when the observed and assumed causal sequences cease to coincide. Both central characteristics of "magic" causal sequences lead Kelley to discuss three concluding questions in which he works out the basic possibilities of concealment, of camouflaging one causal sequence with the other. The application of attribution research to an important everyday phenomenon in this contribution shows the way for future work in the field.

In Part II, "Attributions of Success and Failure," the contributors look into *specific* attributions such as matters related to achievement, which the relevant research has always preferred and has analyzed in the attributional context of both performer and observer.[a] Manfred Hofer and Martin Dobrick present in this part a *theory of social action as illustrated by teacher behavior*, which they try to keep from restrictions that are unifactoral (behavior determined exclusively by attribution) and univariate (regarding the variables of the resulting behavior). Attribution is thus woven into a complex set of relations that can make attribution a central part of a process model that guides mainly the formation of one's expectancies as to a situation's future development (the anticipated "future state") and that determines the actor's motivation and the choice of concrete plans of actions. These are preliminary stages on the way to more accurate prediction and testing for which Hofer and Dobrick include initial results. Achievement becomes one of several topics significant for interaction. Attribution becomes a crucial element among many of a system—of a model that explicitly concerns attribution of others' behavior and the consequences of these attributions for the control of one's own behavior. The ideas in this chapter throw light on interaction in a single direction first, that of the person who is going to act (the teacher), who observes the behavior of others, and who

---

a. The emphasis on this subject has been especially influenced by the work of B. Weiner, who has made the updated concept of his motivation theory available for this American edition of the conference papers. In developing a general theory of human motivation in the new chapter, Weiner makes several additions to his earlier positions. He adds the factor of control to the dimensional structure of perceived causes and revises the role and significance of affects as consequences of attributional analysis and of outcome of actions. The substance of these refinements of the theory is already detectable in the Bielefeld version commented on here.

processes this information according to attributional principles (among others). The addressed person (pupil), his possible reactions, and the corrections and feedback that can emanate from him are only mentioned at first. Further refinements remain to be made, which Weinert's comments programmatically point out.

If we take praise and blame (of a pupil's behavior) as *one* of the teacher's resulting decisions for action, Meyer's contribution[b] presents a systematically useful supplement to the model of Hofer and Dobrick.

To start, Meyer explores the thesis that praise and blame are not only effective reinforcers of behavior; they contain much more information having to do with the information-processing nature of the person praised or blamed. This information results from certain value and cognitive systems present in both persons and is processed accordingly and understood through a series of inferences related to the system. It is, then, not directly understood but, rather, indirectly, because the semantic content of the message is not the only input into the receiver's cognition. The greater part of that input is provided by what the receiver infers about the teacher's opinion concerning the pupil's ability vis-à-vis the difficulty of the task. This information is extracted from the message according to specific rules governing inference through incomplete syllogisms. The direct information, valuations of the sender (praise and blame), remain behaviorally and/or cognitively ineffective. In this process, systems and assigned inference rules match. The respective inference has consequences for the receiver's self-concept of ability and his reaction behavior. Meyer does not test these consequences empirically, but concentrates on the relation that precedes them: the relation between evaluative information (praise/blame) and the receiver's inference of his own ability. To test the prediction based on this relation, Meyer conducts four experiments whose design and sequence of hypotheses are coordinated with each other. The results consistently confirm the relevance of evaluative information (praise and blame)

b. The present volume contains instead the article entitled "An Attributional Analysis of the Relation between Expectancy and Incentive (Affect)" by Wulf-Uwe Meyer and Fritz-Otto Plöger. Herein are reflected some of the consequences of the Bielefeld Symposium, this case concerning the relation between attribution and affect originally treated by Bernard Weiner, Dan Russell, and David Lerman. Meyer and Plöger not only point out weaknesses in the representation of affects and their interrelations as they appear in the Atkinson model, they also show that affects have many relations to cognitions and attributions, of which only one type is considered by the sequence thesis originally proposed.

for the inference of ability, and give clues to possible age trends for these inferences and to the prevalence of ability inferences compared to other inferences. The theoretical system itself is not explicitly tested in Meyer's experiments. This seems at least to suggest that teacher behavior that evaluates or passes comment on achievement also receive attention and be studied further, especially the aspect of unintended information about ability.

In Bielefeld we were part of a larger context and had far closer references and correspondences with each other than we were aware of when studying our colleagues' work. For what becomes of these inferences about ability, which, as Meyer hypothesizes, occur when being blamed or praised? What, according to Hofer and Dobrick, leads the teacher to choose specific attributions for specific aspects of his classroom situation? Which inferences alter my self-concept? Here Stroebe adds a concept similarly made up of parts (at least as far as the process is concerned). Arranged around the central theme of a self-consistency hypothesis, the author cites self-esteem, expectancy of results, and causal attribution as relevant components of the process—relating to the topics of success and failure, which represent the results possible in the areas of achievement and interpersonal encounters. With one unifying concept, Stroebe tries to clarify what determines attributions to success and failure in both areas. Such experiences shall be interpreted according to the criterion of consistency, of compatibility with each individual's self-esteem. A person will take achievement results consistent with his own expectations and attribute them to ability or lack of ability—depending on his individual degree of self-esteem. Analogous experiences in the area of social interaction are similarly processed. Success in the latter case is the positive assessment by or the positive attitude instilled in another person; failure is the negative assessment by or the negative attitude instilled in another person. Stroebe provides an example of how general principles of attribution can divorce themselves from the narrowly defined area of achievement, such as when success or failure are stripped of their connotation specific to the achievement area. He even supports this extension empirically.

At the same time the author supplements the discussion with the consistency criterion that guides the incorporation of ability inferences into one's own self-concept. We assimilate information consistent with our own expectancies and concepts, and we are different from one another in the form these concepts take (or in how high or low our respective self-esteem is). Social reality corrects this interpretation of consistency only if the individual repeatedly has experiences that contradict it. It should not be any different for a person's self-concept than it is for our scientific theories.

Part III, "Attribution and Affect," focuses on central and critical problems of attribution research. Attribution theory significantly furthered and has continued to take part in the "cognitive shift" in psychology. It prefers a rational image of the human being, yet at the same time preserves its fascination for motivational problems and how to create adequate models for them. This is an integral subject for the field, at least as far as achievement concepts are concerned. This unspoken dual commitment confronts attribution theory with emotional factors of experience, which are defined as constructs or treated in *one* possible function—as a consequence of other antecedent factors (like causal attributional cognitions). Emotion thereby has a "chance" in the concept, as witnessed by Bernard Weiner's detailed and reflective essay at the conference centered on a pair of concepts, "Attribution and Affect."[c] Beginning with his model of achievement-motivated behavior, which both loosely establishes the relations of the parts in his system and restricts their content as far as the taxonomy of causes goes, Weiner then turns to the interesting core relation between specific attributional dimensions and resulting affects. With his own recent empirical documentation, the author illustrates here the problematic nature of some earlier theses. The introductory sketch of the model is less insistent as far as the now classic four-field table is concerned. Weiner concedes that circumstances can change the positioning of the main causes in his four-field table, and he restricts their generality by pointing out intercultural differences and other differential conditions. He "breaks the spell" of his scheme and thereby makes it more practical by showing that it is not naive, not universal, not complete (neither in its contents nor in its dimensions), not stable (as far as the relative position of the contents is concerned). At the center of the discussion, however, is a reorientation or extension of cognition toward the periphery zones of emotions. Do locally determined attributions, does the dimension "locus of control" in the attribution of causes

---

c. The present volume contains instead a new chapter by Bernard Weiner, "A Theory of Motivation for Some Classroom Experiences," which develops these initial ideas further. To compare the two positions, please see pp. 54–60, 106, especially parts of the discussion by Meyer and Plöger concerning the role of attribution-mediated affects.

(of achievement results) have specific affective consequences at least on the intensity of affects? In posing these questions of relation, Weiner takes emotions in all their qualitative diversity into the area of legitimate scientific interest, although they remain dependent (they impress one for now only as consequences, not as antecedents in their own right) and lackluster. He treats them initially on the level of "names," on the lexical–semantic level. With these materials his own empirical work shows the need to revise the two-pronged thesis that the intensity of affects is determined by the control dimension in attribution and that the achievement area is restricted to two affects. There are no exclusive or dominant achievement-related affects as far as the content of the affects is concerned and no unspecific increase (or decrease) of intensity of affect corresponding to specific control dimensions. The qualitative dimensions of affects are more decisive and more suited for discriminating the achievement area from other areas.

This study also retains a tendency toward data-reducing taxonomical order, which Weiner's contributions had earlier allowed to dominate. Two taxonomies meet—his expanded field scheme of location is referred to a similarly reduced dimension scheme of emotions by Davitz (1969). This puts emotion and affect in a provocative situation—they seem to be qualitatively richer and functionally more effective than earlier concepts were able to express. Weiner compensates this attraction or challenge—in harmony with the rational image of the human being as naive scientist and with his enlightening emphasis—by means of a *sequence thesis*: emotions *follow* cognitions. These cognitions provide the necessary and sufficient basis for emotions.

In principle, Bernard Weiner's sequence thesis—that emotions follow cognitions[d]—is retained by Ernst Liebhart, who is concerned with postulating the *perception of autonomic changes* as one determinant of emotional behavior. For this behavior, perception is a necessary mediating component. Liebhart is also concerned with articulating this relation in a complex model. The starting assumption is at once limiting and inclusive. It is limiting because the model he introduces is applied explicitly to the clarification of a specific finding, the Valins effect, and because it tries to pinpoint the conditions

---

d. For a further development of this early sequence thesis, see Weiner's new contribution in this volume.

necessary for the occurrence of such effects: it is the correct or incorrect perception of automic changes that is the decisive determinant of emotional behavior and not the changes themselves as Schachter's theory would have it. At the same time, Liebhart's starting assumption is inclusive because the author meritoriously ventures—while also taking into consideration all the preliminaries of such post hoc investigations—to confront his model with the available empirical experimental literature on the subject and even tries to integrate contradictory results, too. This coordinates otherwise disparate individual results, which is helpful and beneficial for our action strategies, which suffer from lack of organization among an increasing amount of information. His concept could have the character of a model in this way as well.

What does the model itself formulate? If I am correct, it is the postulate (and its documentation in the available literature) of four *core conditions*—for the effect of false physiological feedback and, based on this, the postulate of three successively intervening *processes* that in substance quite fulfill the presently global formulation of process as "perception." That is more clarification on the processing of autonomic stimulation than available findings have admitted up to now. What remains is the detail work on the model's "rules of functioning." Are the postulated core conditions (in brief: motivation, accessibility, plausibility, and significance) not merely necessary, but at the same time also sufficient for the occurrence of the Valins effect and of the three mediating processes that precede it? (To what degree are these processes constituted by each of the four conditions cited?) Or are there periphery and additonal conditions, perhaps in the form of inexplicit prerequisites (like the formation of a pattern incongruent with the context) that must be introduced? The answer to these two questions could be used to determine not only the model's validity, as Liebhart does, but its range of generality as well. Is it possible that it cannot "regulate" many more relations than those of the limited Valins situations?

This at least suggests possibilities for future empirical and conceptual investigation to broaden our perspective on emotion, a perspective that we have limited to the sequence thesis.

The fourth and last part of this volume addresses "Methodological Problems and the Social Context of Attribution." Attribution theory has entered its reflective phase. It may often appear to the historian as if early stages of a research area were less scrupulous, more reckless through its fascination for the object of study and would, led by that alone, forget the uniqueness of the path to be traveled—that enquiries about how the results are actually gotten are not made until findings and possible contradictions are compiled. Siegfried Streufert's and Susan Streufert's investigation of "Attribution, Dimensionality, and Measurement" documents this swing back, which began in attribution research referring to conditions of attributions, perhaps as a more process-oriented analysis, by checking how the process of attribution itself elapses. The Streuferts, on the other hand, make us aware of the blurring tints of the medium, the media through which we observe "things" subjected to attribution, to paraphrase Heider's basic title. They wish to demonstrate how instruments of measurement, in this case different rating scales, determine the result of the measurement itself and how that result changes from one instrument (scale) to another. Their findings illustrate this in various degrees. On the path between complete object-representation of our data and data as unreferenced artifacts of methodology, they bring our knowledge closer to the latter; at least they make the dependencies obvious again. This simultaneously outlines another field for research, namely that of also wanting to know what basic component of data and results is nonspecific to certain methods and can, so to speak, be accepted as the common denominator of all techniques. And another question is set up, too, the question of method: Which method for which purpose? The Streuferts' work makes the decision easier. To be sure, the Streuferts leave open the question of which method, which scale should be adopted for making attribution ratings. But just being aware of the consequences such choices have already makes the very act of choosing more conscious.

The second, perhaps more propulsive, side of their contribution is in pointing out that scales not only locate (in the sense of fixing a quantitative impression) but also order—by dimensionally structuring the individual semantic experience: that medium not only "blurs," it can also, to continue the metaphor, increase or decrease the variety and structure of the things mediated (the causal factors in question). Dimensionality (say, causal structures of order and explanation) is thus not only a matter of painstaking research with the certainty that, with enough effort, the exact number of dimensions will be found. Rather, these dimensions will in large part be induced, too.

It may be that in the future cognitive conflict will mark the point at which we ask too much of our experimental subjects, that the structure of everyday thought (which is, after all, the focal point of attribution research) surfaces through contradiction and through the protests of those experimental subjects.

Kenneth Gergen and Mary Gergen broaden the preliminary stand of our attributional self-certainty still further by proposing that the objective basis for attributions is very debatable and that it would be rather more fruitful to consider the statement based on attributions as a special case or as one among other groups of social explanation. To illustrate this and at the same time to outline the conceptual possibilities of a new line of questioning of concern to them, the Gergens cite important contributors in neighboring disciplines. Among these, the interest in everyday life characteristic of ethnomethodology could also touch less specifically on our field. The Gergens try to make clear that even the scientific treatment of attributional questions is partially guided by everyday concepts. The basic thesis, which in a different sense determines or springs from a sociorationalist perspective, denies the objectivity of reality and adheres instead to its primarily social origins. Common sense, also the focus of attribution research, does not reflect or manifest objective reality, but the transcultural or culture-specific products of "contingent ongoing accomplishments of organized artful practices" (Garfinkel 1972: 309). Examined more closely, however, attribution does not thereby lose its abutment in general to what the Gergens consider an unstable reality. Social interpretations do not yet touch the core of attributional explanation. As is otherwise customary in the empirical sciences (in accordance perhaps also with a subtle theory of the fact concept in the sense of Horkheimer, cf. 1934), the independence of the observer from ostensibly "objective" information will be doubted and objectivity will be seen as concordance of an interindividual nature, perhaps typical of a particular society. This does not refer to attribution, though, or to the act of attributing in general—"that" I attribute is not doubted; rather, the Gergens question the objectivity of "how" members of a particular society substantively or factually attribute and, in contrast to this, they try to reveal the character of the social contract.

On the basis of available data, Gergen and Gergen would thus want to assert that there is interindividual concordance in some (or all?)

attributional statements by laymen that is specific for certain societies and that is largely neutral or even arbitrarily linked to relevant objects. With a view to the ontogenetic or sociogenetic perspective, they would add that the determination of the content of attributions (usually or always?) occurs in the course of either cooperative or controversial negotiating. This does not need to compromise or shatter the self-certainty of immediate individual attributions, but is an important addenda to development, to ontogenesis, which otherwise took a back seat as a theme of our conference. As a thesis, its range of validity must still be narrowed down and the renunciation of genetic codes en bloc (as happens in the Gergens' chapter) has to be carefully examined.

The problem with attribution is thus not its *process* or the fact of its existence, but the objectivity of the content used in the explanation. In its *ontogenesis* it is ambiguous, open to the influence of changing social experience. In its *functions* it is less prognostic than profit-oriented (its individual and social benefit). The Gergens see attribution as an optional instrument of interest-guided social behavior that must rely on the assistance of social negotiation because the course and the result of an individual's cognitive processing are hardly reliably known for this individual when he is seeking an explanation. There is an element of reduction, a "nothing-more-than type" formula in the Gergens' concept when they say that we are forced to return to social conventions in our search for explanations because our experience is limited and because reality independent of society cannot be inferred. Which convention do the Gergens follow here? At least socially valid systems of rules, social conventions are brought up for attribution research by their argumentation. How large a role these will play in explaining thematic content will also depend on the degree to which one accepts a graduated system of explanation (ranging from socially accepted and publicly recognized mores to private taboos). Heider reflects on the world and on the basic conditions of its structure for the process of attribution. The Gergens abbreviate on the side of social validity. Attribution includes these perspectives.

SELECTED BIBLIOGRAPHY

Abramson, L.Y., Seligman, M.E.P., and Teasdale, J.D. 1978. Learned helplessness in humans: Critique and reformulation. *Journal of Abnormal Psychology*, 87, 49–74.

Ames, C. 1978. Children's achievement attributions and self-reinforcement: Effects of self-concept and competitive reward structure. *Journal of Educational Psychology*, 70, 345–355.

Ames, R., Ames, C., and Garrison, W. 1977. Children's causal ascriptions for positive and negative interpersonal outcomes. *Psychological Reports*, 41, 595–602.

Anderson, N.H. 1970. Functional measurement and psychological judgment. *Psychological Review*, 77, 153–170.

———. 1965. Averaging versus adding as a stimulus–combination rule in impression formation. *Journal of Experimental Psychology*, 70, 394–400.

Andrews, G.R. and Debus, R.L. 1978. Persistence and causal perception of failure: Modifying cognitive attributions. *Journal of Educational Psychology*, 70, 154–166.

Arkin, R.M. and Duval, S. 1975. Focus of attention and causal attribution of actors and observers. *Journal of Experimental Social Psychology*, 11, 427–438.

Arkin, R.M. and Maruyama, G.M. 1979. Attribution, affect, and college exam performance. *Journal of Educational Psychology*, 71, 85–93.

Aronson, R. and Carlsmith, J.M. 1968. Experimentation in social psychology. In G. Lindzey and E. Aronson (eds.), *The handbook of social psychology*. 2nd edition. Reading, Mass.: Addison-Wesley, 1–79.

Atkinson, J.W. 1964. *An introduction to motivation.* Princeton, N.J.: Van Nostrand.

———. 1957. Motivational determinants of risk-taking behavior. *Psychological Review,* 64, 359–372.

Atkinson, J.W. and Birch, D. 1978. *An introduction to motivation.* New York: Van Nostrand.

———. 1970. *The dynamics of action.* New York: Wiley.

Atkinson, J.W. and Cartwright, D. 1964. Some neglected variables in contemporary conceptions of decision and performance. *Psychological Reports,* 14, 575–590.

Atkinson, J.W. and Litwin, G.H. 1960. Achievement motive and test anxiety conceived as motive to approach success and motive to avoid failure. *Journal of Abnormal and Social Psychology,* 60, 52–63.

Bacon, S.J. 1974. Arousal and the range of cue utilization. *Journal of Experimental Psychology,* 102, 81–87.

Bandura, A., Blanchard, E.B., and Ritter, B. 1969. Relative efficacy of desensitization and modeling approaches for inducing behavioral, affective, and attitudinal changes. *Journal of Personality and Social Psychology,* 13, 173–199.

Barefoot, J.C. and Straub, R.B. 1971. Opportunity for information search and the effect of false heart-rate feedback. *Journal of Personality and Social Psychology,* 17, 154–157.

Barnes, R.D., Ickes, W.J., and Kidd, R.F. 1977. Effects of perceived intentionality and stability of another's dependency on helping behavior: A field experiment. Unpublished manuscript. University of Wisconsin–Madison.

Bar-Tal, D. and Darom, E. 1977. Causal perceptions of pupils' success or failure by teachers and pupils: A comparison. Unpublished manuscript. University of Tel-Aviv, Israel.

Bass, B.M. 1956. Development and evaluation of a scale for measuring social acquiescence. *Journal of Abnormal and Social Psychology,* 53, 269–299.

Beck, A.T. 1976. *Cognitive therapy and the emotional disorders.* New York: International Universities Press.

Becker, H.S. 1963. *Outsiders: Studies in the sociology of deviance.* New York: Free Press.

Beckman, L. 1973. Auswirkungen von schulischen Leistungen auf die Kausalattribuierung von lehrenden und beobachtenden Personen. In M. Hofer and F.E. Weinert (eds.), *Funk-Kolleg Pädagogische Psychologie, Grundlagentexte 2.* Frankfurt: Fischer, 164–176.

Behar, L.B. 1967. The effects of cognitive dissonance on inappropriate emotional reactions. *Journal of Personality,* 35, 505–519.

Bem, D.J. 1972. Self-perception theory. In L. Berkowitz (ed.), *Advances in experimental social psychology.* Vol. 6. New York: Academic Press, 1–62.

Berger, P.L., Berger, R.A., and Kellner, D.B. 1971. *The homeless mind.* Garden City, N.Y.: Doubleday-Anchor.

Berkowitz, L. 1969. Resistance to improper dependency relationships. *Journal of Experimental Social Psychology,* 5, 283–294.

Berkowitz, L., Lepinski, J.P., and Angulo, E.J. 1969. Awareness of own anger level and subsequent aggression. *Journal of Personality and Social Psychology,* 11, 293–300.

Berkowitz, L. and Turner, C. 1974. Perceived anger level, instigating agent, and aggression. In H. London and R.E. Nisbett (eds.), *Thought and feeling: Cognitive alteration of feeling states.* Chicago: Aldine, 174–189.

Berlyne, D.E. 1974. Attention. In E. Carterette and M. Friedman (eds.), *Handbook of perception.* Vol. 1. New York: Academic Press.

——. 1971. *Aesthetics and psychobiology.* New York: Appleton.

——. 1965. *Structure and direction in thinking.* New York: Wiley.

——. 1960. *Conflict, arousal, and curiosity.* New York: McGraw-Hill. (German: *Konflikt, Erregung, Neugier.* Stuttgart: Klett, 1974.)

Billig, M. 1976. *Social psychology and intergroup relations.* London: Academic Press.

Bloemkolk, D., Defares, P., van Enckevort, G., and van Gelderen, M. 1971. Cognitive processing of information on varied physiological arousal. *European Journal of Social Psychology,* 1, 31–46.

Bootzin, R.R., Herman, C.P., and Nicassio, P. 1976. The power of suggestion: Another examination of misattribution and insomnia. *Journal of Personality and Social Psychology,* 34, 673–679.

Borkovec, T.D. 1976. Physiological and cognitive processes in the regulation of anxiety. In G.E. Schwartz and D. Shapiro (eds.), *Consciousness and self-regulation.* New York: Wiley, 261–312.

——. 1973a. The effects of instructional suggestion and physiological cues on analogue fear. *Behavior Therapy,* 4, 185–192.

——. 1973b. The role of expectancy and physiological feedback in fear research: A review with special reference to subject characteristics. *Behavior Therapy,* 4, 491–505.

Borkovec, T.D. and Glasgow, R.E. 1973. Boundary conditions of false heart rate feedback effects on avoidance behavior: A resolution of discrepant results. *Behavior Research and Therapy,* 11, 171–177.

Borkovec, T.D., Grayson, J.B., and Hennings, B.L. 1979. Mitigation of false physiological feedback effects on anxiety via cognitive appraisal. *Cognitive Therapy and Research,* 3, 381–387.

Borkovec, T.D., Wall, R.L., and Stone, N.M. 1974. False physiological feedback and the maintenance of speech anxiety. *Journal of Abnormal Pyschology,* 83, 164–168.

Botto, R.W., Galbraith, G.G., and Stern, R.M. 1974. Effects of false heart rate feedback and sex-guilt upon attitudes toward sexual stimuli. *Psychological Reports,* 35, 267–274.

Bramel, D. 1962. A dissonance theory approach to defensive projection. *Journal of Abnormal and Social Psychology,* 64, 121–129.

Bramel, D., Bell, J.E., and Margulis, S.T. 1965. Attributing danger as a means of explaining one's fear. *Journal of Experimental Social Psychology,* 1, 267–281.

Brehm, J.W. and Behar, L.B. 1966. Sexual arousal, defensiveness, and sex preference in affiliation. *Journal of Experimental Research in Personality,* 1, 195–200.

Brogden, H.E. 1972. Some observations on two methods in psychology. *Psychological Bulletin,* 77, 431–437.

Brophy, J.E. and Good, T.L. 1974. *Teacher-student relationships: Causes and consequences.* New York: Holt, Rinehart and Winston.

───. 1969. Teacher-child dyadic interaction: A manual for coding classroom behavior. University of Texas Report Series No. 27.

Brown, H.A. 1973. Role of expectancy manipulation in systematic desensitization. *Journal of Consulting and Clinical Psychology,* 41, 405–411.

Brown, M. 1963. Factors determining expectancy of success and reaction to success and failure. Unpublished manuscript. University of Michigan.

Buss, A.R. In press. Causes and reasons in attribution theory: A critical perspective. In A.R. Buss (ed.), *The social context of psychological theory. Toward a sociology of psychological knowledge.* New York: Irvington.

───. 1978. Causes and reasons in attribution theory: A conceptual critique. *Journal of Personality and Social Psychology,* 36, 1311–1321.

Cacioppo, J.T. 1979. Effects of exogenous changes in heart rate on facilitation of thought and resistance to persuasion. *Journal of Personality and Social Psychology,* 37, 489–498.

Calvert-Boyanowsky, J. and Leventhal, H. 1975. The role of information in attenuating behavioral responses to stress: A reinterpretation of the misattribution phenomenon. *Journal of Personality and Social Psychology,* 32, 214–221.

Carroll, J.S. and Payne, J.W. 1977. Judgments about crime and the criminal: A model and a method for investigating parole decision. In B.D. Sales (ed.), *Perspectives in law and psychology.* Vol. 1: *The criminal justice system.* New York: Plenum Press.

───. 1976a. The psychology of the parole decision process. In J.S. Carroll and J.W. Payne (eds.), *Eleventh Carnegie symposium on cognition.* Hillsdale, New Jersey: Erlbaum.

───. 1976b. The psychology of the parole decision process: A joint application of attribution theory and information processing psychology. In J.S. Carroll and J.W. Payne (eds.), *Cognition and social behavior.* Hillsdale, New Jersey: Erlbaum.

Cartwright, D. and Harary, F. 1956. Structural balance: A generalization of Heider's theory. *Psychological Review,* 63, 277–293.

Carver, C.S. and Blaney, P.H. 1977a. Perceived arousal, focus of attention, and avoidance behavior. *Journal of Abnormal Psychology*, 86, 154–162.
———. 1977b. Avoidance behavior and perceived arousal. *Motivation and Emotion*, 1, 61–73.
Chapin, M. and Dyck, D.G. 1976. Persistence in children's reading behavior as a function of N length and attribution retraining. *Journal of Abnormal Psychology*, 85, 511–515.
Charlesworth, W.R. 1969. The role of surprise in cognitive development. In D. Elkind and J.H. Flavell (eds.), *Studies in cognitive development*. New York: Oxford University Press, 257–314.
Cicourel, A.V. 1968. *The social organization of juvenile justice*. New York: Wiley.
Clark, M. 1976. Effects of nonveridical heart rate feedback on emotional responding during anticipatory stress. Masters thesis. Kent State University.
Cohen, R., Meyer-Osterkamp, S., and Grusche, A. 1974. Eine Untersuchung zum Einfluβ manipulierter Rückmeldung auf Angst-Reaktionen. *Zeitschrift für Klinische Psychologie*, 3, 143–169.
Conger, J.C., Conger, A.J., and Brehm, S.S. 1976. Fear level as a moderator of false feedback effects in snake phobics. *Journal of Consulting and Clinical Psychology*, 44, 135–141.
Cooper, H.M. and Burger, J.M. 1978. Internality, stability, and personal efficacy: A categorization of free response academic attributions. Unpublished manuscript. University of Missouri—Columbia.
Coopersmith, S. 1967. *The antecedents of self-esteem*. San Francisco: Freeman.
Couch, A. and Keniston, K. 1960. Yeasayers and naysayers: Agreeing response as a personality variable. *Journal of Abnormal and Social Psychology*, 60, 151–174.
Cronbach, L.J. 1950. Further evidence on response sets and test design. *Educational and Psychological Measurement*, 10, 3–31.
———. 1946. Response sets and test validity. *Educational and Psychological Measurement*, 6, 475–494.
Crowne, D.P. and Marlowe, D.A. 1960. A new scale of social desirability independent of psychopathology. *Journal of Consulting Psychology*, 24, 349–351.
Damm, J. 1968. Effects of interpersonal contexts on relationships between goal setting behavior and achievement motivation. *Human Relations*, 21, 213–226.
Davison, G.C., Tsujimoto, R.N., and Glaros, A.G. 1973. Attribution and the maintenance of behavior change in falling asleep. *Journal of Abnormal Psychology*, 82, 124–133.
Davison, G.C. and Wilson, G.T. 1973. Processes of fear-reduction in systematic desensitization: Cognitive and social reinforcement factors in humans. *Behavior Therapy*, 4, 1–21.

Davitz, J.R. 1969. *The language of emotion.* New York: Academic Press.
Decaria, M.D., Proctor, S., and Malloy, T.E. 1974. The effect of false heart rate feedback on self-reports of anxiety and on actual heart rate. *Behavior Research and Therapy,* 12, 251–253.
DeCharms, R. 1968. *Personal causation.* New York: Academic Press.
Deci, E.L. 1975. *Intrinsic motivation.* New York: Plenum.
Defares, P.B., van Enckevort, G.M.W., van Gelderen, M.H., and Schendelaar, J.K.L. 1969. Pseudo-hartslagfeedback in angstreductie. *Nederlands Tijdschrift voor de Psychologie,* 24, 117–135.
Detweiler, R.A. and Zanna, M.P. 1976. Physiological mediation of attitudinal responses. *Journal of Personality and Social Psychology,* 33, 107–116.
Diener, C.I. and Dweck, C.A. 1978. An analysis of learned helplessness: Continuous changes in performance, strategy, and achievement cognitions following failure. *Journal of Personality and Social Psychology,* 36, 451–462.
Dienstbier, R.A., Hillman, D., Lehnhoff, J., Hillman, J., and Valkenaar, M.C. 1975. An emotion-attribution approach to moral behavior: Interfacing cognitive and avoidance theories of moral development. *Psychological Review,* 82, 299–315.
Dweck, C.S. 1975. The role of expectations and attributions in the alleviation of learned helplessness. *Journal of Personality and Social Psychology,* 31, 674–685.
Easterbrook, J.A. 1959. The effect of emotion on cue utilization and the organization of behavior. *Psychological Review,* 66, 183–201.
Edwards, A.L. 1957. *The social desirability variable in personality assessment and research.* New York: Dryden Press.
Elig, T.W. and Frieze, I.H. 1975. A multidimensional scheme for coding and interpreting perceived causality for success and failure events: The Coding Scheme of Perceived Causality (CSPC). JSAS *Catalog of Selected Documents in Psychology,* 5, 313 (Ms. No. 1069).
Epstein, S. 1973. The self-concept revisited. *American Psychologist,* 28, 404–416.
Erdmann, G. and Janke, W. 1977. Interaction between physiological and cognitive determinants of emotional states: Experimental studies on Schachter's theory of emotion. Manuscript.
Eswara, H.S. 1972. Administration of reward and punishment in relation to ability, effort, and performance. *Journal of Social Psychology,* 87, 139–140.
Feather, N.T. 1969. Attribution of responsibility and valence of success and failure in relation to initial confidence and task performance. *Journal of Personality and Social Psychology,* 13, 129–144.
_____. 1967. Valence of outcome and expectation of success in relation to task difficulty and perceived locus of control. *Journal of Personality and Social Psychology,* 7, 372–386.
Feather, N.T. and Simon, J.G. 1973. Fear of success and causal attribution for outcome. *Journal of Personality,* 41, 525–542.

Feather, N.T. and Simon, J.G. 1971a. Causal attributions for success and failure in relation to expectations of success based upon selective or manipulative control. *Journal of Personality*, 39, 527–541.

———. 1971b. Attribution of responsibility and valence of outcome in relation to initial confidence and success and failure of self and other. *Journal of Personality and Social Psychology*, 18, 173–188.

Fenigstein, A. and Carver, C.S. 1978. Self-focusing effects of heartbeat feedback. *Journal of Personality and Social Psychology*, 36, 1241–1250.

Fishbein, M. 1967. A behavior theory approach to the relations between beliefs about an object and the attitude toward that object. In M. Fishbein (ed.), *Readings in attitude theory and measurement*. New York: Wiley.

———. 1965. A consideration of beliefs, attitudes, and their relationships. In I.D. Steiner and M. Fishbein (eds.), *Current studies in social psychology*. New York: Holt, Rinehart and Winston.

———. 1963. An investigation of the relationships between beliefs about an object and the attitude toward that object. *Human Relations*, 16, 233–240.

Fishbein, M. and Ajzen, I. 1972. Attitudes and opinions. In P. Mussen and M. Rosenzweig (eds.), *Annual review of psychology*. Palo Alto, Calif.: Annual Reviews.

Fitch, G. 1970. Effects of self-esteem, perceived performance, and choice on causal attributions. *Journal of Personality and Social Psychology*, 16, 311–315.

Fitts, H.W. 1964. *Tennessee (Department of Mental Health) Self-Concept-Scale*. Nashville, Tenn.: Counselor Recordings and Tests.

Flavell, J.H. 1977. Metacognitive development. Paper presented at the NATO Advanced Study Institute on Structural Process: Theories of Complex Human Behavior. Banff, Alberta, Canada.

Folkes, V.S. 1978. Causal communication in the early stages of affiliative relationships. Unpublished doctoral dissertation. University of California, Los Angeles.

Fontaine, G. 1974. Social comparison and some determinants of expected personal control and expected performance in a novel task situation. *Journal of Personality and Social Psychology*, 29, 487–496.

Frieze, I.H. 1976. Causal attributions and information seeking to explain success and failure. *Journal of Research in Personality*, 10, 293–305.

Frieze, I.H. and Weiner, B. 1971. Cue utilization and attributional judgments for success and failure. *Journal of Personality*, 39, 591–605.

Fromkin, H.L. and Streufert, S. 1974. Laboratory experimentation. In M. Dunnette (ed.), *Handbook of organizational and industrial psychology*. Chicago: Rand McNally.

Garfinkel, H. 1972. Remarks on ethnomethodology. In J.J. Gumperz and D. Hymes (eds.), *Directions in Sociolinguistics. The ethnography of communication*. New York: Holt, Rinehart and Winston.

Garfinkel, H. 1967. *Studies in ethnomethodology.* Englewood Cliffs, N.J.: Prentice-Hall.
Gatchel, R.J., Hatch, J.P., Maynard, A., Turns, R., and Taunton-Blackwood, A. 1979. Comparison of heart rate biofeedback, false biofeedback, and systematic desensitization in reducing speech anxiety: Short- and long-term effectiveness. *Journal of Consulting and Clinical Psychology,* 47, 620–622.
Gatchel, R.J., Hatch, J.P., Watson, P.J., Smith, D., and Gaas, E. 1977. Comparative effectiveness of voluntary heart rate control and muscular relaxation as active coping skills for reducing speech anxiety. *Journal of Consulting and Clinical Psychology,* 45, 1093–1100.
Gaupp, L.A., Stern, R.M., and Galbraith, G.G. 1972. False heart-rate feedback and reciprocal inhibition by aversion relief in the treatment of snake avoidance behavior. *Behavior Therapy,* 3, 7–20.
Geen, R.G. and Pigg, R. 1973. Interpretation of arousal and its effects on motivation. *The Journal of Social Psychology,* 90, 115–123.
Geen, R.G., Rakosky, J.J., and Pigg, R. 1972. Awareness of arousal and its relation to aggression. *British Journal of Social and Clinical Psychology,* 11, 115–121.
Gerard, H.B. 1963. Emotional uncertainty and social comparison. *Journal of Abnormal and Social Psychology,* 66, 568–573.
Gerard, H.B. and Rabbie, J.M. 1961. Fear and social comparison. *Journal of Abnormal and Social Psychology,* 62, 586–592.
Gerdes, E.P. 1979. Autonomic arousal as a cognitive cue in stressful situations. *Journal of Personality,* 47, 677–711.
Gergen, K.J. In press. The positivist image in social psychological theory. In A.R. Buss (ed.), *The social context of psychological theory. Toward a sociology of psychological knowledge.* New York: Irvington.
——. 1977a. Social exchange theory in a world of transient fact. In R.L. Hamblin and J.H. Kunkel (eds.), *Behavior theory in sociology. Essays in honor of George C. Homans.* New Brunswick, N.J.: Transaction Books, 91–114.
——. 1977b. Stability, change, and chance in understanding human development. In N. Datan and H. Reese (eds.), *Life-span developmental psychology: Dialectic perspectives.* New York: Academic Press.
——. 1973. Social psychology as history. *Journal of Personality and Social Psychology,* 26, 309–320.
Gergen, K.J. and Jones, E.E. 1963. Mental illness, predictability, and affective consequences as stimulus factors in person perception. *Journal of Abnormal and Social Psychology,* 67, 95–104.
Giesen, M. and Hendrick, C. 1974. Effects of false positive and negative arousal feedback on persuasion. *Journal of Personality and Social Psychology,* 30, 449–457.

Gilmore, T.M. and Minton, H.L. 1974. Internal versus external attributions of task performance as a function of locus of control, initial confidence, and success-failure outcome. *Journal of Personality, 42,* 159–174.

Girodo, M. 1973. Film-induced arousal, information search, and the attribution process. *Journal of Personality and Social Psychology, 25,* 357–360.

Görlitz, D. 1980. Entwicklungsrichtungen attributionaler Handlungsanalyse. *Bericht über die 5. Tagung für Entwicklungspsychologie.* Berlin: Technische Universität.

――――. 1979. Handlungsrahmen und Handlungsgrenzen attributionstheoretischer Ansätze zur Genese sozialer Kognition. *Bericht über den 31. Kongreßder Deutschen Gesellschaft für Psychologie,* Band 1, Göttingen: Hogrefe, 289–292.

――――. 1974. Motivationshypothesen in der Alltagskommunikation. *Kölner Zeitschrift für Soziologie und Sozialpsychologie, 26,* 539–567.

Görlitz, D., Meyer, W.-U., and Weiner, B. (eds.). 1978. *Bielefelder Symposium über Attribution.* Stuttgart: Klett-Cotta.

Goffman, E. 1963. *Stigma.* Englewood Cliffs, N.J.: Prentice-Hall.

――――. 1961. *Encounters.* Indianapolis, Ind.: Bobbs-Merrill.

――――. 1959. *The presentation of self in everyday life.* Englewood Cliffs, N.J.: Prentice-Hall.

Golding, S.L. and Lichtenstein, E. 1970. Confession of awareness and prior knowledge of deception as a function of interview set and approval motivation. *Journal of Personality and Social Psychology, 14,* 213–223.

Goldstein, D., Fink, D., and Mettee, D.R. 1972. Cognition of arousal and actual arousal as determinants of emotion. *Journal of Personality and Social Psychology, 21,* 41–51.

Gordon, S. 1976. *Lonely in America.* New York: Simon and Schuster.

Gouldner, A.W. 1970. *The coming crisis of western sociology.* New York: Basic Books.

Halisch, F. 1976. Die Selbstregulation leistungsbezogenen Verhaltens: Das Leistungsmotiv als Selbstbekräftigungssystem. In H.-D. Schmalt und W.-U. Meyer (eds.), *Leistungsmotivation und Verhalten.* Stuttgart: Klett, 137–164.

Hamilton, J.O. 1974. Motivation and risk taking behavior. *Journal of Personality and Social Psychology, 29,* 856–864.

Hansen, R.D. and Lowe, C.A. 1976. Distinctiveness and consensus: The influence of behavioral information on actors' and observers' attributions. *Journal of Personality and Social Psychology, 34,* 425–433.

Hanusa, B.H. 1975. An extension of Weiner's attribution approach to social situations: Sex differences in social situations. Paper presented at the 46th Annual Meeting of the Eastern Psychological Association, New York.

Harary, F., Norman, R.Z., and Cartwright, D. 1965. *Structural models: An introduction to the theory of directed graphs.* New York: Wiley.

Hare, R.D. 1972. Cardiovascular components of orienting and defensive responses. *Psychophysiology, 9,* 606–614.

Harré, R. and Secord, P.F. 1972. *The explanation of social behavior.* Oxford: Blackwell.

Harris, V.A. and Jellison, J.M. 1971. Fear-arousing communication, false physiological feedback, and the acceptance of recommendations. *Journal of Experimental Social Psychology,* 7, 269–279.

Harris, V.A. and Katkin, E.S. 1975. Primary and secondary emotional behavior: An analysis of the role of autonomic feedback on affect, arousal, and attribution. *Psychological Bulletin,* 82, 904–916.

Hawk, G. 1975. The effects of false biofeedback on physiological and behavioral responding to pleasant visual stimuli. Masters thesis. Kent State University.

Heckhausen, H. In press. Task-irrelevant cognitions during an examination. Incidence and effects. In H.W. Krohne and L. Laux (eds.), *Achievement, stress, and anxiety.* Washington, D.C.: Hemisphere.

———. 1977a. Motivation: Kognitionspsychologische Aufspaltung eines summarischen Konstrukts. *Psychologische Rundschau,* 28, 175–189.

———. 1977b. Achievement motivation and its constructs: A cognitive model. *Motivation and Emotion,* 1, 283–329.

———. 1976. Relevanz der Psychologie als Austausch zwischen naiver und wissenschaftlicher Verhaltenstheorie. *Psychologische Rundschau,* 27, 1–11.

———. 1975. Effort expenditure, aspiration level, and self evaluation before and after unexpected performance shifts. Unpublished paper. Ruhr-Universität Bochum.

———. 1974. Lehrer-Schüler-Interaktion. Bessere Lernmotivation und neue Lernziele. In F.E. Weiner, C.-F. Graumann, H. Heckhausen, and M. Hofer (eds.), *Pädagogische Psychologie,* Bd. 1. Frankfurt: Fischer, 549–601.

Heffler, D. and Lisman, S.A. 1978. Attribution and insomnia: A replication failure. *Psychological Record,* 28, 123–128.

Heider, F. 1958. *The psychology of interpersonal relations.* New York: Wiley. (German: Psychologie der interpersonalen Beziehungen. Stuttgart: Klett, 1977).

———. 1946. Attitudes and cognitive organization. *Journal of Psychology,* 21, 107–112.

———. 1944. Social perception and phenomenal causality. *Psychological Review,* 51, 358–374.

———. 1926. Ding und Medium. *Symposion,* 1, 109–157.

Heider, F. and Simmel, M. 1944. An experimental study of apparent behavior. *American Journal of Psychology,* 57, 243–259.

Heim, M. 1975. Sex differences in causal attributions for achievement in social tasks. Paper presented at the 46th Annual Meeting of the Eastern Psychological Association, New York.

Hendrick, C. and Giesen, M. 1976. Self-attribution of attitude as a function of belief feedback. *Memory and Cognition,* 4, 150–155.

Hendrick, C., Giesen, M., and Borden, R. 1975. False physiological feedback and persuasion: Effect of fear arousal versus fear reduction on attitude change. *Journal of Personality,* 43, 196–214.

Hirschman, R. 1975. Cross-modal effects of anticipatory bogus heart rate feedback in a negative emotional context. *Journal of Personality and Social Psychology,* 31, 13–19.

Hirschman, R., Clark, M., and Hawk, G. 1977. Relative effects of bogus physiological feedback and control stimuli on autonomic and self report indicants of emotional attribution. *Personality and Social Psychology Bulletin,* 3, 270–275.

Hirschman, R. and Hawk, G. 1978. Emotional responsivity to nonveridical heart rate feedback as a function of anxiety. *Journal of Research in Personality,* 12, 235–242.

Hofer, M. 1974. *Die Schülerpersönlichkeit im Urteil des Lehrers.* Weinheim: Beltz.

Holmes, D. S. 1977. Valins's postdeception dehoaxing revisited. *American Psychologist,* 32, 385.

Holmes, D.S. and Frost, R.O. 1976. Effects of false autonomic feedback on self-reported anxiety, pain perception, and pulse rate. *Behavior Therapy,* 7, 330–334.

Horkheimer, M. 1934. *Dialektischer Materialismus und Psychoanalyse.* Kopenhagen.

Horowitz, I.A. 1972. Attitude change as a function of perceived arousal. *The Journal of Social Psychology,* 87, 117–126.

Ickes, W.J. and Kidd, R.F. 1976. An attributional analysis of helping behavior. In J.H. Harvey, W.J. Ickes, and R.F. Kidd (eds.), *New directions in attribution research.* Vol. 1. Hillsdale, N.J.: Erlbaum, 311–334.

Ickes, W.J., Kidd, R.F., and Berkowitz, L. 1976. Attributional determinants of monetary help-giving. *Journal of Personality,* 44, 163–178.

Ickes, W.J. and Layden, M.A. 1978. Attributional styles. In J.H. Harvey, W.J. Ickes, and R.F. Kidd (eds.), *New directions in attribution research.* Vol. 2. Hillsdale, N.J.: Erlbaum, 119–152.

Izard, C.E. 1977. *Human emotions.* New York: Plenum Press.

Jackson, D.N. and Messick, S. 1963. Response styles and the assessment of psychopathology. In S. Messick and J. Ross (eds.), *Measurement in personality and cognition.* New York: Wiley.

——. 1961. Acquiescence and desirability as response determinants on the MMPI. *Educational and Psychological Measurement,* 21, 779–790.

Janis, I.L. and Field, P.B. 1959. The Janis and Field Personality Questionnaire. In C.I. Hovland and I.L. Janis (eds.), *Personality and persuasibility.* New Haven, Conn.: Yale University Press.

Jones, E.E. and Davis, K.E. 1965. From acts to dispositions: The attribution process in person perception. In L. Berkowitz (ed.), *Advances in experimental social psychology.* Vol. 2. New York: Academic Press.

Jones, E. E., Davis, K. E., and Gergen, K. J. 1961. Role playing variations and their informational value for person perception. *Journal of Abnormal and Social Psychology,* 63, 302–310.

Jones, E. E. and Gerard, H. B. 1967. *Foundations of social psychology.* New York: Wiley.

Jones, E. E. and Harris, V. A. 1967. The attribution of attitudes. *Journal of Experimental Social Psychology,* 3, 1–24.

Jones, E. E., Kanouse, D., Kelley, H. H., Nisbett, R. E., Valins, S., and Weiner, B. (eds.). 1972. *Attribution: Perceiving the causes of behavior.* Morristown, N. J.: General Learning Press.

Jones, E. E. and Nisbett, R. E. 1971. *The actor and the observer: Divergent perceptions of the causes of behavior.* Morristown, N. J.: General Learning Press.

Jones, E. E., Worchel, S., Goethals, G. R., and Grumet, J. F. 1971. Prior expectancy and behavioral extremity as determinants of attitude attribution. *Journal of Experimental Social Psychology,* 7, 59–80.

Jones, S. C. and Panitch, D. 1971. The self-fulfilling prophecy and interpersonal attraction. *Journal of Experimental Social Psychology,* 7, 356–366.

Kanfer, F. H., Karoly, P., and Newman, A. 1974. Source of feedback, observational learning, and attitude change. *Journal of Personality and Social Psychology,* 29, 30–38.

Kanouse, D. E., and Hanson, L. R., Jr. 1972. *Negativity in evaluations.* New York: General Learning Press.

Kaplan, R. M. and Swant, S. G. 1973. Reward characteristics of appraisal of achievement behavior. *Representative Research in Social Psychology,* 4 (2), 11–17.

Karabenick, S. A. 1972. Valence of success and failure as a function of achievement motives and locus of control. *Journal of Personality and Social Psychology,* 21, 101–110.

Katz, D. 1911. *Die Erscheinungsweisen der Farben und ihre Beeinflussung durch die individuelle Erfahrung.* Leipzig: Barth.

Kelley, H. H. 1973. The processes of causal attribution. *American Psychologist,* 28, 107–128.

———. 1972. *Causal schemata and the attribution process.* Morristown, N. J.: General Learning Press.

———. 1971. *Attribution in social interaction.* Morristown, N. J.: General Learning Press.

———. 1967. Attribution theory in social psychology. In D. Levine (ed.), *Nebraska Symposium on Motivation: 1967.* Lincoln: University of Nebraska Press.

Kent, R. N., Wilson, G. T., and Nelson, R. 1972. Effects of false heart-rate feedback on avoidance behavior: An investigation of "cognitive desensitization." *Behavior Therapy,* 3, 1–6.

Kerber, K.W. and Coles, M.G.H. 1978. The role of perceived physiological activity in affective judgments. *Journal of Experimental Social Psychology,* 14, 419–433.

Klein, D.C., Fencil-Morse, E., and Seligman, M.E.P. 1976. Learned helplessness, depression, and the attribution of failure. *Journal of Personality and Social Psychology,* 33, 508–516.

Koenig, K.P. 1973. False emotional feedback and the modification of anxiety. *Behavior Therapy,* 4, 193–202.

Koenig, K.P. and Del Castillo, D. 1969. False feedback and longevity of the conditioned GSR during extinction: Some implications for aversion therapy. *Journal of Abnormal Psychology,* 74, 505–510.

Koenig, K.P. and Henriksen, K. 1974. Cognitive manipulation of GSR extinction: Analogues for conditioning therapies. In H. London and R.E. Nisbett (eds.), *Thought and feeling: Cognitive alteration of feeling states.* Chicago: Aldine, 60–73.

Konecni, V.J. 1975. The mediation of aggressive behavior: Arousal level versus anger and cognitive labeling. *Journal of Personality and Social Psychology,* 32, 706–712.

Krisher, H.P., III, Darley, S.A., and Darley, J.M. 1973. Fear-provoking recommendations, intentions to take preventative actions, and actual preventive actions. *Journal of Personality and Social Psychology,* 26, 301–308.

Krohne, H.W. and Schroder, H.M. 1972. Anxiety defense and complex information processing. *Archiv für Psychologie,* 124, 50–61.

Krug, S. 1971. *Der Einfluss von kognitiven Variablen auf Determinanten leistungsmotivierten Verhaltens.* Unpublished diploma thesis. University of Bochum, West Germany.

Kruglanski, A.W. 1975. The endogenous-exogenous partition in attribution theory. *Psychological Review,* 82, 387–406.

Kukla, A. 1972. Foundations of an attributional theory of performance. *Psychological Review,* 79, 454–470.

Kun, A. and Weiner, B. 1973. Necessary versus sufficient causal schemata for success and failure. *Journal of Research in Personality,* 7, 197–207.

Lacey, J.I. 1967. Somatic response patterning and stress: Some revisions of activation theory. In M.H. Appley and R. Trumbull (eds.), *Psychological stress: Issues in research.* New York: Appleton, 14–39.

Landy, F.J. and Stern, R.M. 1971. Factor analysis of somatic perception questionnaire. *Journal of Psychosomatic Research,* 15, 179–181.

Lanzetta, J.T. 1971. The motivational properties of uncertainty. In H.I. Day, D.E. Berlyne, and D.E. Hunt (eds.), *Intrinsic motivation: A new direction in education.* Toronto: Holt.

Lanzetta, J.T. and Hannah, T.E. 1969. Reinforcing behavior of "naive" trainers. *Journal of Personality and Social Psychology,* 11, 245–252.

Lau. R.R. and Russell, D. 1978. Attributions in the sports pages: A field test of some current hypotheses in attribution research. Unpublished manuscript. University of California, Los Angeles.

Laucken, U. 1974. *Naive Verhaltenstheorie.* Stuttgart: Klett.

Lawrence, D.H. and Festinger, L. 1962. *Deterrents and reinforcement.* Stanford, Calif.: Stanford University Press.

Lefcourt, H.M., von Baeyer, C.L., Ware, E.E., and Cox, D.J. 1978. The multidimensional-multiattributional causality scale: The development of a goal-specific locus of control scale. Unpublished manuscript. University of Waterloo, Ontario, Canada.

Leventhal, G.S. and Michaels, J.W. 1971. Locus of cause and equity motivation as determinants of reward allocation. *Journal of Personality and Social Psychology,* 17, 229–235.

Lewin, K. 1935. *A dynamic theory of personality.* New York: McGraw-Hill.

Lick, J. 1975. Expectancy, false galvanic skin response feedback, and systematic desensitization in the modification of phobic behavior. *Journal of Consulting and Clinical Psychology,* 43, 557–567.

Liebhart, E.H. 1979. Emotion und Einstellungsänderung: Der Einfluß falscher autonomer Rückmeldung und privater Kognitionen. *Zeitschrift für Sozialpsychologie,* 10.

_____. 1977a. Fähigkeit und Anstrengung im Lehrerurteil: Der Einfluß inter- versus intraindividueller Perspektive. *Zeitschrift für Entwicklungspsychologie und Pädagogische Psychologie,* 9, 94–102.

_____. 1977b. Effects of false heart rate feedback and task instructions on information search, attributions, stimulus ratings. *Psychological Research,* 39, 185–202.

_____. 1976. On attributing fictitious cardiac responses. *Perceptual and Motor Skills,* 43, 202.

_____. 1974. Attributionstherapie. Beeinflussung herzneurotischer Beschwerden durch Externalisierung kausaler Zuschreibungen. *Zeitschrift für Klinische Psychologie,* 3, 71–94.

Litman-Adizes, T. 1977. An attributional model of depression: Laboratory and clinical investigations. Unpublished manuscript. University of California, Los Angeles.

Litwin, G.H. 1966. Achievement motivation, expectancy of success, and risk-taking behavior. In J.W. Atkinson and N.T. Feather (eds.), *A theory of achievement motivation.* New York: Wiley, 103–115.

Loftis, J. and Ross, L. 1974. Effects of misattribution of arousal upon the acquisition and extinction of a conditioned emotional response. *Journal of Personality and Social Psychology,* 30, 673–682.

Mandler, G. 1975. *Mind and emotion.* New York: Wiley.

Mandler, G. and Kremen, I. 1958. Autonomic feedback: A correlational study. *Journal of Personality,* 26, 388–399.

Mann, L. 1974. On being a sore loser: How fans react to their team's failure. *Australian Journal of Psychology, 26,* 37–47.

Marcia, J.E., Rubin, B.E., and Efran, J.S. 1969. Systematic desensitization: Expectancy change or counterconditioning. *Journal of Abnormal Psychology, 74,* 382–387.

McClelland, D.C., Atkinson, J.W., Clark, R.A., and Lowell, E.L. 1953. *The achievement motive.* New York: Appleton-Century-Crofts.

McMahan, I.D. 1973. Relationships between causal attributions and expectancy of success. *Journal of Personality and Social Psychology, 28,* 108–114.

McMartin, J.A. and Shaw, J.I. 1971. Effects of ability level and outcome severity on the degree of responsibility assigned for a happy accident. *Proceedings 80th Annual Convention of the American Psychological Association.*

Meyer, J.P. 1978. Dimensions of causal attribution for success and failure: A multivariate investigation. Unpublished doctoral dissertation. University of Western Ontario, London, Canada.

Meyer, W.-U. 1978. Der Einfluß von Sanktionen auf Begabungsperzeptionen. In D. Görlitz, W.-U. Meyer, and B. Weiner (eds.), *Bielefelder Symposium über Attribution.* Stuttgart: Klett, 71–87.

_____. 1976. Leistungsorientiertes Verhalten als Funktion von wahrgenommener Begabung und wahrgenommener Aufgabenschwierigkeit. In H.-D. Schmalt and W.-U. Meyer (eds.), *Leistungsmotivation und Verhalten.* Stuttgart: Klett, 101–135.

_____. 1973. *Leistungsmotiv und Ursachenerklärung von Erfolg und Mißerfolg.* Stuttgart: Klett.

_____. 1970. Selbstverantwortlichkeit und Leistungsmotivation. Unpublished doctoral dissertation. Ruhr-Universität Bochum, West Germany.

Meyer, W.-U., Bachmann, M., Biermann, M., Plöger, F.-O., and Spiller, H. 1977. Lob und Tadel unter dem Gesichtspunkt der Information: Der Einfluß von Sanktionen auf Begabungsperzeptionen. Unpublished manuscript. Abteilung Psychologie der Universität Bielefeld.

Meyer, W.-U. and Butzkamm, A. 1975. Ursachenerklärungen von Rechennoten: I. Lehrerattribuierungen. *Zeitschrift für Entwicklungspsychologie und Pädagogische Psychologie, 7,* 53–66.

Meyer, W.-U., Folkes, V.S., and Weiner, B. 1976. The perceived information value and affective consequences of choice behavior and intermediate difficulty task selection. *Journal of Research in Personality, 10,* 410–423.

Meyer, W.-U. and Plöger, F.-O. 1978. Auswirkungen von Sanktionen auf die Wahrnehmung der eigenen Begabung. In S.-H. Fillip (ed.), *Selbstkonzept-Forschung: Probleme, Befunde, Perspektiven.* Stuttgart: Klett-Cotta.

Michela, J., Peplau, L.A., and Weeks, D. 1978. Perceived dimensions and consequences of attributions for loneliness. Unpublished manuscript. University of California, Los Angeles.

Miller, D.T. 1976. Ego involvement and attributions for success and failure. *Journal of Personality and Social Psychology, 34,* 901–906.

Miller, G.A. 1962. *Psychology: The science of mental life.* New York: Harper & Row.

―――. 1956. The magical number seven, plus or minus two: Some limits on our capacity to process information. *Psychological Review,* 63, 81–97.

Miller, G.A., Galanter, E., and Pribram, K.H. 1960. *Plans and structure of behavior.* New York: Holt, Rinehart and Winston. (German: *Strategien des Handelns.* Stuttgart: Klett, 1973).

Mischel, W. 1973. Toward a cognitive social learning reconceptualization of personality. *Psychological Review,* 80, 252–283.

Misovich, S. 1974. Some effects of arousal and false GSR feedback on affective judgments. *Psychological Report,* 34, 351–358.

Misovich, S. and Charis, P.C. 1974. Information need, affect, and cognition of autonomic activity. *Journal of Experimental Social Psychology,* 10, 274–283.

Misovich, S. and Sosik, T.P. 1975. Effects of cognition of autonomic activity on information searching and affective change. Unpublished manuscript.

Neisser, U. 1967. *Cognitive psychology.* New York: Appleton-Century-Crofts. (German: *Kognitive Psychologie.* Stuttgart: Klett, 1974).

Nisbett, R.E., Caputo, G.C., Legant, P., and Maracek, J. 1973. Behavior as viewed by the actor and as viewed by the observed. *Journal of Personality and Social Psychology,* 27, 154–164.

Nisbett, R.E. and Schachter, S. 1966. Cognitive manipulation of pain. *Journal of Experimental Social Psychology,* 2, 227–236.

Nisbett, R.E. and Valins, S. 1971. *Perceiving the causes of one's own behavior.* New York: General Learning Press.

Nisbett, R.E. and Wilson, T.D. 1977. Telling more than we can know: Verbal reports on mental processes. *Psychological Review,* 84, 231–259.

Nissen, H.W. 1954. The nature of drive as innate determinant of behavioral organization. In M.R. Jones (ed.), *Nebraska Symposium on Motivation: 1954.* Lincoln: University of Nebraska Press.

Nuttin, J.R. 1973. Pleasure and reward in motivation and learning. In D. Berlyne (ed.), *Pleasure, reward, preference.* New York: Academic Press.

O'Brien, E.J. and Epstein, S. 1975. Naturally occurring changes in self-esteem. Paper presented at the meeting of the American Psychological Association, New Orleans, La.

Ostrove, N. 1978. Expectations for success on effort-determined tasks as a function of incentive and performance feedback. *Journal of Personality and Social Psychology,* 36, 909–916.

Pancer, S.M. and Eiser, J.R. 1975. Expectations, aspirations, and evaluations as influenced by another's attributions for success and failure. Paper presented at the 83rd Annual Meeting of the American Psychological Association. Chicago.

Passer, M.W. 1977. Perceiving the causes of success and failure revisited: A multidimensional scaling approach. Unpublished doctoral dissertation. University of California, Los Angeles.
Patten, R.L. and White, L.A. 1977. Independent effects of achievement motivation and overt attribution on achievement behavior. *Motivation and Emotion*, 1, 39−59.
Peplau, L.A., Russell, D., and Heim, M. In press. An attributional analysis of loneliness. In I. Frieze, D. Bar-Tal, and J. Carroll (eds.), *Attribution theory: Applications to social problems*. San Francisco: Jossey-Bass.
Peters, R.S. 1958. *The concept of motivation*. London: Routledge and Kegan Paul.
Phares, E.J. 1978. Locus of control. In H. London and J.E. Exner, Jr. (eds.), *Dimensions of personality*. New York: Wiley.
———. 1957. Expectancy changes in skill and chance situations. *Journal of Abnormal and Social Psychology*, 54, 339−342.
Piaget, J. 1952. *The origins of intelligence in children*. New York: International Universities Press.
———. 1932. *The moral judgment of the child*. New York: Harcourt Brace.
Piccione, A. and Veitch, R. 1974. The impact of false-arousal feedback on interpersonal attraction. *The Journal of Social Psychology*, 108, 233−240.
Piliavin, I.M., Rodin, J., and Piliavin, J.A. 1969. Good samaritanism: An underground phenomenon? *Journal of Personality and Social Psychology*, 13, 289−299.
Plon, M. 1974. On the meaning of the notion of conflict and its study in social psychology. *European Journal of Social Psychology*, 4, 389−436.
Raynor, J.O. 1974. Future orientation in the study of achievement motivation. In J.W. Atkinson and J.O. Raynor (eds.), *Motivation and achievement*. Washington, D.C.: Winston, 121−154.
Reisman, S., Insko, C.A., and Valins, S. 1970. Triadic consistency and false heart-rate feedback. *Journal of Personality*, 38, 629−640.
Rest, S. 1976. Schedules of reinforcement: An attributional analysis. In J.H. Harvey, W.J. Ickes, and R.F. Kidd (eds.), *New directions in attribution research*, Vol. 1. Hillsdale, N.J.: Erlbaum.
Rest, S., Nierenberg, R., Weiner, B., and Heckhausen, H. 1973. Further evidence concerning the effects of perceptions of effort and ability on achievement evaluation. *Journal of Personality and Social Psychology*, 28, 187−191.
Rheinberg, F. 1977. Bezugsnorm-Orientierung − Versuch einer Integration motivierungsbedeutsamer Lehrervariable. In W.H. Tack (ed.), Bericht über den 30. Kongreß der Deutschen Gesellschaft für Psychologie. Band 2. Göttingen: Hogrefe, 318−319.
———. 1975. Zeitstabilität und Steuerbarkeit von Ursachen schulischer Leistung in der Sicht des Lehrers. *Zeitschrift für Entwicklungspsychologie und Pädagogische Psychologie*, 7, 180−194.

Riemer, B.S. 1975. Influence of causal beliefs on affect and expectancy. *Journal of Personality and Social Psychology,* 31, 1163−1167.

Robinson, E.J. and Robinson, W.P. 1976. The young child's understanding of communication. *Developmental Psychology,* 12, 328−333.

Rogers, R.W. and Deckner, C.W. 1975. Effects of fear appeals and physiological arousal upon emotion, attitudes, and cigarette smoking. *Journal of Personality and Social Psychology,* 32, 222−230.

Rosen, G.M., Rosen, E., and Reid, J.B. 1972. Cognitive desensitization and avoidance behavior: A reevaluation. *Journal of Abnormal Psychology,* 80, 176−182.

Rosenbaum, R.M. 1972. A dimensional analysis of the perceived causes of success and failure. Unpublished doctoral dissertation. University of Caliornia, Los Angeles.

Ross, L. 1977. The intuitive psychologist and his shortcomings: Distortions in the attribution process. In L. Berkowitz (ed.), *Advances in experimental social psychology.* Vol. 10. New York: Academic Press.

Ross, L., Lepper, M.R., and Hubbard, M. 1975. Perseverance in self-perception and social perception: Biased attributional processes in the debriefing paradigm. *Journal of Personality and Social Psychology,* 32, 880−892.

Ross, M., Insko, C.A., and Ross, H.S. 1971. Self-attribution of attitude. *Journal of Personality and Social Psychology,* 17, 292−297.

Rotter, J.B. 1964. *Clinical psychology.* Englewood Cliffs, N.J.: Prentice-Hall.

——. 1966. Generalized expectancies for internal versus external control of reinforcement. *Psychological Monographs,* 80, (1, Whole No. 609).

Ryle, G. 1949. *The concept of mind.* London: Hutchinson.

Schachter, S. 1964. The interaction of cognitive and physiological determinants of emotional state. In L. Berkowitz (ed.), *Advances in experimental social psychology.* Vol. 1. New York: Academic Press.

Schachter, S. and Singer, J.E. 1962. Cognitive, social, and physiological determinants of emotional state. *Psychological Review,* 69, 379−399.

Schachter, S. and Wheeler, L. 1962. Epinephrine, chlorpromazine, and amusement. *Journal of Abnormal and Social Psychology,* 65, 121−128.

Schaefer, H.H., Tregerthan, G.J., and Colgan, H.H. 1976. Measured and self-estimated penile erection. *Behavior Therapy,* 7, 1−7.

Scheier, M.F., Carver, C.S., and Gibbons, F.X. 1979. Self-directed attention, awareness of bodily states, and suggestibility. *Journal of Personality and Social Psychology,* 37, 1576−1588.

Schmalt, H.-D. and Meyer, W.-U. (eds.). 1976. *Leistungsmotivation und Verhalten.* Stuttgart: Klett.

Schneider, K. 1973. *Motivation unter Erfolgsrisiko.* Göttingen: Hogrefe.

——. 1971. Leistungs- und Risikoverhalten in Abhängigkeit von situativen und überdauernden Komponenten der Leistungsmotivation: Kritische Untersuchungen zu einem Verhaltensmodell. Unpublished doctoral dissertation. University of Bochum, West Germany.

Schopler, J. and Matthews, M.W. 1965. The influence of the perceived causal locus of partner's dependence of the use of interpersonal power. *Journal of Personality and Social Psychology*, 2, 609–612.

Schütz, A. 1967. *Collected papers. I. The problem of social reality.* The Hague: Martinus Nijhoff.

Secord, P.F. and Backman, C.W. 1965. An interpersonal approach to personality. In B. Maher (ed.), *Progress in experimental personality research.* Vol. 2. New York: Academic Press.

Seligman, M.E.P. 1975. *Helplessness: On depression, development, and death.* San Francisco: Freeman.

Shaver, K.G. 1975. *An introduction to attribution processes.* Cambridge, Mass.: Winthrop.

_____. 1970. Defensive attribution: Effects of severity and relevance on the responsibility assigned for an accident. *Journal of Personality and Social Psychology*, 14, 101–113.

Shaw, J.I. and Skolnick, P. 1971. Attribution of responsibility for a happy accident. *Journal of Personality and Social Psychology*, 18, 380–383.

Shaw, M.E. and Sulzer, J.L. 1964. An empirical test of Heider's levels of attribution of responsibility. *Journal of Abnormal and Social Psychology*, 69, 39–46.

Silberman, M. 1969. Behavioral expression of teacher's attitudes toward elementary school students. *Journal of Educational Psychology*, 60, 402–407.

Simon, J.G. and Feather, N.T. 1973. Causal attributions for success and failure at university examinations. *Journal of Educational Psychology*, 64, 46–56.

Simon, P. and Weiner, B. In press. Dimensions of causal attributions related to helping judgments. *Personality and Social Psychology Bulletin*.

Singerman, K.J., Borkovec, T.D., and Baron, R.S. 1976. Failure of a "misattribution therapy" manipulation with a clinically relevant target behavior. *Behavior Therapy*, 7, 306–313.

Skinner, B.F. 1975. The steep and thorny way to a science of behavior. *American Psychologist*, 30, 42–49.

Smedslund, J. 1972. *Becoming a psychologist.* Oslo: Universitetsforlaget.

_____. 1970. Circular relation between understanding and logic. *Scandinavian Journal of Psychology*, 11, 217–219.

Sogin, S.R. and Pallak, M.S. 1976. Bad decisions, responsibility, and attitude change: Effects of volition, foreseeability, and locus of causality of negative consequences. *Journal of Personality and Social Psychology*, 33, 300–306.

Spence, J.T., Helmreich, R., and Stapp, J. 1975. Likability, sex-role congruence of interest and competence: It all depends on how you ask. *Journal of Applied Social Psychology*, 5, 93–109.

Stein, A.H. and Bailey, M.M. 1973. The socialization of achievement orientation in females. *Psychological Bulletin*, 80, 345–366.

Steiner, I.D. 1970. Perceived freedom. In L. Berkowitz (ed.), *Advances in experimental social psychology.* Vol. 5. New York: Academic Press.

Stern, R.M., Botto, R.W., and Herrick, C.D. 1972. Behavioral and physiological effects of false heart-rate feedback: A replication and extension. *Psychophysiology*, 9, 21–29.

Streufert, S., Kliger, S.C., Castore, C.H., and Driver, M.J. 1967. Tactical and negotiations game for analysis of decision integration across decision areas. *Psychological Reports*, 20, 155–157.

Streufert, S. and Nogami, G.Y. 1973. Time effects on the attribution process: Does attribution of causality differ from attribution of responsibility? Purdue University: ONR Technical Report No. 16.

Streufert, S. and Streufert, S.C. 1978. *Behavior in the complex environment*. New York: Winston and Sons and Halstead Division, John Wiley.

―――. 1969. Effects of conceptual structure, failure, and success on attribution of causality and interpersonal attitudes. *Journal of Personality and Social Psychology*, 11, 138–147.

Streufert, S., Streufert, S.C. and Nogami, G.Y. 1973. Effects of time on causal attributions. Purdue University: ONR Technical Report No. 13.

Stroebe, W., Eagly, A.H., and Stroebe, M.S. 1977. Friendly or just polite? The effect of self-esteem on attributions. *European Journal of Social Psychology*, 7, 265–274.

Sushinsky, L.W. 1969. Cognitive desensitization as a model of systematic desensitization. Unpublished masters thesis. Northwestern University.

Sushinsky, L.W. and Bootzin, R.R. 1970. Cognitive desensitization as a model of systematic desensitization. *Behavior Research and Therapy*, 8, 29–33.

Szasz, T.S. 1960. The myth of mental illness. *American Psychologist*, 15, 113–118.

Tannenbaum, P.H. and Zillmann, D. 1975. Emotional arousal in the facilitation of aggression through communication. In L. Berkowitz (ed.), *Advances in experimental social psychology*. Vol. 8. New York: Academic Press, 149–192.

Taylor, S. and Fiske, S.T. 1975. Point of view and perceptions of causality. *Journal of Personality and Social Psychology*, 32, 439–445.

Taylor, S.E. 1975. On inferring one's attitudes from one's behavior: Some delimiting conditions. *Journal of Personality and Social Psychology*, 31, 126–131.

Tennen, H. and Eller, S.J. 1977. Attributional components of learned helplessness and facilitation. *Journal of Personality and Social Psychology*, 35, 265–271.

Thibaut, J.W. and Kelley, H.H. 1959. *The social psychology of groups*. New York: Wiley.

Thibaut, J.W. and Riecken, H.W. 1955. Some determinants and consequences of the perception of social causality. *Journal of Personality*, 24, 113–133.

Thornton, E.W. and Hagan, P.J. 1976. A failure to explain the effects of false heart-rate feedback on affect by induced changes in physiological response. *British Journal of Psychology*, 67, 359–365.

Toulmin, S. 1961. *Foresight and understanding.* New York: Harper & Row.
Triandis, H.C. 1972. *The analysis of subjective culture.* New York: Wiley-Interscience.
Tversky, A. and Kahneman, D. 1973. Availability: A heuristic for judging frequency and probability. *Cognitive Psychology,* 5, 207–232.
Valins, S. 1974. Persistent effects of information about internal reactions: Ineffectiveness of debriefing. In H. London and R.E. Nisbett (eds.), *Thought and feeling: Cognitive modification of feeling states.* Chicago: Aldine, 116–124.
_____. 1970. The perception and labeling of bodily changes as determinants of emotional behavior. In P. Black (ed.), *Physiological correlates of emotion.* New York: Academic Press, 229–243.
_____. 1967. Emotionality and information concerning internal reactions. *Journal of Personality and Social Psychology,* 6, 458–463.
_____. 1966. Cognitive effects of false heart-rate feedback. *Journal of Personality and Social Psychology,* 4, 400–408.
Valins, S. and Ray, A.A. 1967. Effects of cognitive desensitization on avoidance behavior. *Journal of Personality and Social Psychology,* 7, 345–350.
Valle, V.A. 1974. Attributions of stability as a mediator in the changing of expectations. Unpublished doctoral dissertation. University of Pittsburgh.
Valle, V.A. and Frieze, I.H. 1976. Stability of causal attributions as a mediator in changing expectations for success. *Journal of Personality and Social Psychology,* 33, 579–587.
Veroff, J. 1957. Development and validation of a projective measure of power motivation. *Journal of Abnormal and Social Psychology,* 54, 1–8.
Walsh, N.A., Meister, L.A., and Kleinke, C.L. 1977. Interpersonal attraction and visual behavior as a function of perceived arousal and evaluation by an opposite sex person. *The Journal of Social Psychology,* 103, 65–74.
Walster, E. 1966. Assignment of responsibility for an accident. *Journal of Personality and Social Psychology,* 3, 73–79.
Watson, J.S. 1967. Memory and "contingency analysis" in infant learning. *Merrill-Palmer Quarterly,* 13(1), 55–76.
_____. 1966. The development and generalization of "contingency awareness" in early infancy: Some hypotheses. *Merrill-Palmer Quarterly,* 12(2), 123–135.
Weiner, B. 1977. Attribution and affect: Comments on Sohn's critique. *Journal of Educational Psychology,* 69, 506–511.
_____. 1976a. Attributionstheoretische Analyse von Erwartung X Nutzen-Theorien. In H.-D. Schmalt und W.-U. Meyer (eds.), *Leistungsmotivation und Verhalten.* Stuttgart: Klett, 81–100.
_____. 1976b. An attributional approach for educational psychology. In L. Shulman (ed.), *Review of research in education.* Vol. 4. Itasca, Ill.: Peacock.

_____. 1975a. *Die Wirkung von Erfolg und Mißerfolg auf die Leistung.* Stuttgart: Klett.

_____. 1975b. An attributional interpretation of expectancy-value theory. In B. Weiner (ed.), *Cognitive views of human motivation.* New York: Academic Press.

_____. (ed.). 1974a. *Achievement motivation and attribution theory.* Morristown, N.J.: General Learning Press.

_____. 1974b. Achievement motivation as conceptualized by an attribution theorist. In B. Weiner (ed.), *Achievement motivation and attribution theory.* Morristown, N.J.: General Learning Press, 3–48.

_____. 1972. *Theories of motivation: From mechanism to cognition.* Chicago: Rand McNally. (German: *Theorien der Motivation.* Stuttgart: Klett, 1976).

Weiner, B., Frieze, I.H., Kukla, A., Reed, L., Rest, S., and Rosenbaum, R.M. 1971, 1972. Perceiving the causes of success and failure. In E.E. Jones, D.E. Kanouse, H.H. Kelley, R.E. Nisbett, S. Valins, and B. Weiner (eds.), *Attribution: Perceiving the causes of behavior.* Morristown, N.J.: General Learning Press.

Weiner, B. and Kukla, A. 1970. An attributional analysis of achievement motivation. *Journal of Personality and Social Psychology,* 15, 1–20.

Weiner, B. and Kun, A. 1977. The development of causal attributions and the growth of achievement and social motivation. In S. Feldman and D. Bush (eds.), *Cognitive development and social development.* Potomac: Erlbaum.

Weiner, B., Kun, A., and Weiner, M.B. In press. The development of mastery, emotions, and morality from an attributional perspective. In W.A. Collins (ed.), *Minnesota symposia on child development.* Vol. 13. Hillsdale: Erlbaum.

Weiner, B. and Litman-Adizes, T. In press. An attributional, expectancy-value analysis of learned helplessness and depression. In J. Garber and M.E.P. Seligman (eds.), *Human control.* New York: Academic Press.

Weiner, B., Nierenberg, R., and Goldstein, M. 1976. Social learning (locus of control) versus attributional (causal stability) interpretations of expectancy of success. *Journal of Personality,* 44, 52–68.

Weiner, B. and Peter, N. 1973. A cognitive-developmental analysis of achievement and moral judgments. *Developmental Psychology,* 9, 290–309.

Weiner, B. and Potepan, P.A. 1970. Personality characteristics and affective reactions towards exams of superior and failing college students. *Journal of Educational Psychology,* 61, 144–151.

Weiner, B., Russell, D., and Lerman, D. 1979. The cognition-emotion process in achievement-related contexts. *Journal of Personality and Social Psychology,* 37, 1211–1220.

_____. 1978a. Affective consequences of causal ascriptions. In J.H. Harvey, W.J. Ickes, and R.F. Kidd (eds.), *New directions in attribution research.* Vol. 2. Hillsdale, N.J.: Erlbaum, 59–90.

_____. 1978b. Affektive Auswirkungen von Attributionen. In D. Görlitz, W.-U. Meyer, and B. Weiner (eds.), *Bielefelder Symposium über Attribution.* Stuttgart: Klett-Cotta, 139-173.
Weiner, B. and Sierad, J. 1975. Misattribution for failure and enhancement of achievement strivings. *Journal of Personality and Social Psychology,* 31, 415-421.
Whalen, C.K. and Henker, B. 1976. Psychostimulants and children: A review and analysis. *Psychological Bulletin,* 83, 1113-1130.
White, M.D. and Wilkins, W. 1973. Bogus physiological feedback and response thresholds of repressors and sensitizers. *Journal of Research in Personality,* 7, 78-87.
White, R.W. 1959. Motivation reconsidered: The concept of competence. *Psychological Review,* 66, 297-333.
Wilkins, W. 1971. Perceptual distortion to account for arousal. *Journal of Abnormal Psychology,* 78, 252-257.
Wilson, G.T. 1973. Effects of false feedback on avoidance behavior: "Cognitive" desensitization revisited. *Journal of Personality and Social Psychology,* 28, 115-122.
Wilson, G.T. and Lawson, D.M. 1978. Expectancies, alcohol, and sexual arousal in women. *Journal of Abnormal Psychology,* 87, 358-367.
Wilson, T.P. 1970. Conceptions of interaction and forms of sociological explanation. *American Sociological Review,* 35, 697-710.
Wimer, S.W. and Peplau, L.A. 1978. Determinants of reactions to lonely others. Paper presented at the 58th Annual Meeting of the Western Psychological Association, San Francisco.
Woll, S.B. and McFall, M.E. 1979. The effects of false feedback on attributed arousal and rated attractiveness in female subjects. *Journal of Personality,* 47, 214-229.
Wyer, R.S. 1976. An investigation of the relations among probability estimates. *Organizational Behavior and Human Performance,* 15, 1-18.

AUTHOR INDEX

Abramson, L.Y., 46, 73
Ajzen, I., 172
Ames, C., 52
Ames, R., 52
Anderson, N.H., 110, 160
Andrews, G.R., 53
Angulo, E.J., 128, 136, 145, 146
Anscombe, G.E.M., 207
Arkin, R.M., 58, 91
Aronson, R., 159
Atkinson, J.W., 38, 48, 54, 55, 95, 96, 97, 98, 102, 105, 223
Austin, J.L., 207

Backman, C.W., 109
Bacon, S.J., 136
Baeyer von, C.L., 50
Bailey, M.M., 72
Bandura, A., 139
Barefoot, J.C., 129, 135, 136
Barnes, R.D., 62
Baron, R.S., 134
Bar-Tal, D., 41, 42
Bass, B.M., 159
Bayes, Th., 144
Beck, A.T., 72
Becker, H.S., 198
Beckman, L., 84

Behar, L.B., 127, 128, 138, 146, 150
Bell, J.E., 128, 136, 143, 146, 150
Bem, D.J., 134, 148, 153, 155
Berger, P.L., 199
Berger, R.A., 199
Berkowitz, L., 61, 128, 136, 145, 146, 149
Berlyne, D.E., 126, 137, 153
Billig, M., 199
Birch, D., 96
Blanchard, E.B., 139
Blaney, P.H., 130, 138
Bloemkolk, D., 127, 129, 130, 137, 138, 152
Bootzin, R.R., 123, 132, 138
Borden, R., 139, 146, 147, 150, 151
Borkovec, T.D., 124, 126, 127, 128, 129, 132, 134, 135, 136, 140, 141, 143, 144, 150, 151, 152
Botto, R.W., 129, 130, 152, 153
Bramel, D., 128, 136, 143, 146, 150
Brehm, J.W., 128, 132, 135, 138, 146, 153, 154
Brogden, H.E., 160
Brophy, J.E., 78, 83, 84
Brown, H.A., 136
Brown, M., 96
Brunswik, E., 4, 6

255

Burger, J.M., 41, 42
Buss, A.R., 209, 210
Butzkamm, A., 84

Capioppo, J.T., 124
Calvert-Boyanowsky, J., 123
Caputo, C., 195
Carlsmith, J.M., 159
Carroll, J.S., 63, 69, 70, 71, 75
Cartwright, D., 15, 17, 96
Carver, C.S., 130, 133, 135, 138, 142, 148, 149
Castore, C.H., 163, 164
Chapin, M., 53
Charis, P.C., 127, 129, 138, 152
Charlesworth, W.R., 106
Cicourel, A.V., 198
Clark, M., 151, 153
Clark, R.A., 54
Cohen, R., 133, 135, 136, 140, 148, 151, 154
Coles, M.G.H., 128, 129, 134, 152
Colgan, H.H., 124
Conger, A.J., 132, 135, 153, 154
Conger, J.C., 132, 135, 153, 154
Cooper, H.M., 41, 42
Coopersmith, S., 109
Couch, A., 159
Cox, D.J., 50
Cronbach, L.J., 159

Damm, J., 98
Darley, J.M., 148
Darley, S.A., 148
Darom, E., 41, 42
Darwin, Ch., 203
Davis, K.E., 60, 111, 115, 195, 196
Davison, G.C., 132, 137, 138
Davitz, J.R., 226
Debus, R.L., 53
Decaria, M.D., 129, 137, 145, 151
DeCharms, R., 5, 43, 60, 65
Deci, E.L., 43
Deckner, C.W., 123
Defares, P., 127, 129, 130, 132, 137, 138, 152, 154
Del Castillo, D., 138
Detweiler, R.A., 127, 130, 144, 146, 152
Diener, C.I., 40, 53
Dienstbier, R.A., 75, 123

Dobrick, M., 222, 223, 224
Driver, M.J., 163, 164
Duval, S., 91
Dweck, C.S., 40, 53
Dyck, D.G., 53

Eagly, A.H., 116, 118
Easterbrook, J.A., 136
Efran, J.S., 136
Eiser, J.R., 49
Elig, T.W., 41
Eller, S.J., 73
van Enckevort, G., 127, 129, 130, 132, 137, 138, 152, 154
Epstein, S., 109, 110, 119
Erdmann, G., 123, 124
Eswara, H.S., 63
Euclid 13

Feather, N.T., 51, 96, 107, 110, 111, 112, 113
Fencil-Morse, E., 73
Fenigstein, A., 130, 135, 142
Festinger, L., 53
Field, P.B., 112, 116
Fink, D., 129, 133, 142, 143, 152, 153, 155, 156
Fishbein, M., 172
Fiske, S.T., 91
Fitch, G., 52, 111, 112
Fitts, H.W., 112
Flavell, J.H., 93
Folkes, V.S., 40, 72
Fontaine, G., 49
Freud, S., 72, 214
Frieze, I.H., 40, 41, 42, 44, 48, 49, 51, 52, 53, 54, 55, 61, 102, 114, 177, 196
Fromkin, H.L., 159, 164
Frost, R.O., 146, 148, 151

Gaas, E., 140
Galanter, E., 92
Galbraith, G.G., 129, 132, 152
Garfinkel, H., 198, 229
Garrison, W., 52
Gatchel, R.J., 140
Gaupp, L.A., 132, 152
Geen, R.G., 146, 155
van Gelderen, M., 127, 129, 130, 132, 137, 138, 152, 154

Gerard, H.B., 127, 132, 142, 151
Gerdes, E.P., 123, 128, 132, 134, 138, 147, 151
Gergen, K.J., 195, 197, 203, 208, 229, 230
Gergen, M., 229, 230
Gibbons, F.X., 130, 133, 148, 149
Giesen, M., 130, 131, 139, 141, 146, 147, 150, 151
Gilmore, T.M., 52
Girodo, M., 127
Glaros, A.G., 137
Glasgow, R.E., 134, 135, 141, 143, 152
Goethals, G.R., 115
Goffman, E., 199, 202
Golding, S.L., 129, 131
Goldstein, D., 49, 50, 51, 129, 133, 142, 143, 152, 153, 155, 156
Good, T.L., 78, 83, 84
Gordon, S., 72
Gouldner, A.W., 199
Grayson, J.B., 126, 150, 151
Grumet, J.F., 115
Grusche, A., 133, 135, 136, 140, 148, 151, 154

Hagan, P.J., 130, 138, 151
Hamilton, J.O., 98
Hannah, T.E., 195
Hansen, R.D., 142, 146
Hanson, L.R., Jr., 138, 140
Hanusa, B.H., 72
Hårary, F., 15, 17
Hare, R.D., 130
Harré, R., 206, 208
Harris, V.A., 115, 139, 143, 146, 148, 150, 151, 155, 156
Hatch, J.P., 140
Hawk, G., 138, 151, 152, 153
Heckhausen, H., 63, 76, 191, 216
Heffler, D., 123
Hegel, G.W.F., 197
Heider, F., 3, 5, 11, 12, 20, 40, 41, 42, 43, 44, 60, 75, 102, 142, 163, 195, 214, 220, 221, 230
Heim, M., 64, 72
Helmreich, R., 159, 172
Hendrick, C., 130, 131, 139, 141, 146, 147, 150, 151
Henker, B., 67, 68

Hennings, B.L., 126, 150
Henriksen, K., 138, 150
Herman, C.P., 123
Herrick, C.D., 129, 130, 152, 153
Hillman, D., 75, 123
Hillman, J., 75, 123
Hirschman, R., 136, 138, 143, 151, 152, 153
Hofer, M., 78, 222, 223, 224
Holmes, D.S., 126, 146, 148, 151
Horkheimer, M., 229
Horowitz, I.A., 155
Hubbard, M., 126
Hume, D., 206
Husserl, E., 197

Ickes, W.J., 52, 61, 62, 75
Insko, C.A., 129, 138, 145, 146
Izard, C.E., 106

Janis, I.L., 112, 116
Janke, W., 123, 124
Jellison, J.M., 139, 143, 146, 150, 155
Jones, E.E., 60, 111, 115, 119, 195, 196
Jones, S.C., 119

Kahnemann, D., 147, 148
Kanfer, F.H., 127, 128, 129, 131, 153
Kanouse, D.E., 138, 140
Kant, I., 197, 214
Kaplan, R.M., 63
Karabenick, S.A., 96
Karoly, P., 127, 128, 129, 131, 153
Katkin, E.S., 148, 151, 156
Katz, D., 12
Kelley, H.H., 43, 47, 60, 81, 87, 131, 142, 144, 147, 148, 149, 196, 214, 221, 222
Kellner, D.B., 199
Keniston, K., 159
Kent, R.N., 132, 134, 138, 148
Kerber, K.W., 128, 129, 134, 152
Kidd, R.F., 61, 62, 75
Klein, D.C., 73
Kleinke, C.L., 150, 151
Kliger, S.C., 163, 164
Koenig, K.P., 132, 138, 140, 150
Konecni, V.J., 124
Kremen, I., 124
Krisher, H.P., 148

Krohne, H.W., 136
Kruglanski, A.W., 209
Kukla, A., 40, 44, 48, 53, 54, 55, 61, 63, 96, 102, 113, 114, 177, 195, 196
Kun, A., 68, 93

Lacey, J.I., 124, 127
Landy, F.J., 146
Lanzetta, J.T., 126, 130, 195
Lau, R.R., 40
Lawrence, D.H., 53
Lawson, D.M., 124
Layden, M.A., 52
Lefcourt, H.M., 50
Legant, P., 195
Lehnhoff, J., 75, 123
Lepinski, J.P., 128, 136, 145, 146
Lepper, M.R., 126
Lerman, D., 41, 55, 56, 57, 58, 87, 105, 106, 107, 223
Leventhal, G.S., 123
Lewin, K., 48
Lichtenstein, E., 129, 130
Lick, J., 136
Liebhart, E.H., 84, 91, 123, 127, 134, 138, 139, 141, 145, 147, 149, 152, 226, 227
Lisman, S.A., 123
Litman-Adizes, T., 45, 73
Litwin, G.H., 96, 98
Loftis, J., 132
Lowe, C.A., 142, 146
Lowell, E.L., 54

Malloy, T.E., 129, 137, 145, 151
Mandler, G., 124, 147, 204
Mann, L., 42
Mannheim, K., 199
Maracek, J., 195
Marcia, J.E., 136
Margulis, S.T., 128, 136, 143, 146, 150
Maruyama, G.M., 58
Marx, K., 197, 199
Matthews, M.W., 61
Maynard, A., 140
McClelland, D.C., 54
McFall, M.E., 129, 133, 137, 152
McMahan, I.D., 49, 51
McMartin, J.A., 162

Mead, G.H., 198
Meinong, A., 3
Meister, L.A., 150, 151
Mettee, D.R., 129, 133, 142, 143, 152, 153, 155, 156
Meyer, J., 46, 47, 48, 49
Meyer, W.-U., 40, 49, 75, 84, 96, 97, 107, 109, 113, 114, 177, 188, 219, 223, 224, 225
Meyer-Osterkamp, S., 133, 135, 136, 140, 148, 151, 154
Michela, J., 46, 47, 64, 72
Miller, D.T., 190
Miller, G.A., 92, 162, 204
Minton, H.L., 52
Mischel, W., 80, 81, 87
Misovich, S., 127, 129, 138, 152

Neisser, U., 204
Nelson, R., 132, 134, 138, 148
Newman, A., 127, 128, 129, 131, 153
Nicassio, P., 123
Nierenberg, R., 49, 50, 51, 63
Nisbett, R.E., 123, 126, 132, 147, 195, 196, 203, 204, 215
Nissen, H.W., 68
Nogami, G.Y., 163, 164, 168, 169, 171
Norman, R.Z., 17
Nuttin, J.R., 68

O'Brien, E.J., 110
Ostrove, N., 49

Pallak, M.S., 195
Pancer, S.M., 49
Panitch, D., 119
Passer, M.W., 46, 47
Patten, R.L., 188
Payne, J.W., 63, 69, 70, 71, 75
Peplau, L.A., 46, 47, 64, 72
Peter, N., 63
Peters, R.S., 207
Phares, E.J., 50, 53
Piaget, J., 5, 6, 106, 163, 215
Piccione, A., 129, 138, 149
Pigg, R., 146, 155
Piliavin, I.M., 61, 62
Piliavin, J.A., 61, 62
Plöger, F.-O., 97, 223, 225
Plon, M., 199

Potepan, P.A., 113
Pribram, K.H., 92
Proctor, S., 129, 137, 145, 151

Rabbie, J.M., 127, 132
Rakosky, J.J., 146, 155
Ray, A.A., 132, 138, 148, 154
Raynor, J.O., 96
Reed, L., 40, 44, 48, 53, 54, 55, 61, 102, 114, 177, 196
Reid, J.B., 128, 132, 143, 145, 148, 151
Reisman, S., 129, 138, 145
Rest, S., 40, 44, 48, 52, 53, 54, 55, 61, 63, 102, 114, 177, 196
Rheinberg, F., 75, 84, 86
Riecken, H.W., 195
Riemer, B.S., 44
Ritter, B., 139
Robinson, E.J., 93
Robinson, W.P., 93
Rodin, J., 61, 62
Rogers, R.W., 123
Rosen, E., 128, 132, 143, 145, 148, 151
Rosen, G.M., 128, 132, 143, 145, 148, 151
Rosenbaum, R.M., 40, 44, 45, 48, 49, 53, 54, 55, 61, 102, 114, 177, 189, 196
Ross, H.S., 146
Ross, L., 126, 131, 132
Ross, M., 146
Rotter, J.B., 43, 44, 65, 82
Rubin, B.E., 136
Russell, D., 40, 41, 55, 56, 57, 58, 64, 72, 87, 105, 106, 107, 223
Ryle, G., 203, 207

Schachter, S., 121, 123, 124, 126, 128, 132, 135, 151, 152, 227
Schaefer, H.H., 124
Scheier, M.F., 130, 133, 148, 149
Schendelaar, J.K.L., 132, 154
Schneider, K., 96
Schopler, J., 61
Schroder, H.M., 136
Schütz, A., 48, 197
Secord, P.F., 109, 206, 208
Seligman, M.E.P., 46, 65, 72, 73
Shaver, K.G., 162, 163, 171, 196, 201

Shaw, J.I., 162
Shaw, M.E., 162
Silberman, M., 78
Simmel, M., 11, 12
Simon, P., 51, 62, 63, 110, 113
Singer, J.E., 123, 128
Singerman, K.J., 134
Skinner, B.F., 200, 206, 216
Skolnick, P., 162
Smedslund, J., 214
Smith, D., 140
Sogin, S.R., 195
Sosik, T.P., 127, 129
Spence, J.T., 159, 172
Spinoza, B., 13, 14, 15
Stapp, J., 159, 172
Stein, A.H., 72
Steiner, I.D., 65
Stern, R.M., 129, 130, 132, 146, 152, 153
Stone, N.M., 129, 136, 140, 151
Straub, R.B., 129, 135, 136
Streufert, Siegfried, 159, 163, 164, 165, 166, 168, 169, 171, 174, 175, 180, 228
Streufert, Susan, 163, 166, 168, 175, 180, 228
Stroebe, M.S., 116, 118
Stroebe, W., 116, 118, 224
Sulzer, J.L., 162
Sushinsky, L.W., 132, 134, 138
Swant, S.G., 63
Szasz, T.S., 200

Tannenbaum, P.H., 123
Taunton-Blackwood, A., 140
Taylor, S., 91
Taylor, S.E., 127, 129, 130, 151
Teasdale, J.D., 46, 73
Tennen, H., 73
Thibaut, J.W., 81, 195
Thornton, E.W., 130, 138, 151
Tolman, E.C., 216
Toulmin, St., 203
Tregerthan, G.J., 124
Triandis, H.C., 42
Tsujimoto, R.N., 137
Turner, C., 128, 145, 146, 149
Turns, R., 140
Tversky, A., 147, 148
Twain, M., 34

Valins, S., 123, 124, 126, 129, 132, 137, 138, 145, 148, 149, 151, 154, 155
Valkenaar, M.C., 75, 123
Valle, V.A., 44, 49, 51, 52
Veitch, R., 129, 138, 149

Wall, R.L., 129, 136, 150, 151
Walsh, N.A., 150, 151
Walster, E., 162, 163, 171
Ware, E.E., 50
Watson, J.S., 69
Watson, P.J., 140
Weeks, D., 46, 47, 64, 72
Weiner, B., 39, 40, 41, 43, 44, 45, 48, 49, 50, 51, 53, 54, 55, 56, 57, 58, 61, 62, 63, 64, 67, 68, 73, 75, 85, 87, 93, 102, 105, 106, 107, 113, 114, 162, 172, 177, 178, 181, 184, 188, 189, 195, 196, 219, 220, 222, 225, 226
Weiner, M.B., 68

Weinert, F.E., 223
Wertheimer, M., 12, 13, 14, 15
Whalen, C.K., 67, 68
Wheeler, L., 123
White, L.A., 188
White, M.D., 137
White, R.W., 68
Whitehead, A.N., 5
Wilkins, W., 128, 137
Wilson, G.T., 124, 132, 134, 136, 138, 141, 148
Wilson, T.D., 147, 203, 204, 215
Wilson, T.P., 203
Wimer, S.W., 64
Wittgenstein, L., 207
Woll, S.B., 129, 133, 137, 152
Worchel, S., 115
Wyer, S., 144

Zanna, M.P., 127, 130, 144, 146, 152
Zillmann, D., 123

SUBJECT INDEX

Ability, 41, 45, 47, 63ff., 99, 101f., 177ff., 185, 189, 190
Acceptance-rejection, 109ff.
Achievement, change programs, 52ff.
Achievement motivation theory, 95ff., 105
Achievement performance, factors for, 41ff.
Act
 motivation to, 86
 pressure to, 86
Action
 competence for, 81
 concepts of, 81ff.
Actor-observer differences, 210
Actual state, 81
Affect, 54ff., 65f., 225f.
 and atrribution, relations between, 55, 56ff., 103ff.
 and outcome, 55ff.
 and stability, 58
 sources of in achievement situations, 57f.
 study of, 59
Affective life in the classroom, 59
Affects
 anticipated as incentives, 95ff., 98ff., 102ff.
 primary, 106f.
 secondary, 107
Affiliation, 72
Aggression, 145, 149
Altruism in the classroom, 62
Amazement, 100, 103, 104, 105, 106, 107
Ambiguity, 129, 130, 137, 138
Anxiety, 132, 139, 140, 146
Apparent Causal Sequence (ACS).
 See Causal sequence, apparent
Arousal, level of, 128, 132
"As-if models", 147
Attention, 127, 149, 150, 152, 153
Attitude change, 124, 128, 141, 143, 147, 152
Attitudes, 14f., 16f., 172
Attribution, 3ff., 9ff., 77ff., 109, 144f., 195, 200ff.
 and affect, relations between 55ff., 100, 103ff., 106f.
 and person perception, 11, 12, 18
 behavioral impact of, 146ff.
 defensive, 162
 external, 110, 112, 114f., 116f., 162, 177f., 180f., 200, 201, 204, 208, 209f.
 instruction, 134, 139

261

SUBJECT INDEX

internal, 110, 112f., 114f., 116f., 162, 177f., 180f., 185, 200, 201, 204f., 208f.
management of, 19ff., 34f.
of failure, 37f., 109ff., 111ff., 114ff., 118f., 222f.
of success, 37f., 98f., 101f., 109ff., 111ff., 114ff., 118f., 222f.
plausibility of, 141ff.
processes, 125, 195, 200, 201f.
Attribution theory, central assumption, 40
Audience, 21ff., 24
Availability, 148
of causal factors, 93
Awareness of mental processes, 147, 203ff.

Balance, 7, 9ff., 220f.
Behavior
approach, 128
avoidance, 132, 136, 151f.
control of, 75ff.
model of social, 76ff.
Blame, 223f.
Brain washing, 201

Causal attribution
act of, 188
and other models, relation between, 83ff.
Causal dimensions and psychological affects, linkage between, 65
Causal explanation, teacher's . . . of pupil actions, 76
Causal factors, 161f., 177f., 180f.
accessibility of, 93
Causal hierarchy, 4ff.
Causal properties, consequences of, 48ff.
Causal schemata, 144ff., 214
Causal sequence, 21ff.
apparent (ACS), 21ff., 24ff., 26ff., 29f., 31ff.
real (RCS), 21ff., 24ff., 26f., 29f., 31ff.
concealment of, 31ff.
elements of, 29ff.
Causality, 206
attributions of, 162ff., 200, 205f.
dimensions of, 43ff., 65

phenomenal, 12f., 15f.
pleasure, 68
psychological consequences of perceived, 43ff.
Cause-effect
expectations (violations of), 27ff.
sequences, 27ff.
Causes
and reasons, distinction between, 206f., 208ff.
modification of, 86
of success and failure, 40ff., 63f., 65f., 72, 177f.
perceived, 148ff.
taxonomy of, 43ff.
type of effect of, 87
Ceiling effects, 185
Changes, autonomic, 123ff., 132, 151, 226f.
Classification, 148
Classroom experiences, 39ff., 65
Cognition-emotion sequence in achievement contexts, 58f.
Cognitive processes, inferences of, 69
Competence, 68f.
Competence-incompetence, 109ff.
Complexity, 137f.
Confidence games, 24ff.
Consensus information, 150
Consequences of causal properties, 48ff.
Consistency information, 149, 150
Constancy phenomena, 5, 12
Context (*See also* Information, accessibility of context-), 125, 132ff., 135ff., 142
Control, 38, 45, 47, 60ff., 72
and locus, concepts, 44
as causal dimension, consequences of, 60ff.
self-perception of, 64f.
Cost, level of, 83
Covariation, 142f.
Crime, 69ff.
Cross-cultural study, 42

Depression, 65, 72ff.
Desensitization, cognitive, 124, 132, 134, 139, 149, 154
Diagnosticity, 190

Dimensionality, 160ff., 163, 171, 173, 176, 185f., 228f.
Dimensions
  attributional . . . of the experimenter and the subject, 176ff.
  of causal factors, 161f., 177f.
  of causality, 43ff., 65
Disposition, 150
Distinctiveness information, 148f.
Drug treatment, 67
Drunkenness, 62

Effort, 41, 45, 47, 63f., 65, 99, 101, 102, 177ff., 181ff., 185, 189
Effort regulation, 191
Embarrassment, 95
Emotion, 225f.
  theory of, 121, 123, 124, 151, 152
Emotions
  for failure, 56ff.
  for success, 56ff.
Entity properties, 28ff.
Entropy, 8
Equivalence of real and fictitious autonomic changes, 155f.
Ethnography, 208ff.
Ethnomethodological, 198f.
Evaluation, 63f.
  moral and control aspects of, 64
Expectancies of the situation's future development, 78f.
Expectancy, 49, 50
  and incentive, 96f.
  of success, 48f.
  of the effect of action, 82
  shifts, 49, 51, 52f., 61
Expectations
  of outcome, 110, 111ff., 118f., 128
  of success and failure, 95ff.
Experiments and reality, 6
Explanandum, 126, 153
Explanation, social, 200, 201f., 203, 205f., 211
Explanation search, 40ff., 106f., 125, 126ff.
  motivations for, 126ff.
Explanatory option, 210
Explanatory uncertainty. (*See also* Subjective uncertainty), 128ff.
Extinction, 138
  resistance to, 52ff.

Factor-analytic procedures, 46, 47f.
Failure (*See also* Attribution of failure) 49, 55f., 109ff., 177, 179, 180ff., 185, 188, 190
  emotions for, 56f., 58
  experience of, 109, 111
  incentive value of, 95
Feedback
  interoceptive, 132
  parameters, 129, 131
Feelings, 59
Flexibility, attributional, 137
Future state, 80ff.

Gestalt, laws of, 12ff.
Globality, 46, 65
Goal dimension, 80ff.
Goal expectancies, determinants of, 49

Happiness, 100, 102, 104, 105
Heart rate, 125, 128, 129, 130, 145
Heisenberg type effect, 188, 193
Helping behavior, 61ff.
Helplessness, attributional framework for, 73
Hyperactivity, 67f.

Illness, 62
  mental, 200, 203, 214f.
Importance. *See* Subjective importance
Incentives
  and expectancy, 96f.
  and subjective probability of success, 96, 105
  assessment of, 96
  of success and failure, 95ff.
Incongruity, 125, 127, 130
Index state, 80f.
Indifference, 100, 102
Inference, attributional, 40
Information, accessibility of context-, 135ff.
Information-processing, 144
Information-seeking, 60
Instructions, experimental, 171
Intent, 167, 172, 202
Intention(ality), 44, 45, 46, 65, 172, 189, 201, 202, 205
  vs. control, 45, 46, 47
Interference hypothesis, 138f.

Internality, 44, 47, 55, 162, 177, 178, 180, 181, 189
Interpersonal relations, 9ff.

Joy, 100, 103ff.

Label, 146
Learned helplessness, 72ff.
Locus, 37
 and control, concepts of, 44
 as causal dimension, consequences of, 54ff., 65, 72
Locus of causality, affective consequences, 54ff.
Locus of control controversy, 50f.
Logic, rules of, 214
Loneliness, 47, 64, 72
Luck, 41, 42, 45, 47, 54, 99, 101, 102, 103, 105, 177ff., 180ff., 185
 attribution to . . . and feelings of surprise, 106f.

Magic
 and science, relation between, 26
 real, 24ff.
"Magic" events, nature of, 26ff.
Magic tricks, 19ff., 221f.
 properties of, 21ff.
 "The Whispering Queen," 21ff., 29
Magician, 20, 21ff.
Mastery, 68f.
Measurement problems in attribution psychology, 159ff.
Mental processes. See Awareness of mental processes
Metacognition, 93
Methodological problems, 157ff., 227ff.
Minimum data pattern, 142
Mood, 47
Moral evaluation (See also Evaluation, moral and control aspects of), 214
Motivation, theory of, 39ff., 95ff.
Multidimensional scaling, 46, 47

Naive psychology and scientific psychology, 43
Naive theories, teacher's, 78
Negativity bias(es), 138
Negligence, 167, 172
Negotiation, 197f., 200f., 203, 206
Newspaper, 7f.

Observer. See Audience
 See Actor-observer differences
"Origin," 60
Outcomes, attributions of interpersonal, 52, 114ff.

Parole decisions, 69ff.
 process, 70
Perception, 3ff., 177
 and attribution, 3ff., 18, 220
 ecology of, 4
Persistence, 126
Person Perception, 10ff.
 and attribution, 11f.
Philosophy, analytic, 196, 206ff., 210
Plausibility, 141ff.
Positivist perspective, 196, 197, 206, 210
"Prägnanz," law of, 13
Praise, 223
Prediction, 201, 203
Press, 7
Pride, 54, 59, 95ff., 100, 102, 104, 105
Probability (See also Subjective probability)
 of success and failure, subjective, 95ff.
Psychophysiology, naive, 145f.
Psychostimulants, 67f.
Punishment and reward
 determinants of, 63f.
 information value of, 223f.

Range of generality, 91
Real causal sequence (RCS).
 See Causal sequence, real
Reasons and causes, distinction between, 206ff., 209
Reattribution, 132
Reference norms, 190f.
Reinforcement
 contingencies, 216
 schedules, 53, 54, 216
Reliability, 176, 184, 186
Relief, 100, 102, 104
Reorganization, 14
Response-produced stimuli, 140f.
Responsibility, 161, 162ff., 188, 195, 202, 209
 and causality, attributions of, 162ff.

SUBJECT INDEX

attributions of, 162ff.
   vs. attributions of causality, 163, 165ff., 169ff.
   for crimes, 71
Reward and punishment, determinants of, 63f.
Risk, 71
Routine behavior, 92

Salience, 129, 145, 148
   of feedback, 129f.
   of (perceived) causal factors, 125, 148
   vs. subjective importance, 131
Satisfaction, 100, 102, 104f.
Scales, 159ff., 162ff., 227f.
   bipolar, 161, 166f., 168ff., 173f., 176, 185, 187, 188
   characteristics of, 184f.
   forced-choice, 161, 162ff., 166f., 168ff., 172f., 176, 178. 179f., 181ff., 185
   non-forced-choice, 161, 162f., 166f., 168ff., 172f., 176, 178, 180f., 184f.
   percentage, 161, 166, 168ff., 173f., 176, 185, 187
   types of, 161ff., 184f., 187, 188
Science, 25f.
   and magic, relation between, 26
Search for causes. See Explanation search
Self-assessment, 110ff., 118f.
Self-concept, 109, 116, 119
   and social reality, 118f.
   maintenance of, 51f.
   of ability, 51, 113, 223f.
Self-consistency hypothesis, 111, 113f., 116f., 119, 224
Self-esteem, 38, 58, 109ff., 116ff., 224
   and causal explanation in achievement, 111ff.
   and causal explanation in personal relations, 114ff.
Self-perception, 60
Self-perception theory, 146
Self-responsibility, 190
Self-theory, 119
Sentiments, 64
Shame, 54, 59, 95ff.

Significance, ascription of, 78
Situation
   and causal explanation, 84f.
   perceived, 78
Social perception, 60
Social psychology, 10f.
Sociology of knowledge, 199
Sociorationalism, 196, 197ff., 229
Stability (See also Time, stability over), 37, 44, 46f., 65, 72, 85, 162, 177, 181, 189
   and affect, 58
   as causal dimension, consequences of, 48ff.
Story as property of magic tricks, 23f.
Subjective importance (See also Salience), 130ff., 145
Subjective probability, 125, 144, 146
Subjective uncertainty (See also Explanatory uncertainty), 126, 130
Success (See also Attribution of success), 41, 49f., 55f., 109ff., 177, 179f., 181ff., 185, 190
   anticipated, 82
   emotions for, 57
   expectancy of, 48ff.
   expectation of, 112ff.
   experience of, 109, 111
   incentive value of, 95, 105
   level of, 81ff.
Subjective probability of, 98, 105
Success and failure
   expectations of, 95ff.
   incentives of, 95ff.
   perceived causes of, 40, 41f., 63, 65, 72
   subjective probability of, 95
Supernatural, 24, 27, 29, 35
Surprise, 100, 103f., 105ff.
Sympathy, 64

Tactical and negotiations game (TNG), 164, 174, 179
Task difficulty, 41f., 44, 45, 47, 99, 101f., 177ff., 180f., 183, 185, 190f.
TAT–type measure, 172
Teacher, 47
Teacher's behavior, 75ff., 222, 223f.
   prediction of, 90

Theory of motivation, attributional, 66
application of, 65ff.
Thing-medium ("Ding und Medium") distinction, 5, 28f., 30
Time, stability over, 85
Time effect(s) (*See also* Warm-up effect), 168, 174f., 176, 179, 185, 187f., 193
Trick, magic. See Magic Tricks

Uncertainty.
See Subjective uncertainty
See Explanatory uncertainty

Unconsciousness (*See also* Awareness of mental processes), 147
Unit-formation, 12, 14, 18
Units of analysis, 91

Validity, 163f., 171, 173, 175, 176
Valins effect, 121, 124, 125, 130, 151, 153, 226f.
Voluntary, 209

Warm-up effects, 169, 175
Why-questions, 35, 40, 107

ABOUT THE CONTRIBUTORS

Martin Dobrick holds degrees in both education and psychology. Employed in the Department of Education of the University of Braunschweig, he has been involved since 1975 in research on individualizing teacher behavior. He is especially concerned with cognitive social psychological issues in the school environment.

Kenneth Gergen is Professor of Psychology at Swarthmore College. Most recently, he and Mary Gergen have been carrying out extensive research on the process of social explanation. This work attempts to foster a relationship between the traditional attribution research in social psychology and current developments in the philosophy of social science. Kenneth Gergen has authored or edited six books and over eighty research articles on a wide range of subjects in social psychology. He has taught at Harvard University, the University of Marburg, and the University of Paris.

Mary Gergen is a Research Associate in the Psychology Department at Swarthmore College. Her recent research interests have focused on the impact of attributional styles on psychological aspects of aging. She is co-author, with Kenneth J. Gergen, of a new textbook, *Social Psychology*, and has also collaborated with him on many other research projects and publications at Swarthmore and at Harvard University.

ABOUT THE CONTRIBUTORS

Dietmar Görlitz is Professor of Developmental Psychology at the Technical University of Berlin (West). Since his 1972 dissertation on nonverbal communication (published as [*Problems and Results of Nonverbal Communication*], in German), he has concentrated on motivation psychology. His current research deals with attributional judgments in the context of social-cognitive development and with mapping the development of attributional processes in verbal and nonverbal communication.

Heinz Heckhausen has broad interests in motivation, personality, and development and their educational-psychological applications. Since 1964 he has been Professor of Psychology at the recently founded Ruhr-University Bochum, where he has built up the department of psychology as well as a productive research group. He has published several books on motivation in German and in English, including *The Anatomy of Achievement Motivation.*

Fritz Heider, Distinguished Professor Emeritus of the University of Kansas, is regarded as the founder of the field of research to which the present book is devoted: attribution theory. He received his doctorate from the University of Graz in Austria in 1920, coming to the United States in 1930. He has published numerous articles on problems of interpersonal behavior but is best known for his 1958 book, *The Psychology of Interpersonal Relations*, which is the main source of the topics *balance* and *attribution*, the subjects of an increasing number of theoretical and experimental studies.

Manfred Hofer, a psychologist, is Professor of Education at the University of Braunschweig, where his research is devoted mainly to cognitive aspects of teacher behavior and to teacher-pupil interaction. He is co-author of a televised course on educational psychology and of a textbook on statistical theory.

Harold Kelley has been prominent in developing attribution theory. The author/co-author of *The Social Psychology of Groups; Interpersonal Relations: A Theory of Interdependence;* and *Personal Relationships*, contributes to the present volume a chapter on "magic tricks" that reflects his interest in perceptual and attributional processes in interpersonal interaction. He is Professor of Psychology at the University of California, Los Angeles.

Ernst H. Liebhart is Professor of Social Psychology at the University of Marburg, where his research activities center on attribution and intuitive prediction, with particular attention to cognitive processes, close relationships, and clinical applications.

Wulf-Uwe Meyer, Professor of Psychology at the University of Bielefeld, is involved in research in achievement motivation, attribution, and self-concept of ability. His publications include *Leistungsmotiv und Ursachenerklärung von Erfolg und Mißerfolg*, and, together with Heinz-Dieter Schmalt, *Leistungsmotivation und Verhalten.*

Siegfried Streufert, who has held positions at Princeton, Rutgers, Purdue, and Bielefeld universities and at the National Institutes of Health, now holds a professorship at the Pennsylvania State University Medical School. Known for a number of theories related to behavior in complex environments, he is founding editor of the *Journal of Applied Social Psychology* and has published several books and a great many articles on decisionmaking, attitudes, attributions, complex research methods, and behavioral medicine.

Susan C. Streufert has held positions at Purdue and Bielefeld and at the National Institutes of Health. At present she is a health scientist administrator who reviews grant applications submitted to the NIH in behavioral medicine. Her research and many publications have been concerned with complexity theory, attributions, decisions, effects of information on complex behavior, and with behavioral medicine.

Wolfgang Stroebe, Professor of Social Psychology at the University of Tübingen, has published numerous articles in European and American journals, most recently on counterattitudinal advocacy and social support, effects of bereavement on mortality and morbidity, and integration of economics and psychology, and epistemological bases of social psychology. His books include *Categorization and Social Judgement* (with J.R. Eiser) and *Grundlagen der Sozialpsychologie I.*

Bernard Weiner is Professor of Psychology at the University of California, Los Angeles. He is interested in motivation and personality, with more specific focus on the development of an attributional theory of motivation and emotion. His most recent books are *Human Motivation, Cognitive Views of Human Motivation*, and *Achievement Motivation and Attribution Theory*.

Franz E. Weinert has been Professor of Psychology at the University of Heidelberg since 1968, after serving some years as teacher for elementary and secondary schools. His current research interests focus on problems of human learning, cognitive development, and on some issues of instructional psychology.